BUSINESS
of
BANKING

BUSINESS
of
BANKING

Don Wright

& Wally Valentine

Northcote House

Northcote House Publishers Ltd
Harper & Row House
Estover Road
Plymouth PL6 7PZ, United Kingdom
Tel: Plymouth (0752) 705251   Telex: 45635
Fax: (0752) 777603

First edition 1986
Reprinted August 1987
Reprinted November 1987
Second edition 1988

© 1986 and 1988 by Don Wright & Wally Valentine

British Library Cataloguing in Publication Data

Wright, Don,   1940-
  Business of banking. — 2nd ed.
  1. Great Britain. Banking
  I. Title II. Valentine, Wally
  332.1'0941

ISBN 0-7463-0535-4

Typesetting and Artwork by K-DEE Typesetters

Printed and bound in Great Britain
by A. Wheaton & Co. Ltd, Exeter

Contents

Table of Cases

Table of Statutes

1

The Business of Banking

One of the main objectives of this book is to introduce you to the fascinating and changing world of banking. For years banks and bankers have been seen as part of a staid and solid, if not downright boring, profession. Security and stability were the order of the day.

Today's banking profession is somewhat different. It is one of enormous *change and competition*; banking professionals will have to adapt quickly to deal with the fierce competition found on every high street today.

To be able to do this you need *to know the business of banking* for without this up-to-date knowledge you will be unable to deal with the two key components of our business:

MONEY and PEOPLE

KNOWING THE BUSINESS

The book is meant to provide a general appreciation and understanding of the role of banks, their relations with customers and the competition they face.

Hopefully, it will show that banks (and other financial institutions) are not organisations that hardly ever affect ordinary people. They are involved in almost every aspect of modern life. If you know and understand what services are available, and how to make best use of them, everyday life can become easier and certainly more profitable.

Banking has become an enormous business, and whatever the past may have been, banking in particular, and finance in general, have become exciting and vibrant activities, the more so with all the new technology available today. The book, therefore, will start you off on this road to understanding.

We have already said that the business is about change: you must *keep up to date*. You can do this by

Reading a quality newspaper
All quality newspapers have sections on business and finance which keep their readers abreast with day to day events. In addition they regularly print articles about changes

in the financial scene, special events, and explanations of how the 'business' works.

Regular reading is crucial if you are to keep up to date and widen your knowledge of the financial world.

Certainly books like this cannot go into the detail of specific services and rates of interest and hope to be up to date. Banking and financial markets and services are changing daily. Use your newspaper reading to supplement the information in this book and keep you really on top of the subject.

Remember, too, that newspapers carry advertisements. Read them; they are excellent sources of financial information and demonstrate the wide variety of services on offer.

Using TV and radio
Whilst most of us watch and listen mainly for entertainment remember that these media are tremendous sources of information on the financial scene. Make sure that you listen to and/or watch the special 'money' programmes broadcast regularly on both radio and TV. Try and take in one major newscast every day. You'll be surprised at how much of the news is financial news.

Professional publications
There are many professional publications available which will widen your knowledge of the financial world; take every opportunity to read these specialist publications.

Bankers, however, *must* read the Institute of Bankers magazine *Banking World*. The objective of this magazine is to keep bankers up to date with what is going on in the banking and financial world and to publish articles of special relevance both to bankers and to banking students.

Walk the High Street
Take some time to walk along your local high street; look at what is on offer in the banks, building societies, moneyshops, post offices, and even retail outlets. They all publish brochures detailing their services. Try and make a collection of these — they are a vital source of information.

USING THIS BOOK

When you move onto the next chapters you will notice they include certain features, namely:
— objectives
— text
— pattern note summaries
— summary notes in the text
— check out questions

The chapters are laid out this way to help you to get the most you can out of the book and to make your studying easier and more effective.

The objectives

We start each chapter by summarising what you will learn. This will help you know what you are going to cover and what you should achieve.

Unless you know what you are supposed to achieve it is impossible to measure whether you have been successful or not.

In all studying you need to ask:
— What do I need to learn?
— Have I learned it?

The objectives section deals with the first point.

Before you start to read each chapter, quickly flick over the whole chapter

- to get a feel for the overall content.
- get an idea of how long each section will take to cover.

The text

The text gives you the facts and details for an understanding of the subject.

Although we do include some summary notes it is important that you make your *own* notes as you are reading. Making your own notes not only helps you understand the subject, it helps you to memorise the detail more quickly.

Do not just rely on the summaries we have given; they are not meant to be comprehensive notes.

One other point about notemaking. Remember to make notes when

- reading a newspaper
- listening to radio
- watching TV

Don't *just* rely on memory; there is always the chance you will forget!

Pattern notes

These diagrams provide an overview of the whole area. They give you a chance to view each topic from a different perspective, and should be a positive aid to understanding and recall. They can be used in conjunction with the summary notes at the end of each chapter — particularly at final revision where you can use them to talk your way through the subject.

Summary notes

We have provided summary notes to help you when you come to revise the subject. By revision we do not just mean the final revision that you do immediately before the examination. You should revise each subject *throughout the year*. These summary notes can be used

- immediately on completion of the chapter
- a month after the reading
- 'term end' revision at Christmas/Easter
- final revision

Once again — remember to make your own notes, too.

Check out questions

We have already said how important it is for you to know *whether* you have learned what you set out to learn.

The Check Out question will help you do this. There is a temptation when you have finished reading to close the book and get on with something else. Please do not do this! You will be missing a key stage in your learning process — a stage that will help *you*.

Check that you have understood what you have been studying, otherwise you will have difficulty with following chapters and final revision will be almost impossible.

Set aside some time to work through the Check Out questions. They are not difficult and they will not take long. This will help build your confidence.

This introductory chapter has tried to set the scene and we hope that when you have studied the rest of the book you will not only have learned about, but that you will also feel as excited as we do about the *Business of Banking*.

2
Money

On completion of this chapter you will know

— why and how money developed
— the main functions performed by money
— the features by which we recognise money
— why money needs to be stable in value
— how changes in the value of money can be measured
— the part coins have played in the development of money
— how banknotes have developed
— what constitutes legal tender
— how to distinguish between money and other assets ('near money')
— the various types of plastic money which exist.

INTRODUCTION

We can describe money as anything which is generally acceptable for the settlement of a debt. We shall be looking at money in our modern economy in due course. Because we are so used to money, and often take it for granted, we first need to go back in time to establish why money came to be needed in society and how it has developed as society has become more complex and sophisticated.

For thousands of years Man had no use for money at all. In his very primitive state he had to be self-sufficient. Everything that a person required to live — food, clothes, shelter, tools — had to be produced by that person or his family. The basic family unit lived in isolation and fended for itself; anything which the family could not produce or obtain themselves they had to do without, a situation which lasted until about 5,000 years ago.

About that time Man started to live in communities, and began to trade. All individuals have certain skills and talents which make them better at some things than others. In those early days some men were good at making arrows and axe-heads, others at fishing, others at hunting, others at building and so on. Soon Man began to discover the advantages of basic specialisation.

Barter

Although Man was still self-sufficient, limited trading did take place. This occurred through a system known as barter — a system where goods or services were directly exchanged for other goods and services. This system of payment in kind continued long after money was introduced to overcome the problems and difficulties of the barter system.

Although barter enabled Man to exchange goods surplus to his requirements for goods and services which he needed, and could not provide himself, there were drawbacks.

(a) Double coincidence of wants

The main problem of barter is that you have to find someone who has what you want, and is willing to exchange it for what you have to offer. A man with a sheep to exchange may quickly find someone who wants a sheep, but that someone may only be offering tools in exchange. Trade cannot take place if the man with the sheep is actually looking for clothes, not tools. Both parties must have what the other wants and be willing to trade. This is known as a 'double coincidence of wants'.

(b) Exchange rates

Assuming a man is found who is willing to exchange his spare tools for a sheep, both men now face the second main problem with a barter system — how many tools equal one sheep? If they cannot agree a suitable rate of one for another, trade cannot take place. The problem extends beyond merely agreeing how many tools equal one sheep. Standards have to be set so that sheep of different ages and sizes can be compared, and also tools of different quality and design. You would need different rates for sheep of different ages, and tools of different sizes. We can begin to see just how difficult such a system is to maintain.

(c) Change

Let us assume the man with the sheep eventually meets a man with spare tools. After long negotiations they agree an exchange rate of ten arrows and three axes for the sheep. But what if the man with the sheep only wants five arrows and two axes? How does the second man give him change? Only if the man with the sheep is willing to take something else as well will the transaction be satisfactory.

(d) Time

Barter as a system of exchange is often handicapped by the need to exchange goods within a specific period of time. An obvious example would be the exchange of goods which were perishable, such as milk or meat.

Money

The method of overcoming all these problems was to introduce a system of money.

The development of Man from primitive cave-dweller to sophisticated urban high-technology user was based upon increasing specialisation and the division of labour.

Specialisation in the task a person is most skilled at results in large increases of output. Any surplus output can be exchanged for money and with that money people can buy the goods and services they need. The result of this would be better standards of living and a much wider variety of better produced goods and services for people.

Quite obviously, specialising in one task meant that a person could not afford to spend valuable time searching for others with whom to exchange goods.

For this system to work money must be generally acceptable throughout society. It is no good if only a few people will accept money in exchange for goods and services. To obtain the full benefits of money *everyone* has to accept money all the time.

Money has taken many interesting shapes and forms over the years; we shall look at some of them later. However, no matter what form it takes, money must fulfil certain functions and have certain characteristics.

FUNCTIONS OF MONEY

Medium of exchange

Exchange is the function of money which has enabled us to develop from a primitive barter system to a modern economy, governed by specialisation and the division of labour. As long as everyone in the economy accepts money in payment for debts we do not have the problems, inconvenience and worries associated with simple barter. It is hard to estimate the full impact that money has had on our lives but certainly our freedom has been increased because of it. We are free to *choose* when to buy and sell our goods and services.

Unit of account

We saw earlier that measurement of value posed a problem in the barter system: there was no objective yardstick against which to value sheep and tools, for example. Money fulfils this function.

Now that we have a common denominator we can compare the prices of all goods and services. We can now value sheep not only against tools, but against all other goods or services that exist because they are all measured in the same units. Once an individual knows the *money* value of all goods and services on offer, he can choose the right combinations of goods — and in the right quantities — to get the best possible value for his money.

Since money is used here as a measure for comparison we have been able to develop accounting records. The ability to record payments and receipts, and to make forecasts and plans, has had a tremendous impact on society. Try to imagine what the accountancy or banking professions would be like if there was no money to act as a unit of account!

Store of value

Under a system of barter we noticed that some goods (such as meat, milk and other perishable goods) had to be exchanged and used quickly. Many of the goods available could, therefore, not be stored for the future due to their perishability. Money, however, *can* be used as a store of value or wealth to be used in the future. Thus, money can be saved for emergencies or to pay for expensive goods and services some time in the future. This obviously gives the individual more freedom of choice in the way he can dispose of his wealth.

Standard of deferred payments

Under this heading we can introduce a time element. A monetary system allows for exchanges of goods to be made in one time period with payments in another time period (or spread over a series of periods). This is an extremely important function and has enabled societies to develop sophisticated financial systems.

Using a simple example, a builder undertakes to build a house for a client at a cost of £50,000. To save such a sum would take the client decades; by that time house prices would have risen, possibly beyond the client's reach. The client will have the added problem of finding and paying for somewhere to live whilst he is saving! How do we overcome this problem? The answer is that the client pays the builder by *instalments* over a period of time. Very simply, the client moves into the house as soon as it is built and pays the builder over a period of years. Money here is being used to provide *credit* for transactions.

Everything is fine so long as the people who supply the builder with his materials (bricks, mortar, wood and tiles) will accept payment by instalments from the builder. However, for small amounts people usually demand payment immediately. If the builder has to pay his suppliers immediately, but will not receive the full amount from his client for the house for many years, how can the system operate?

As we noticed before, the Industrial Revolution hinged on the division of labour and increased specialisation. The same principle applies here where the commodity concerned is not wood, nails, or bricks, but *money*. Institutions were formed and grew to satisfy the need we have identified. Banks grew because they could lend money deposited with them for safe-keeping to people who needed it to purchase goods and services; these loans were paid back over a period of time.

We will look at this process, known as *credit creation,* in a later chapter. Other institutions, even more specialised than banks, grew out of recognising that money could act as a standard of deferred payment. Building societies for example were formed specifically for people who needed large amounts of money to buy houses. In our example, the builder's client would borrow the money from a building society in the form of a mortgage for £50,000 to pay the builder; he would then pay back the £50,000 to the building society over a period of many years, usually 25.

Money, acting as an objective standard over time, enables society to develop a system of credit based on specialised institutions such as banks, building societies, and finance houses. We have seen how the builder can carry on his business — building and selling houses and paying his suppliers. We have seen that the client can borrow from a building society and purchase his dream home. We need to answer two final questions to complete the picture:

1.　How do the building societies (and other financial institutions) obtain their money?
2.　How do the financial institutions make a profit?

The answer to both is the charging of *interest*. Many people have spare money at various times which they do not need for immediate purchases. Coupled with this, at any one time many other people will require money to make purchases.

We need, therefore, a mechanism to bring the two together. This mechanism is the financial institution, such as the bank or building society, and the rate of interest it pays and charges.

In order to attract funds the bank pays customers interest on money deposited with it, and charges interest on money it lends to those who require it. The bank's profit comes from paying a rate of interest to depositors *smaller* than the rate charged to borrowers.

CHARACTERISTICS OF MONEY

From this explanation we can begin to see how important money is to any economy. We have examined what money *does* earlier in this Chapter, but what *is* money? It seems almost too simple to say that money is anything which fulfils the functions of money, but in fact this is so. Over the centuries and throughout the world many different articles have been used as money. This list is almost endless — all sorts of animals, feathers, beans, axeheads, shells, sharks' teeth, metal, stones, decorated paper, cigarettes, chocolate and even pieces of plastic!

Whatever article or commodity is used, it will have certain features that are more or less common throughout time or place.

Acceptability
Money has to be generally acceptable as a means of settling debts between people. Money will only be useful if everyone is confident that, having accepted it in exchange for the goods they wish to sell, they can themselves exchange the money with others for goods and services they wish to purchase. If people begin to lose confidence in their money, their society quickly degenerates to a barter system.

As money developed, it had for a long time a value in itself, quite aside from its exchange value. This was its *intrinsic* value. This is why money in many societies took the form of precious metals such as gold or precious stones such as diamonds. Other commodities such as livestock obviously have an intrinsic value; even today the Masai tribesmen of Africa count their wealth in terms of cattle. Even if the tribesmen stopped accepting cattle in settlement of debts the cattle would still have a use aside from 'money' — they would provide food and skins for their owners.

There have been notable occasions in history when people were reluctant to accept 'official' money. These are two examples:

(i)   in England during Tudor times the paring or clipping of coins — or even the debasing of coins (mixing the gold with a cheaper base metal) — resulted in people being unwilling to accept coins for goods and services.

(ii)   in Germany between the two World Wars a terrible inflation resulted in people refusing to accept German banknotes because they lost value daily. They bought goods immediately and used these goods as money for future purchases. Money in Germany lost its value so fast at one point that it was more effective to burn banknotes to heat a room, than to try and buy coal with the money.

In both cases money was still used. All that happened was the *form* that the money took changed. The official form of money (coins and banknotes) became unacceptable to society and another form, for example cigarettes in Germany, became more acceptable as a means of settling debts.

Homogeneity

Every unit of money must be uniform or identical in every respect (homogeneous) to all other units of money. In Britain, all 50p pieces must look and feel the same and be made of the same metals in the same quantities. All £5 notes must be identical (except for the serial number), and so on.

Why must this be so? Let us look again at the primitive society which uses cattle for money. Unless all the cattle are identical difficulties can arise in exchanges. After all, no two beasts are identical, and arguments could arise between buyer and seller about the cattle; the beast offered in exchange for maize this month may be thinner and less healthy than the one offered last month. Once this happens the 'money' will become less acceptable and people will begin to find alternatives.

Sir Thomas Gresham, the Elizabethan merchant and founder of the Royal Exchange in London, understood the problem of having a non-uniform system of money. Elizabethan England suffered from a metal currency which had been severely clipped and debased. New issues of gold coins of full purity (or fineness) and weight quickly disappeared from circulation. This was because, as Gresham explained to Queen Elizabeth I, people kept the new full-weight coins and continued to pass on the clipped and debased ones. As Gresham pointed out, this was only natural, since the new coins were more valuable.

Gresham's famous 'Law' stated that 'bad money drives out good'. The only way to avoid such a situation was to ensure that *all* units of money were identical.

Divisibility

An efficient system of money must be divisible into different units to cater for transactions of different value. When we consider that today transactions are carried out for amounts varying between a few pence and many millions of pounds the need for units of different value is vital.

Different value units not only allow *exact* amounts of money to be paid but also enable *change* to be given. In modern economies where we use notes and coins this is a simple and straightforward task. But where other types of money are used, such as shells or cattle, the problem of giving change is a major one.

Durability

All things are subject to wear and tear as they are used. An efficient system of money needs to utilise articles that are durable, so as to limit the cost of replacement (in Britain £1 notes were changed to £1 coins precisely for this reason). Foodstuffs and livestock are clearly not ideal units of money because they deteriorate with time. Gold is almost ideal because gold coins can last for centuries with normal use.

Portability

An important characteristic of money is that it should be small and easily carried about. It should combine high value with lightness. Even though modern banknotes are small and light and carry high values (e.g. £50) you would still need considerable quantities of them to make large purchases such as a car or house. Compare this with the cheque — a single piece of paper worth whatever you have in your account, a few pounds or many millions.

However, not all economies have used money which was easily portable. The island of Yap in the South Pacific used stone money often nearly 2 feet in diameter. Although such a system lost out on portability, the 'money' was certainly difficult to steal!

Scarcity

Whatever is being used as money should be relatively scarce, so that it possesses *value*. Value is determined by supply and demand. Generally speaking reductions in supply will lead to increases in price, and vice versa. Take the recent history of oil. In the 1970s and 1980s Saudi Arabia tried to enforce oil agreements on oil producers in two ways. Firstly, it tried reducing supplies of oil onto the market. This forced up oil prices and created massive inflation all over the world. Secondly, more recently, Saudi Arabia has tried the opposite method to obtain an agreement. They have flooded oil onto the market so there is more than people need. This has forced the price of oil right down from $35 a barrel to $10 a barrel.

The same process occurs on the demand side. Increases in demand for a product will increase its price; reductions in demand will reduce its price.

So it is with the supply of and demand for money. Make it too scarce (reduce supply) and its price goes up. Make it too freely available (increase the money supply) and you can, if the supply of goods and services does not rise with it, create inflation. We will be examining this in more detail later when we look at the role of the Bank of England in the economy.

Recognisability

To allow exchanges to take place, money has to be easily recognisable by all who use it. It must be familiar to them so they know the size, shape and feel of all the coins and notes. People will begin to refuse to accept money if they are not certain that they recognise it. People using Scottish banknotes in England often come up against this problem.

The Government always engages in a big publicity campaign whenever it introduces a new coin or banknote. The introduction of decimal currency saw a huge campaign in schools, offices, shops to show people what the new currency would look and feel like. Recent changes such as the £1 coin and £50 note highlight this point. Shape, weight and 'feel' are additionally important for certain groups in society. Coins need to be different shapes (10p and 50p) and weights (2p and £1) and notes different sizes so that blind people for example can recognise them by touch. Some banks have even produced plastic note guides by which a blind person can tell which note he has.

Notes today appear with very intricate designs on specially watermarked paper. This is not only aesthetically pleasing but serves the very useful purpose of making the notes very difficult to forge.

THE FUNCTIONS	THE CHARACTERISTICS	
Store of Value	Security	(scarcity)
Unit of Account	Prevents	(portable)
Medium of Exchange	Unfortunate	(uniform)
Standard of Deferred Payment	Damage	(divisible)
	Robbers	(recognisable)
	Are	(acceptable)
	Dangerous	(durable)

2.1 The Money Make Up

MONEY STABILITY

We have looked at money's functions and in particular its function as a store of wealth. In this section we will see what happens if money becomes unstable in value. We can have variations in money's stability in two ways — inflation, or deflation.

Inflation

We call inflation the situation which occurs when the general level of prices in an economy is rising rapidly. For example, if the prices of goods and services rise by 10% over a given period then, with a given amount of money, a person would be able to purchase 10% *fewer* goods and services at the end of the period than at the beginning. The purchasing power of that person's money has been eroded.

Periods of rapid or high inflation in an economy are said to be bad because of the uncertainty and instability they create. We have already seen that once the functions of money break down people revert to a barter system, and that such a system is unable to produce and maintain a very sophisticated economy — no or little specialisation, no mass production, reduction in choice of goods.

When rapid inflation occurs prices rise so quickly that the business community cannot keep pace. The economy starts to get out of control with prices and wages spiralling to ever higher levels until hyper-inflation is reached. Here money as a medium of exchange begins to collapse as people turn towards holding goods rather than money; the Government finds it difficult to borrow money and its income from taxes falls in value creating a financial crisis which filters through to the rest of the financial system. Such inflation has existed in several (especially South American) countries and has contributed much to their political instability. Britain, along with other European economies, faced alarmingly high levels of inflation (over 25% at one point) in the early 1970s.

There are three possible explanations for inflation.

(i) *Monetarists.* Monetarists believe that inflation occurs because of excessive increases in the money supply. The Government needs to reduce the money supply, thus increasing the value of money and reducing the rate of increase in the prices of goods and services so as to restore the confidence of investors and entrepreneurs. This is carried out by a variety of measures:

— stop printing money
— increase interest rates
— impose lending restrictions on banks
— sell long-dated Government debt.

(ii) *Cost-Push.* This type of inflation occurs when rising production costs push up prices to consumers. Labour costs rise due to scarce skills or strong trade unions utilising negotiating powers to the full; capital costs rise due to changes in interest rates or government policy; and raw material costs may rise due to shortages in the supply industries, inflation in other sectors of the economy, changes in world prices, changes in tastes and fashions, and the weather (agriculture).

(iii) *Demand-Pull.* This occurs when demand for goods and services outstrips the ability of the economy to supply them. Demand exceeds supply. This can be caused by lower interest rates which encourage spending, by changes in taxation giving people more spending power, or by government action to reduce unemployment.

Whatever type of inflation we have it will have important effects:

— Those on fixed incomes such as pensioners, will suffer as the value of their real incomes declines
— It will erode the value of savings
— Rising production costs often result in lower output and rising unemployment
— Debtors tend to gain because they pay back less in real terms
— Creditors tend to lose because they see the real value of the returns they receive falling

Deflation

Deflation is a situation where the general price level is falling. Deflation is typified by falling prices, rising bankruptcies and liquidations, and rising unemployment. It stems largely from demand deficiency within the economy (falling demand relative to supply). Falling demand can be caused by:

— changing tastes and fashions
— falling expectations about future profits exhibited by firms
— Government policy to prevent inflation.

Deflation tends to get worse and worse if left unchecked. Sales fall, so firms cut back on output which results in still lower employment, lower income and fewer sales. It becomes a vicious circle.

One way of recovery is for the Government to intervene to stimulate demand, creating jobs, thus increasing income and boosting sales. Firms take on more labour to meet this extra demand, and so incomes rise and the upward cycle starts again.

Monetary stability

It is important that we know of any variations in the value of money. Without such knowledge it would be impossible for the Government to take action to reduce inflation, stimulate the economy when deflation sets in, and generally to keep the economy stable.

For many years now we have used a system of index numbers to monitor changes in the value of money. A quantity or 'basket' of goods and services are selected which feature most prominently in the average household's list of purchases. Since we do not spend exactly the same amount of money on all goods or services we purchase, a *weighting* has to be given to each of the goods and services in the basket. This weighting is determined by the importance of those goods or services in the overall pattern of the household's expenditure. In order for the index to function all the prices are taken at a base point in time. This is known as the base year (or month or week) and is given the figure 100.

Subsequent changes are worked out via the system of weighting. A figure above 100 illustrates increases in prices and reductions in purchasing power; figures below 100 show falling prices or increases in the amount of goods and services a given amount of money will purchase compared with earlier periods.

Many attempts have been made to construct such indices, some dating back to the beginning of this century. These include:

(i)   *Retail Price Index (RPI)*. This was introduced in January 1974 and included items such as food, clothing, fuel and light, transport and household durables.

(ii)   *Tax and Price Index (TPI)*. This was introduced in 1979 and tried to take into account the effect of direct taxation upon income.

(iii)   *Wholesale Price Index (WPI)*. This attempts to measure changes in the price of materials used in industry. It can be said to be a reasonable predictor of changes in retail prices since changes in the price of materials will be reflected in changes in retail prices after a time-lag.

Although such indices are useful there are certain points to consider:

Size of Sample. A sample number of households is taken. Is the number a representative number?

Contents of basket. The limited number of items in the basket may not accurately reflect the average household's consumption pattern.

Items may become out of date. People change their spending habits over time. New products appear on the market. The index needs to be constantly updated to remain relevant. However, a current index can quickly bear little resemblance to the original. If that happens the index becomes meaningless because it is not comparing the same basket of goods and services.

Limited in Scope. An index may not cover all possible items. The TPI was introduced to show the effect on taxpayers. However, large numbers of people do not pay tax. The more limited in scope an index, the less useful it is.

Weights. Not only do the items have to be regularly updated but the respective weights given to each have to be checked to reflect changing tastes and fashions.

COINS

Precious metals soon became the first form of money used which we can readily recognise today. Metals such as gold and silver had many of the characteristics and carried out many of the functions of those things we regard as money. For example, metals such as gold were always in high demand; gold tended to have a stable price and was easily recognised. It was very durable and so lasted a long time; and, perhaps one of the most important functions, it was readily accepted as a method of paying debts.

Originally these precious metals appeared in the form of bars. Whenever a transaction was carried out the bars had to be weighed and pieces cut off and the weight checked again on scales. We can imagine how difficult and time-consuming this process was. It soon became clear that something smaller and more convenient was needed — and so came about the first coins.

Coins have obvious advantages over metal bars in terms of portability and uniformity. However, there were certain problems which were quickly recognised.

The first one of these concerned purity or, as it was called, 'fineness'. Fineness can be described as the percentage of pure metal to any alloy that is mixed with it. People quickly realised that the economic well-being of their societies depended largely on how sound their currency was. Confidence in the currency was very important — if confidence was lost trade became difficult, even impossible. What was needed, therefore, was some form of guarantee that the coins in circulation were in fact pure gold or pure silver.

This guarantee was usually provided by the ruling monarch. Coins were stamped with the image of the monarch on them to provide this guarantee of purity. It acted as a seal of approval much in the same way as the monarch sealed in wax his imprint on great legal documents. For example, the gold sovereign was guaranteed to be 11/12ths fine. This meant that 11/12ths of the total weight of the coin was made up of gold, the other 12th being made up of an alloy which was mixed with the gold to make it more hardwearing.

Debasement

Basically debasement involves the reduction of the *quantity* of the precious metal in the coin involved. This can be done in several ways:

   (i)   Clipping. Often unscrupulous people, which sometimes included the monarch, began clipping the edges of the gold coins. All these tiny clippings would be collected, melted down and made into new coins. Gradually a solution to this problem was found when edges of coins were milled. This meant that anyone could tell whether a coin had been tampered with or not. These milled edges can still be seen on some of our coins today, notably the 5p and 10p pieces and the new £1 coin. This is an historical note only since the 'silver' coins of today are no longer pure silver. They are in fact 'token coins': the value of the metal involved in making the coin is much less than its face value.

   (ii)   Sweating. This involved reducing the quantity of the precious metal in the coin by using chemicals which corroded it.

(iii)   Abrasion. This involved vigorously shaking gold or silver coins together and collecting the tiny pieces which were rubbed from the coins. This was an extremely time-consuming process and, like the other forms of debasement above, gradually ceased when coins became token money.

(iv)   State Action. Very often in order to pay for very expensive wars monarchs would debase the coinage by reducing the purity or fineness of the coins in circulation. As we have already seen Sir Thomas Gresham had warned Elizabeth I of the dangers of debasing the coinage in this way.

History of coins

Iron bar coinage existed in Britain almost 2,000 years ago. Things soon changed, however, when the Romans invaded Britain and brought with them their own system of coinage. But it was not until the eighth century, long after the Romans had left Britain, that we see the British form of coinage being introduced. This was based on the pound weight of silver. One pound weight of silver could be divided into 240 silver coins. These silver pennies were marked so they could be cut in half (hence the half-penny) and cut into quarters (hence farthing, or fourth-thing). Although the metal changed over the years, the idea that 240 pennies equalled one pound stayed with us for over nine centuries until the introduction of decimal currency in 1971 (when 100 pennies equalled one pound).

Silver remained the principal coinage in circulation in Britain at that time and after 1066 William the Conqueror introduced a new standard, that of sterling silver. Silver was guaranteed to be 925/1000ths pure. It was not until the reign of Henry VIII in the sixteenth century that the gold sovereign was introduced. This gold sovereign was to have a value equivalent to one pound of silver. Charles II introduced the guinea in 1664 and in 1672 the copper penny replaced the silver penny. The silver standard continued to operate until 1816.

The Coinage Act of 1816 saw the sovereign replace the guinea. This formalised the operation of the gold standard and the sovereign became the major currency for settling international debts. The gold standard continued until 1914 when it was suspended due to the outbreak of the First World War (1914-18). Britain returned to the gold standard in 1925 but this eventually broke down in 1931 when Britain came off the gold standard. The price of gold was kept at a fixed level. The Mint would accept gold for coins at a rate of £3 17s 10½d per ounce, 11/12ths fine. This meant that the gold sovereign contained 123.27447 grains of standard gold 11/12ths fine.

Royal Mint

The Royal Mint has been in existence for more than 1,000 years. Originally there were mints all over England, designed to manufacture and supply coins. However, as communications improved over the years the number of mints reduced until by the thirteenth century most minting took place in the Tower of London. There it remained for almost six centuries when it moved, not far away, to premises built on Tower Hill.

Minting only ended at Tower Hill just over ten years ago when the Royal Mint moved to Llantrisant in Wales. The Mint produces up to 2,000,000,000 coins annually, the vast majority of which are exported abroad to the many countries which the Royal Mint supplies. Apart from producing Britain's coins and the coins for nearly seventy countries around the world, the Royal Mint also produces many coins for the collector's market. One third of its sales are in this area.

BANKNOTES

The Goldsmiths

The goldsmiths of the seventeenth century in London became the precursors of the modern day banks. In order to carry out their business, the goldsmiths required very secure premises with vaults in which to store precious metal such as gold. People began asking the goldsmiths to store their surplus gold. This was a convenient, secure and inexpensive way to store valuables.

In return for this service the goldsmiths charged a fee. They would issue the depositor with a *receipt* stating how much gold had been deposited with them. These receipts were in fact *promissory notes*. In other words the receipt was a promise to pay upon demand a certain quantity of gold. When people needed gold for transactions they went along to their goldsmith, handed in the receipt and received the gold in return. They then exchanged the gold for goods and services. The person who had received the gold would then take that and deposit it with *his* goldsmith. In fact, the gold was often deposited with the *same* goldsmith it had been withdrawn from only a few hours earlier. People soon realised that there was no need physically to withdraw and deposit gold time after time in order to settle debts. They began endorsing the back of the receipt from the goldsmith and by doing so handed over the title to the gold to a third party. The third party could then take the receipt along to the goldsmith and receive gold for it in return. This had the advantages that it saved time, and was much less risky.

Very soon the goldsmiths began issuing *notes* for fixed amounts, for example £10, £50, £100, instead of receipts for varying amounts. Also, unlike the original receipts given, these notes were payable to the *bearer* instead of to a named individual. Thus there was no need to endorse the back of the receipt anymore.

The goldsmiths quickly realised that because people were happy to pass round these promissory notes in exchange for debts very little of the gold deposited with them actually left their vaults. The goldsmiths therefore began lending this surplus gold to customers. We will look at this in greater detail later on.

From this time on they were no longer simply goldsmiths — they were bankers.

Growth of banks

From these humble and ordinary beginnings the number of banks in Britain grew until by 1821 there were 781 'country' banks. Many of these banks were issuing their own notes. The main point to remember about this period in the development of the banknote and the bank was the fundamental importance of the *standing* of the bank which issued the note. Anyone who accepted a banker's note in settlement of a debt was in fact relying on the honesty and good business acumen of the banker who issued it. Any loss in confidence that the bank could meet its debts by converting these banknotes into gold upon request, would result in a 'run' on the bank. If the banker had insufficient gold to meet all the demands of people who presented their notes asking for gold, he would then go bankrupt and depositors would lose their money.

Several financial crises occurred between 1800 and 1825, the result of which was the bankruptcy of almost 300 banks. The public demanded control of the note issue. A series of banking acts, for example, the 1844 Bank Charter Act, gradually reduced the powers of the banks to issue their own notes. This helped end the runs on the banks of the early nineteenth century, but also had an extra advantage. The Bank of England had always enjoyed a privileged position in English banking and the placing of the sole responsibility for issuing notes helped formalise its central position in English banking. Its position as sole issuer of banknotes in England and Wales was reached in 1921 when the last private bank, Fox, Fowler and Company, became part of Lloyds Bank.

Fiduciary issue

For a long time Britain operated a 'convertible' banknote system. The banknotes that were issued were backed by gold and were freely convertible on demand into gold. So long as people had confidence in the banks the banknotes were regarded as 'good as gold'. Since Britain left the gold standard in 1931 it has had an inconvertible banknote system. Notes are no longer backed by gold; the promise to pay which can be seen on banknotes today is merely a promise to pay another banknote. Since notes were no longer backed by gold it was pointless maintaining a coinage system which had a high intrinsic value. Gold sovereigns thus went out of use in 1914 and the 'silver' coins, although still minted, no longer contained silver. Cupro-nickel is now used as a substitute for silver. Today, both notes and coins in England and Wales are simply a token currency.

We saw earlier how the goldsmiths quickly realised that, as only a small percentage of the gold deposited with them actually left their vaults, they could lend to people who required money. This was achieved by issuing *more* promissory notes than they had gold to back those notes. This meant that the currency was a 'fractionally backed' currency. In other words, people could take their notes to the banks and have them converted into gold on demand. But if everyone who held notes had gone to the banks at the same time and demanded gold in exchange, the banks could not have met those demands.

As we have seen this system works well so long as people retain confidence in the banknotes that are issued. Thus notes that were issued not backed by gold were issued on trust. This is called a fiduciary issue.

The 1844 Bank Charter Act limited the fiduciary element that the Bank of England could issue to £14 million. The fiduciary element was backed by Government securities and any notes issued above this amount had to be backed fully by gold and silver. The fiduciary amount has gradually been increased over the years. The 1928 Currency and Bank Notes Act allowed a fiduciary issue of £260 million, and this has grown until today when the note issue of around £12 billion is entirely fiduciary. No notes are backed by gold.

MODERN MONEY

Legal tender

Before we examine more closely what constitutes money today, it would be useful to distinguish between legal tender and money. The distinction is this:

(i) Legal tender is any means of payment which must be accepted by law in settlement of a debt.

(ii) Money is anything that is generally acceptable as a method of settling a debt.

We have seen earlier in this chapter the variety of things that have been used as money. Today, cheques are so generally acceptable that they too can almost be regarded as money. The difference between a cheque and a £5 note is that no-one can be *compelled* to accept a cheque as a means of settling a debt but you *are* legally bound to accept a £5 note. To be precise, no-one can refuse to accept a £5 note in the settlement of a debt worth £5. What most of the general public do not realise is that the *exact* money must be given when settling a debt or the seller could refuse to accept it. A £5 note offered to purchase a newspaper could in fact be refused by the newsagent. Not only does a person have to supply the correct amount of legal tender but also has to use the right amount of currency:

> Bank of England notes — up to any amount
> Bronze coins — up to 20p
> Cupro-nickel coins — up to £5
> 50p coins — up to £10
> £1 coins — up to any amount

We can say, therefore, that the £1 coin and banknotes are *unlimited* legal tender, whereas the bronze coins, cupro-nickel coins and 50p coins are all *limited* legal tender.

Bank deposits

When the banks realised how little of the money deposited with them ever left their vaults they began to indulge in a process known as *credit creation*. This will be discussed later, but briefly the banks lent money in excess of what they could actually cover with the money deposited in their vaults. As long as only a few bank customers wanted to take their money out of the bank at any one time, the bank could indulge in this process of credit creation. It was only if a large number of the bank's customers arrived at the same time to withdraw their money that a run on the bank might occur.

Today bank deposits make up by far the largest proportion of the total money supply in the UK economy. For example, in the first quarter of 1986 there were £13 billion worth of notes and coins in circulation. Bank deposits however, totalled a massive £140 billion. This was made up of roughly £51 billion in sight deposits, £69 billion in time deposits, and £20 billion in deposits in other currencies. Bank deposits of today are regarded as money, especially sight deposits. *Sight deposits* are those accounts which can be drawn upon immediately, usually by use of a cheque. It was inevitable that bank accounts would one day become regarded as money, because an account such as a cheque account not only fulfilled many of the functions of money but also had certain advantages over banknotes. These advantages include:

— More convenient to carry than large amounts of notes and coins
— Fewer problems with potential theft
— Safer to post than notes and coins
— Notes and coins could only be obtained from a bank whilst it was open, cheques could be used to make payments outside banking hours. The recent advent of cash dispensers which are available even when the bank is closed has reduced this advantage.

Two things ought to be borne in mind. Bank deposits are not legal tender; no-one can be compelled to accept them in payment of a debt. Second, whereas the bank deposit is regarded as money the cheque is not. The cheque is in essence an *order* from someone who has a deposit with a bank to his bank to pay over a specified sum of money from his account to a named third party. The cheque therefore is merely a *claim* to the money — not money itself.

Near/quasi-money

A range of assets exist which do not fulfil all the functions of money. These are known as near or quasi-money. The distinction between money and near money hinges on the word *liquidity*. Liquidity can be defined as the ease with which an asset can be converted into cash without significant loss of interest or capital. Notes and coins are therefore 100% liquid. Sight or demand deposits (cheque account) are also regarded as liquid.

Let us look at some of those items which are regarded as near or quasi-money.

(i) Time deposits. These are deposits where a period of notice has to be given before withdrawals are made, usually seven days. Withdrawals within seven days can often be made, however, but it usually involves a loss of interest on that money. This time factor coupled with the loss of interest firmly place this asset in the category of near money.

(ii) Building Society deposits. These accounts are in the name of the account holder only; they cannot be transferred to third parties. The only way this form of account can be used to settle debts is for the account holder to turn that account into cash and pay the third party with that cash.

(iii) Bills of exchange. The use of bills of exchange pre-dated the use of cheques as money and was used widely in trade and commerce. The bill of exchange is used mainly today in foreign trade. A manufacturer in England buying machinery from a German supplier could pay for it with a bill of exchange. This is *a promise to pay on a specified date a certain sum of money.* Upon delivery of the goods or at a certain time specified afterwards the bill would be presented to the importer's bank for payment. To reduce the possibility of default these bills were often underwritten by a merchant bank who thus guaranteed payment to the foreign supplier. Such bills are not generally acceptable by the public and therefore cannot be regarded as money.

(iv) Postal orders. These are used to make payments between two people. However, they have to be bought with money and, upon receipt, converted back into money.

(v) Stocks and shares. Although stocks and shares can often be accepted as a method of settling debts the conversion of those stocks and shares into cash may involve loss,

since the price of stocks and shares can go down as well as up.

(vi) Savings stamps. Savings stamps can be used to settle certain forms of debts e.g. TV Licences. This acceptability is obviously only very limited.

(vii) Premium bonds. Premium bonds are registered in the name of the holder and so cannot be passed on and encashed by third parties.

(viii) Luncheon vouchers. Only certain shops will accept luncheon vouchers in payment for food. They lack therefore general acceptability, and their conversion into cash is severely limited.

Plastic money

It was once thought, about 20 years ago, that the introduction of plastic cards would gradually replace cash altogether. Although these cards have in fact replaced cash as a method of payment in many cases, notes and coins are likely to be used for small purchases for some time to come.

Plastic money takes several forms. Below are listed some of the plastic cards that have had a significant impact.

(i) Cheque Guarantee Card. These cards were first issued in Britain in the mid-sixties by the commercial banks. They were used to guarantee payment of cheques up to a value of £30. This limit has subsequently been increased and now cheque guarantee cards guarantee cheques up to £50 per cheque. This makes the cheque more acceptable to shops because the shopkeeper knows that payment of the cheque is guaranteed by the bank.

(ii) Credit Card. These cards are issued by the banks to enable customers to purchase goods and services at certain specified shops, hotels, restaurants and so on. A statement is sent every month and the customer then has the option of paying off the total amount outstanding or paying off the amount over a period of time. If the second option is chosen the customer pays a rate of interest on the amount outstanding. The two main cards which exist at the moment are Access and Visa.

Not all shops accept these cards; those which do, carry the relevant symbol on the door of the shop. The network of outlets which accept credit cards is however fairly extensive — well over 200,000 in the UK alone. The recent trend has been for credit cards to be used for more than one function, e.g. for use with ATMs. TSB Trustcards and Barclaycards can be used as both credit cards and cheque guarantee cards.

(iii) Bank Cash Card. These cards are issued by the banks to enable customers to obtain cash from dispensers. These cash dispensers are situated inside and outside the banks (through the wall machines). They function not only while the bank is open but also outside banking hours. Modern machines supply other services as well as dispensing cash and we shall be looking at these in a later section.

(iv) Charge Card. Charge cards (or as they are sometimes known entertainment and travel cards) are like bank credit cards but have a slightly more specialised use.

The two most famous ones are Diners Club and American Express. The Diners Club card was first introduced into the UK in 1951. There are over 250,000 of these cards in the UK today. American Express was introduced in England in 1963. It has presently over 750,000 cards in the UK.

Like credit card companies, the charge card companies levy a commission on the outlets which accept their cards. However, charge cards differ in several respects from credit cards. When you receive your statement from the charge card company the whole of the amount of the statement is due for payment. Second, charge cards have an enrolment fee in order to join, and lastly there is usually a membership fee.

(v) Shop Credit Cards. These cards are issued by individual companies such as John Lewis, Fenwicks, and Marks & Spencer so that customers can make purchases within their stores without having to use cash.

An application for one of these cards is made by simply filling in a form which can be obtained from the shop. For example, the Marks & Spencer card, known as Chargecard, can be obtained by filling in details such as name, address, occupation, gross income, credit limits requested, and bank details. When you receive the card you can use that card to purchase anything that Marks & Spencer sell including food. You have an agreed credit limit and, as with bank credit cards, have 25 days after the receipt of your monthly statement to pay the amount outstanding. Alternatively you can make payments over a period of months. Interest is charged at so much per month on outstanding balances. Cards such as these make purchasing very easy indeed, easier even than writing a cheque.

A monthly statement keeps you up to date as to what you owe. However, outstanding balances are charged at a fairly high Annual Percentage Rate (APR). If large amounts are left outstanding for any long period of time it may be cheaper to obtain a personal loan from a bank than to use this method of credit. Even if you wish to spread payments over a period of time there is a minimum which must be paid every month, usually 5% of the outstanding balance or £10 whichever is the greater.

The following are the main users of Visa, Access and store cards:

Visa	*Access*
Bank of Scotland	Bank of Ireland
Barclaycard	Clydesdale
Cooperative Bank	Midland
Girobank	Lloyds
Lloyds	NatWest
Robert Fleming/Save & Prosper	Royal Bank of Scotland
Standard Chartered	
TSB Trustcard	

Store cards

Boots	John Lewis
Burton Group	Littlewoods
Debenhams	Marks & Spencer
House of Fraser	Sears

One interesting recent development is that Lloyds Bank, who were one of the original Access banks, have also joined Visa. One possible reason for this is that Lloyds would be issuing their own debit card similar to the Barclays Connect card and, as Visa merchants should accept the Connect card, Lloyds may feel that launching their own card under the Visa banner would be easier than starting a new launch through Access.

(vi) Discount Cards. These cards, such as the Countdown card, offer discounts on a wide range of goods and services when the card is shown at the time of purchase. The customer receives a booklet containing a list of names and addresses of all the shops, restaurants and other outlets which participate in the scheme.

(vii) Eurocheque Card. These cards are used by customers who are going abroad, in conjunction with a book of Eurocheques. The card carries the distinctive EC symbol and is used like a normal cheque guarantee card. There are over 29 million in circulation. It has three main uses: a customer can

(1) obtain cash at over 200,000 branches in 39 countries,

(2) make payments at over 5 million retail outlets all of which carry the symbol, and

(3) obtain cash and other services through a newly established ATM network both at home and abroad.

SUMMARY

DEVELOPMENT OF MONEY
- Early man had to be self-sufficient.
- Grouping into primitive societies resulted in trade developing.
- Exchanges took the form of one good for another, in other words barter.
- Barter was limiting because it
  — relied on both parties having exactly what each other wanted in correct quantities (double coincidence of wants)
  — caused problems by fixing the exchange rate of one good for another
  — caused a problem of giving change
  — caused a problem in relation to perishable goods.
- Money developed to solve these problems and make exchanges more efficient.

MONEY
- Is anything which is generally accepted as a method of settling debts.
- To be called money the item must fulfil certain *functions:*
  — *medium of exchange* — efficient method by which we can exchange one good for another

- — *unit of account* — acts as a measurement of value so we can compare prices of all goods and services
- — *store of value* — money, unlike perishable goods, can be kept for future purchases thus increasing the freedom of choice of the individual
- — *standard of deferred payment* — enables society to have a system of credit — goods bought in one period can be paid for in another.
- ● Whatever is used, money will be distinguishable by some or all of the following *characteristics:*
  - — *generally acceptable* — maintained by confidence in money fulfilling its functions
  - — *uniform* — all money of similar value is identical
  - — *divisible* so that transactions of varying value can be catered for — enables change to be given
  - — *durable* to give sense of permanence and enhance confidence
  - — *portable* so that it can be easily carried to where the transactions take place
  - — *scarce* — its relative rarity gives money its value
  - — *recognisable,* otherwise people would refuse to accept it.
- ● Money must be *stable in value* over time.
- ● *Inflation* is a general increase in the prices of goods and services in society
  - — various types: excess money supply, cost-push, demand-pull
  - — whatever type it has important effects on:
    fixed-income earners (pensioners)
    value of savings
    employment
    debtors
    creditors
- ● *Deflation* is a general fall in the prices of goods and services in society typified by
  - — falling output
  - — rising unemployment
  - — rising bankruptcies
- ● Monetary stability is measured by use of an index. The price of a basket of 'typical' goods is checked over time and changes in prices are reflected by changes in the index number. Examples of an index: Retail Price Index (RPI), Tax and Price Index (TPI).

HISTORY OF COINS AND BANKNOTES

- ● *Coins*
  - — Coins developed from the use of *bars of precious metals* which were bulky and inconvenient to use.
  - — Confidence was maintained by the ruler stamping his image on coins to guarantee their purity *(fineness).*
  - — Problems arose due to *debasement* of coinage, i.e. reduction in volume of previous metal in the coin.
  - — This occurred by clipping, sweating, abrasion, and state action.

— *Sterling* silver standard established by William the Conqueror, guaranteed purity (925/1000ths pure).
— Coinage Act 1816 established the *gold standard,* and the sovereign became the major currency for settling international debts.
— Britain left the gold standard in 1914, returned temporarily in 1925 and left it permanently in 1931.
— The *Royal Mint* is the sole issuer of coins in England and Wales.

● *Banknotes*
— Banknotes developed from London *goldsmiths' receipts* given to customers who deposited valuables for safekeeping.
— These receipts were soon passed on to third parties to settle debts (by *endorsing* the receipt).
— This was more convenient and safer than taking gold out of the goldsmiths' vaults.
— Receipts soon issued to *bearer* for fixed amounts. Therefore, no more need for endorsement.
— By lending surplus gold the goldsmiths became *bankers.*
— Rapid *expansion* of the banks occurred throughout the nineteenth century.
— Banks issued more *promissory notes* than were backed by gold.
— The issue of notes not backed by gold was called a *fiduciary* issue.
— Money today is all fiduciary — *none* of it is backed by gold.
— *Runs* on the banks due to lack of confidence prompted government action.
— 1844 Bank Charter Act restricted fiduciary issue of Bank of England to £14m.

MODERN MONEY

● *Legal Tender*
— Anything which by law must be accepted in the settlement of a debt.
    Debtors have a responsibility to present the correct amount
    Limits to quantity of certain denominations acceptable (bronze 20p, cupro-nickel £5, 50p pieces £10).

● *Bank Deposits*
— Most money is in the form of bank deposits (£13 billion notes and coin, £140 billion bank deposits).
— This has resulted because of *credit creation,* and the use of *cheques* as a method of settling debts.
— Bank deposits are money but *not* legal tender.
— The cheque is not money but a claim on money (bank deposit).

● *Near Money*
— Assets which perform *some* of the functions of money but not all.
— Examples:
    Time deposits (bank and building society)
    Bills of exchange

Postal orders
Stocks and shares
Savings stamps
Premium Bonds
Luncheon vouchers

● *Plastic Money*
— Developed to make payments *easier* or to provide *specialist* services.
— Examples:
Cheque guarantee card
Credit card
Cash card
Charge card
Shop credit card
Discount card
Eurocheque card
— Some designed to replace carrying cash or cheques (credit cards).
— Others enable cash withdrawals (and access to other services) outside banking
hours.

CHECK OUT QUESTIONS

1. Define money
2. What is barter?
3. How did barter develop?
4. What is meant by 'a double coincidence of wants'?
5. List two other disadvantages of barter.
6. Name three items which have been used as money.
7. List four functions of money.
8. List six characteristics of money.
9. Define inflation.
10. Define deflation.
11. What is meant by demand-pull inflation?
12. Give two consequences of inflation.
13. Give two consequences of deflation.
14. How do you measure the stability of money over time?
15. Give an example.
16. What is fineness?
17. What coin was 11/12ths fine?
18. Define debasement.
19. Give two examples of debasement.
20. How did goldsmiths develop into bankers?
21. How were goldsmiths' receipts passed to third parties?
22. What was a 'run' on a bank?
23. What is meant by a fiduciary issue?

24. What Act limited this to £14 million?
25. Define legal tender.
26. Why is a cheque not legal tender?
27. What is the difference between sight and time deposits?
28. What is quasi money?
29. Give an example of a charge card.
30. How do charge cards differ from bank credit cards?

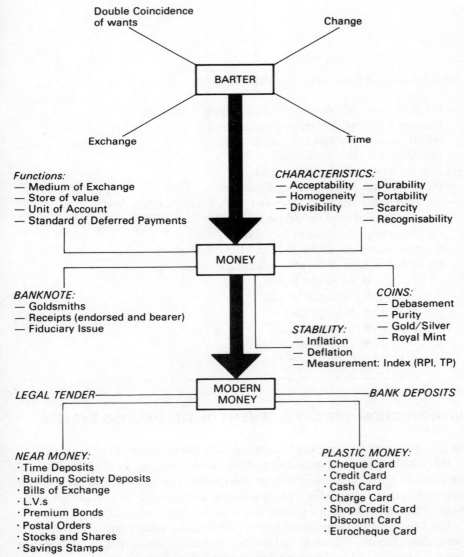

2.2 From Barter to Modern Money

3

Development of the Banking System

On completion of this chapter you will know:

— the main financial institutions which operate in the City.
— the main functions of these institutions.
— which financial markets exist in the City.
— how the retail banks developed.
— how the banks can "create" credit.
— the major Acts which have regulated bank activity.
— the main items which are contained in the banks' balance sheet.
— how the Bank of England developed.
— the functions of the Bank of England.
— the main provisions of the 1979 and 1987 Banking Acts.
— the main functions of the other main banks including:
  - Merchant Banks
  - Discount Houses
  - Foreign Banks
  - Overseas Banks
  - Consortium Banks

INTRODUCTION: THE DEVELOPMENT OF THE BANKING SYSTEM

In this chapter we will be examining the growth and development of banking.

When we hear someone mention "the City" we immediately think of "banks" and the picture we imagine is one of the high street banks. The high street banks are indeed prevalent in the "Square Mile" which makes up the City of London and all have their head offices there but such a picture would be too simple and misleading.

The City is a vast complicated network of financial institutions all carrying out particular functions. We saw in the previous chapter that specialisation had important benefits for society. The City institutions have developed specialisation to a very high degree of sophistication. The high street banks perform a wide range of services, but some financial institutions offer only a very limited number of services to only a few customers.

In this chapter we will define and differentiate these institutions and their functions and look at their relationship to one another.

Such a vast array of different institutions needs effective supervision to protect borrowers and lenders, and to regulate activity according to certain rules and practices.

This is the role undertaken by the Bank of England. The Bank of England has, since its inception, held a very special place in British banking. Later in this chapter we will see how the Bank of England watches over the whole financial network.

First of all, let us look briefly at the composition of the money markets in order to obtain an overview of the UK financial system, and in particular:

— the financial institutions which comprise the money markets;
— the various markets themselves;
— the commodities (known as financial instruments) bought and sold in these markets.

FINANCIAL INSTITUTIONS

Just like any market, there are many different institutions carrying out different functions. Very often the names can be confusing. For example, the high street banks, retail banks, clearing banks, joint stock commercial banks are, with one or two exceptions, all names for the same banks — Lloyds, Barclays, National Westminster, Midland, the TSB, Yorkshire Bank, and Co-operative Bank.

However, no matter what name we give to "banks" they all perform the same basic function: they provide a link between borrowers and lenders, those who have surplus money they do not wish to spend immediately and those who do not have surplus money and wish to borrow. Basically, by charging a rate of interest to borrowers slightly higher than they pay to lenders, the banks make their profit. This is known as financial intermediation.

Lord Wilson, the ex-Prime Minister, headed a committee which investigated the workings of the financial system. His committee reported: "The financial system is a complex network embracing payments mechanisms and the borrowing and lending of funds. Though they also have other important functions, the key role played by the financial institutions in the system . . . is to act as financial intermediaries channelling funds from those with income in excess of their needs to those wishing to borrow."

To understand how and why they do this is crucial to an understanding of why banks exist.

If I wish to borrow some money I can either borrow directly from a member of my family or a friend, or use a financial intermediary (a bank). Why is it better to use financial intermediaries?

(a)   They have access to large amounts of deposits and so have funds available when required by borrowers.

(b)   They minimise the risk of loss if the borrower does not repay the loan. They can do this because of their large reserves.

(c)   Large scale operations. The financial intermediaries operate on a very large scale and so gain economies of scale, enabling them to pass on savings to borrowers.

(d)   Maturity transformation. Lenders often want fairly immediate access to their deposits. Borrowers often want to borrow for long periods of time. Unless there were financial intermediaries this problem could not be overcome. Deposits are made daily by millions of people and organisations. Financial intermediaries use their skill to make long term loans to customers, keeping enough liquid assets on hand to meet the demands of depositors.

Today, banks are divided into two main categories — Bank Financial Intermediaries (BFIs) and Non-Bank Financial Intermediaries (NBFIs). The BFIs are often referred to as *primary banks* and the NBFIs as *secondary banks*. The general distinction between the two is that the primary banks provide a money transmission service (discussed in later chapters) whilst the secondary banks concentrate on term deposits.

Financial intermediaries include:

	Commercial Banks
BFIs	The TSB
	National Girobank
	National Savings Bank
	Other Banks
	Building Societies
	Finance Houses
NFBIs	Insurance Companies
	Pension Funds
	Unit Trust Companies
	Investment Trust Companies

The 1979 Banking Act attempted to define "banks" more closely when a distinction was made between

(i)   Recognised Banks and
(ii)   Licensed Deposit Takers (LDTs)

Under this definition banks such as Barclays, Lloyds, National Westminster and Midland are "recognised Banks" and Unit Trust and Investment Trust companies are LDTs. Certain institutions listed above fall into neither category; these are exempt from the provisions of the 1979 Act — building societies, National Girobank, National Savings Bank, insurance companies, pension funds and the Banking Department of the Bank of England.

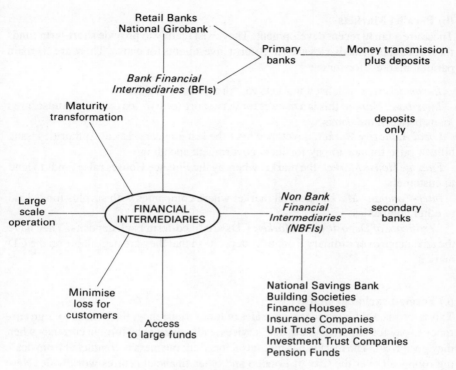

3.1 Financial Intermediaries

MONEY MARKETS

However complicated and strange the money markets seem, they all perform the same function — they are the means whereby buyers and sellers are brought together in order to transact business, to buy and to sell. The main difference between a money market and, say, a vegetable market is that the commodity "bought" and "sold" on the former is money.

For the sake of simplicity the markets for money can be divided into two sections, Short Term Money Markets, and Long Term Capital Markets.

Short-term money markets

There are four main short-term markets for money:

(a) Discount Market

This market is operated by the Discount Houses in conjunction with the banks and the Bank of England. It involves the discounting of commercial bills and purchases of the government's Treasury Bills through the Bank of England. We will be examining the relationship between the Discount Houses and Bank of England in more detail later in this chapter.

(b) Parallel Markets

These are a fairly recent development. They exist mainly to provide short-term funds for financial intermediaries and short-term investments for banks. There are six main parallel markets for funds:

Euromarkets: specialised markets for foreign currency funds.

Inter-bank Market: this is a market for very short-term (often overnight) unsecured loans between the banks.

Local Authority Market: developed over the last 30 years. Local Authorities issue bills to raise finance to pay for local government spending.

Finance House Market: the market whereby the Finance Houses raise funds to lend to customers.

Inter-Company Market: a small market where companies with surplus funds lend to other companies.

Certificate of Deposit (CD) Market: CDs are fixed-term bank deposits. They have the advantage over ordinary bank time deposits in that they are negotiable on the CD market.

(c) Foreign exchange market

This is the market for purchases and sales of foreign currency. Firms need foreign currency to pay for imported goods and services; individuals need foreign currency when they go abroad. The market has no central location; business is conducted from dealing rooms all over the City of London and other financial centres worldwide (New York, Paris, Rome, Hong Kong). Although there are independent dealers, most operate from within the banks.

(d) London International Financial Futures Exchange (LIFFE)

This market is one of the more recent developments in the London money markets. Opened in 1982 it exists to provide a market for "financial futures". This is where transactions occur *today* in deals to purchase finance at a fixed price at some *future* date. Since interest rates vary over time, people saw the opportunity of smoothing out changes in interest rates by providing fixed interest rates on future loans.

Just as dealers on the commodity markets (wheat, coffee, tin) speculate as to the future price of commodities, so LIFFE dealers speculate on the future price of finance. This enables firms to borrow now without having to worry whether interest rates will rise six or nine months from now.

Long-term capital markets — Stock Exchange

The main mechanism through which long-term capital is raised is the Stock Exchange.

At any one time the Government, industry and commerce need huge amounts of capital. The Government needs funds to finance its projects. Very often taxation does not produce all the money when it is needed. When this happens the Government must borrow. This is also done at local government level.

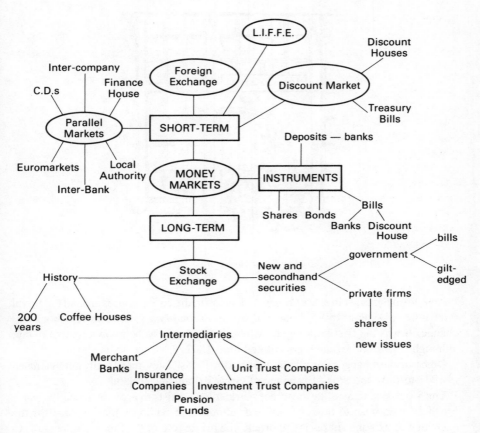

3.2 The Money Markets

Equally, industry and commerce need to raise capital

- to start up
- to expand
- to carry out research

The Stock Exchange exists to bring together those with funds to invest, and those who need such capital. The Stock Exchange has been in existence for over 200 years. In the 18th century trading was something of an adventure, involving sending cargo ships to distant lands.

Various merchants would take 'shares' in an enterprise and divide up the profits at the end of the voyage. Gradually, merchants realised that it was not necessary, at the end of such a venture, to break up the association. If there was a way in which the original backers could get their money back (i.e. by selling their 'share' to someone else) the association, or company, could carry on.

3.3 New Jonathan's Coffee House

An informal market in shares began to develop in the coffee houses around the Royal Exchange in London. In 1773 one of them, *New Jonathan's,* became The Stock Exchange. It was the first building anywhere in the world to be known by that name, although it was not formally constituted until 1802.

Other local exchanges grew up throughout the British Isles; they finally amalgamated in 1973 to form the Stock Exchange of Great Britain and Ireland.

The Stock Exchange, like any other marketplace, exists to provide a meeting place for those who wish to buy and sell and, although providing a marketplace for the exchange of existing shares is important, the prime role of the Stock Exchange is to allow companies to raise money from investors. This role has been highlighted by the Government's privatisation of companies such as British Telecom, British Gas, Rolls Royce, British Airports Authority, and BP.

The Exchange's main functions today are to

- enable new capital to be raised through the issue of new 'securities' (i.e. stocks and shares);
- facilitate the transfer of existing stocks and shares between buyers and sellers.

Once a company has raised money through the initial issue of its shares the fluctuations in the price of its secondhand shares are not of great short-term significance as they do not receive any more money simply because a trade has taken place in the shares.

The great benefit to companies of this secondhand market is that it guarantees that shareholders can always sell their shares at a price on the market without having to seek out a buyer. Shareholders always know what their shares are worth as the price of each quoted company share is given each day in the financial pages of the newspapers.

Without this secondhand market companies could find that raising money by selling shares to the public could be very difficult indeed.

The Big Bang

In October 1986 the City of London in general, and the Stock Exchange in particular, underwent a major change in the way that it transacted its business. This change was known as the *Big Bang*. Prior to this event, if a customer wanted to deal in shares they had to ask a Stockbroker to arrange for the shares to be bought. The Stockbroker could not go direct to the Stock Exchange floor but had to instruct a Jobber to buy (or sell) the shares. Stockbrokers could not act as Jobbers and vice versa. In addition, commissions charged on these transactions were on a fixed scale which meant that competition was limited.

The system introduced in 1986 did away with fixed commissions and the restriction that a firm could only act as Broker or Jobber. Each member firm of the Stock Exchange could now be

— a *market maker*, who must quote and deal in a list of shares, i.e. act as a jobber
— an *agency broker*, who carries out the function of stockbroking
— a *dealer/broker*, who combines the above functions.

One other major change of the Big Bang was that the barriers to entry into the market were lifted, allowing banks and other financial intermediaries to deal direct in stocks and shares. The result of this was a series of acquisitions, mergers and takeovers of stockbrokers and jobbers to form big new financial houses, many of whom set up computerised dealing rooms to allow them to deal away from the floor of the Stock Exchange, e.g. Barclays de Zoete Wedd (BZW), which was formed by Barclays Bank merging activities with de Zoete (stockbrokers) and Wedd Durlacher (jobbers). This move was helped by the introduction of the Stock Exchange Automated Quotation service, which records all deals through a computer.

A further significant change took place in the dealings in British Government Stock, whereby the Bank of England now deals with gilt market makers who are mainly banks. These market makers have *lender of last resort* access to the Bank and this, plus some other changes, has had an impact on the operation of the *Discount Houses* (see pages 53−4).

RETAIL BANKS

As we have seen, retail banks have several different names. Not all the retail banks are clearers (members of the Committee of London & Scottish Bankers. Not all the retail banks are joint stock commercial banks (plcs or public limited companies), for example National Girobank. Nor were all the retail banks recognised banks under the terms of the 1979 Banking Act (National Girobank was exempt).

This apparent confusion can hopefully be dispelled if we look at the basic *functions* offered by these organisations. What links all these banks is that they offer:

- payments services — especially cheque facilities, standing orders, direct debits.
- deposit services — a range of bank deposits available for customers in which to store part or all of their wealth.
- lending facilities — to provide loans or credit for customers wishing to make purchases large and small.

These functions, and especially payments services, distinguish the high street or retail banks from others such as merchant banks. Other distinguishing features are the large branch networks which the high street banks have — some 12,000 branches in England and Wales alone — and their emphasis on retail lending to individuals and small businesses.

These retail banks are enormously important in the British economy. Their range of services is extensive and growing — moving into related financial areas rather than 'pure' banking, as witness Lloyds Bank's recent move into estate agency.

They have formed large financial groups by setting up, merging with, or taking over institutions providing related services — among them merchant banks, insurance brokers, unit trust companies and leasing companies.

The banks today have between them

- 30 million customers
- deposits of more than £140 billion
- more than 330,000 employees

How did the banks come to be such large institutions?

History of retail banks

We have seen in the previous chapter how money developed and how the goldsmiths were the forerunners of modern banks. Goldsmiths' receipts became the first banknotes; depositors could issue notes instructing the goldsmiths to pay a certain amount of gold to third parties. This prompted the advent of the modern cheque.

The goldsmiths saw that, because of the use of their receipts and their customers' confidence in the system, little gold ever actually left their vaults. The goldsmiths could lend this gold at a rate of interest to others by issuing more notes. As long as all noteholders did not arrive at the same time and demand gold for their notes, there was enough gold to meet the day-to-day demands of those few customers who actually wanted gold from the vaults.

This process is known as *credit creation*. A simple example will illustrate the point. Let us assume that there is only one goldsmith, with initial deposits of £1000. Let us also assume that money not being used for transactions (i.e. savings) is deposited with the goldsmith. Finally let us assume that only 10% of the gold in the vaults is ever taken out at any one time. The goldsmith's initial balance sheet would look like this:

Liabilities		*Assets*	
Deposits (gold)	£1000	Gold coins	£1000
	£1000		£1000

Knowing that only £100 (10%) of the gold will be taken out of the vault, the goldsmith can now lend the *other* £900 to someone else and charge him interest on the loan. Such a person arrives on his doorstep and negotiates a loan of £900. The balance sheet now looks like this:

Liabilities		Assets	
Deposits (gold)	£1000	Gold coins	£100
		Loans	£900
	£1000		£1000

The customer takes the £900 of gold and spends it. The person who receives the gold goes to the goldsmith and deposits the £900 of gold. The balance sheet now looks like this:

Liabilities		Assets	
Deposits (gold)	£1000	Gold coins	£100
Deposits (gold)	£900	Gold coins	£900
		Loans	£900
	£1900		£1900

Of this new deposit of £900 the goldsmith needs to keep £90 (10% available for over the counter transactions) but can lend the remaining £810.

This process will continue even further, until the balance sheet looks like this:

Liabilities		Assets	
Deposits (gold)	£10 000	Gold coins	£1000
		Loans	£9000
	£10 000		£10 000

The goldsmith has 'created' £9000 worth of credit from an initial deposit of £1000. Checking back we can see that he still has 10% of his total assets in the form of gold coin for withdrawal from the vaults.

Even if there were hundreds of goldsmiths, and each loan was spent and deposited with a different goldsmith, the process of credit creation would continue just the same.

It was this ability to create credit, and earn extra interest, which led to the great expansion of banking in the 18th and 19th centuries. Throughout the 18th century the development of banks took two forms:

- London banks
- Private country banks

Modern banking had begun in London with the goldsmiths, but two factors had limited their expansion:

- poor transport and communications;
- the Bank of England Act 1709 which restricted banks other than the Bank of England to partnerships with no more than six partners.

Banks outside London, the country banks, were formed in provincial cities by local merchants, issuing their own notes. By 1750 there were a dozen or so of these country banks.

The period 1750-1850 saw a tremendous expansion in industrialisation in Britain (the 'Industrial Revolution'). As industry expanded the factory system and towns grew rapidly, producing a greater demand for finance. In the fifty years from 1750 the number of country banks grew to over 700.

However, individual banks overstretched themselves by expanding their fiduciary issue of notes through this credit creation process. The early years of the 19th century saw an alarming number of bank failures after a succession of runs on various banks.

To restore confidence in the banking system, a series of Acts were passed to bring more control and regulation. The most important of these were:

(a) Bank Act 1826

This Act allowed banks to become joint-stock banks but only 65 miles or more from London. This strengthened the privileged position of the Bank of England which continued to be the only joint-stock bank in the City.

(b) Bank Charter Act 1833

Under increasing pressure from London banks, the government extended the principle of joint-stock banking to banks in London. Banks could operate within the former 65-mile radius with joint stock status, but by doing so forfeited their right to issue notes. This was not such a blow since the system of credit creation enabled banks to expand their scale of activities.

(c) Bank Charter Act 1844

By 1844 there were 105 joint-stock banks; the 1844 Act further restricted the note-issuing powers of the banks. All new banks or amalgamations of banks lost the right to issue notes. The Act also limited the Fiduciary Issue by the Bank of England to £14m. Note issues over £14m had to be backed by gold and silver at the Bank of England.

(d) Companies Act 1862

This Act provided for limited liability for banks. In the event of the bank being unable to meet its debts the shareholders were only liable for a limited amount, the amount they originally invested in the company.

(e) Bills of Exchange Act 1882

This Act was an important stage in the development of banking: it codified the law relating to bills of exchange and cheques, and established a means of protection for banks and customers against theft or fraud.

This legislation enabled the process of growth to continue throughout the century. By 1866 there were 154 joint-stock banks with 850 branches compared with 246 private banks with 376 branches. By 1900 the joint-stock banks had 3757 branches compared with only 19 private banks.

Amalgamations took place in the joint-stock banks. In 1900 there were 77 and by 1914 there were 16 clearing banks, this reducing to 11 by 1920. The inter-war years (1918-39) saw the banks concentrating on developing their branch network structure.

The 1960s saw the advent of 'mergermania'. The Labour Government (1964-70) encouraged the growth of organisations to compete with large multi-national firms. British Leyland, for example, was formed from a series of mergers and takeovers of smaller car firms. The banks followed suit; by 1968 we had the emergence of the 'Big Four' after the merger of National Provincial and Westminster Banks (Barclays, Lloyds, Midland, National Westminster). Another 'super-merger' in 1968, that between Barclays, Lloyds and Martins, was referred to the Monopolies Commission which turned down the proposal, though it agreed that either Barclays or Lloyds could take over Martins (Barclays did).

Since the 1960s the banks have consolidated their position and extended their range of services so that they act as 'financial supermarkets' — all the financial services a customer could want being within one organisation.

The last twenty years has seen the growth of other banks, most notably the TSB, Co-operative, National Girobank and Yorkshire Bank (owned by Barclays, Lloyds, National Westminster and Williams and Glyn's).

Bank balance sheet

To get a general picture of the main areas of the retail banks' operations, and the scale of their activities, we need to look at their balance sheet. Basically, any balance sheet comprises two sections:

● Liabilities
● Assets

The liabilities show what the bank owes to others, whilst the assets are what, in the main, others owe to the bank. As they are in fact opposite sides of the same coin the two will always balance.

Like any organisation a bank needs to make a profit if it is to continue and grow. We mentioned earlier that banks make a profit by charging more to people who wish to borrow than they pay to people who deposit money with them. But successful banking is not simply about lending as much money as possible. As we have seen from earliest times they needed to protect themselves against a run on the bank by holding cash (liquid assets) in their vaults in order to meet the demands of depositors.

Banks are therefore faced with 'liquidity/profitability' dilemma. On the one hand they must keep some of their assets in liquid forms such as cash. On the other, they have to make a profit. The most profitable form of lending is long-term loans (advances) but of course they are the least liquid.

The banks, therefore, have to monitor their balance sheets carefully to achieve the correct balance between liquid assets (such as cash in the tills, which does not earn any profit for the bank), and profits for growth from very illiquid assets such as advances. They do this by having a sliding scale of assets — a whole range of assets which vary from totally liquid (cash) to totally illiquid (advances). If they are faced with increased demands for cash by customers, the banks can convert their assets into more liquid forms by, for example, calling in loans from the Discount Market which are instantly repayable.

Let us list the main items of the retail banks' balance sheet:

(a) Liabilities

The liabilities side of the balance sheet can be divided into two main sections, Capital/Reserves, and Deposits.

Capital and Reserves represents the money which the bank owes to its shareholders. The capital is the money which has been raised by issuing shares; reserves represent the money which has been built up from previous profits and not distributed to shareholders.

Deposits. There are four main types of deposit which make up this element of the balance sheet:

1. *Sight Deposits.* These are mainly current accounts. They are often called *demand deposits* because they are payable on demand to the account holder.
2. *Time Deposits.* These are all those accounts which require notice of withdrawal before a customer has access.
3. *Certificates of Deposit.* These are deposits for a fixed term, and for large amounts. They are payable to the bearer and, therefore, have a very good second-hand value.
4. *Foreign Currency Deposits.* Since controls on the holding of foreign currency by individuals and companies were ended in 1979 these deposits have grown; people and firms buy and hold foreign currency to take advantage of favourable exchange rates.

(b) Assets

The assets of the retail banks can be divided into the following:

Notes and Coin. This item refers to the amount of notes and coin kept in the banks' tills for over-the-counter transactions. Currently the banks hold £2.3 billion. This money earns no profit for the bank; they naturally like to keep as little as possible in this form.

Balances with the Bank of England. These are kept mainly to settle differences between the banks which occur through the clearing system (£477m for example in March 1988). Again, like cash in the tills, these balances earn no profit for the banks; this is why they are relatively small. Banks also maintain other balances (cash ratio deposits), explained more fully when we look at the Bank of England later in this chapter.

Market Loans. These loans are made to the money markets for short periods of time and are very easily turned into cash. They can be 'at call' (overnight) or 'short notice' (up to 14 days) to the Discount Houses, to local authorities, on the CD Market, overseas, or the inter-bank market. Currently figures for each are as follows:

Discount Houses	£5.9 billion
Inter-Bank	£18.4 billion
C.D.s	£3.8 billion
Local Authorities	£0.9 billion
Overseas	£4.0 billion

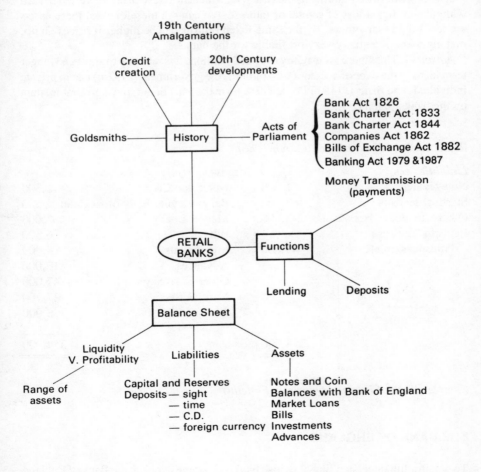

3.4 The Retail (high street) Banks

Since they are issued for short periods of time they earn some interest for the banks whilst retaining a high degree of liquidity should the need to obtain cash arise.

Bills. These are very liquid, short term, and secure. Only the government, the banks themselves, or the most reputable companies, issue them. There are three main types:
— Treasury Bills issued by the government;
— Local Authority Bills;
— Eligible Bank Bills (bills 'accepted' or bought by the banks).

Investments. These are mainly investments by the banks in government stocks ('gilt-edged' stocks because they are very secure) which are long term fixed interest loans £6.3 billion). The price of these stocks can rise or fall in the market and therefore the investment could return a capital loss if converted into cash.

Earlier we defined liquidity as the ease with which an asset can be converted to cash without significant loss of capital or interest. We can see therefore that these assets are less liquid than others. By the same token returns can be higher if prices go up, making them potentially very profitable for the banks.

Advances. This figure is currently over £124 billion. It is made up of short and longer term loans to the overseas sector (£4.4 billion), the government (£792m) and to private individuals and firms (£119 billion). These form the least liquid, most profitable, item on the banks' balance sheets.

Retail Banks' Balance Sheet (March 1988)

Liabilities (£m)		Assets (£m)	
Notes issued	1,000	Notes and Coin	2,300
Sterling deposits	167,000	Balances with Bank of England	500
Other Currency Deposits	43,000	Market Loans	33,000
Items in Suspense,		Bills	6,500
Transmission etc.	43,000	Investments	16,000
		Advances	113,000
		Other Currency	47,000
		Misc. Assets	27,700
		Acceptances	8,000
	254,000		254,000

(Source: *Bank of England Quarterly Bulletin*).

THE BANK OF ENGLAND

To obtain a full understanding of British banking, we must look at the Bank of England and its role in the financial system. As we shall see, it truly occupies a *central* position in British banking. In a very complex, expanding and ever changing financial system the Bank of England is affectionately called the Old Lady of Threadneedle Street — because of the number of years it has existed, not because it is unable to supervise the banking system effectively.

The Bank has successfully controlled, monitored and advised the banking system for many years. It has done so largely through informal means (discussions, advice, publishing information) rather than by its stringent legal powers — a testament to the flexibility of the system the Bank itself has helped create.

History of the bank

The Bank of England was founded when it received a Royal Charter from William III on 27th July 1694. A Court of Directors (equivalent to a modern company's Board of Directors) was established comprising a Governor (Sir John Houblon), a Deputy Governor and 24 Directors.

It was founded because William III was short of money to finance his war against France. William Paterson, a wealthy merchant, put forward the idea of setting up a bank so that its capital could be lent to the government. There were 1268 subscribers, who raised £1.2m to be repaid after 1706 at £100,000 per year interest.

From the beginning the Bank of England was associated with the government and its special position in English banking was maintained and reinforced. It was the only bank to be established as a joint stock company; all other banks had to be partnerships (Act of 1709). The 1826 Act excluded all banks except the Bank of England from issuing their own notes within a 65 mile radius of London.

The 1844 Bank Charter Act was a further step in regulating the note issue in Britain. The Bank of England was to have an Issue Department separate from its Banking Department. It was allowed a fiduciary issue of £14m, and no new banks were able to issue notes. Those who merged lost their note-issuing powers. The Bank finally became the sole issuer of notes under the terms of the 1928 Currency and Bank Notes Act, taking over from the Treasury the issue of 10 shilling and £1 notes. Bank notes are now printed at the Bank's printing works in Debden, Essex.

The Bank's central role was firmly established in the late 19th century. A series of crises had led to loss of confidence in several large banks; disaster was averted by the Bank of England stepping in to lend money to stop the crises spreading to all banks, and so to restore confidence in the banking system.

After the Bank had helped Barings in 1890 it announced that it would in future be willing to purchase certain bills from the discount market. This, in essence, meant the Bank would act as 'lender of the last resort' to provide funds for the system whenever necessary. This confirmed its central role.

After 250 years of belonging to private stockholders, the Bank of England was nationalised under the 1946 Bank of England Act. This Act did not radically alter the position of the Bank but, by taking over its stock, the government highlighted the importance and central role of the Bank of England in British and world banking. The Court of Directors was reduced to 16. The Governor and Deputy Governor, each elected for five years, and four others, were to be 'executive' Directors. The other Directors were to be drawn from various walks of life — merchant bankers, trade union leaders, industrialists.

The Act also conferred upon the Bank the power to request information from the banks and, if necessary, to 'issue directions to any banker'. This clause gave effective legal control over the banks to the Bank of England.

However, because of the long-established, friendly relations which have existed between itself and the other banks, the Bank of England has never resorted to using its directing powers.

The 1979 Banking Act was a far-reaching piece of legislation concerning the Bank, which came about as a result of three factors:

(i)   A call from the EEC for member nations to establish a system of authorisation of all deposit taking institutions.

(ii)   The growth of the financial markets and the number of new institutions in them which were outside the control of the Bank. Leading bankers argued it was time for closer supervision of *all* institutions, not just the main banks.

(iii)   The 'secondary banking' crisis of the early 1970s. By 1970 many institutions which accepted deposits were outside the control of the Bank. These were known as secondary banks. This called into question the exact definition of the word 'bank' and the effectiveness of the Bank of England's supervisory powers over the banking system in general. A number of these secondary banks got into financial difficulties in 1973. In an attempt to prevent the loss of confidence of their depositors spreading throughout the rest of the banking sector, the Bank of England and the clearing banks put together a support package of £1,300m, which became known as the 'lifeboat'.

The Banking Act 1979 was the result mainly of this crisis. It was an attempt to try and differentiate all the institutions which operated in the City and called themselves 'banks'. The Act introduced two categories of institution:

1.   Recognised banks.
2.   Licensed Deposit Takers (LDTs).

(i)   To be regarded as a bank and use the title 'bank' an institution had to satisfy certain criteria. It had to have a high reputation and standing in the community over a long period of time; and it had to provide a specialised service (assets of £250,000) or a wide range of banking services (assets £5m) to include:

> current and deposit accounts
> loans and overdrafts
> foreign exchange
> financial advice
> purchase and sale of securities for customers

(ii)   To be regarded as a licensed deposit-taking institution an organisation must safeguard depositors interests (net assets of £250,000); maintain adequate liquid assets; and maintain adequate provision for bad debts and possible emergencies.

(iii)   Some institutions were given exemption status, e.g. building societies, National Girobank, and they were allowed to conduct banking business because they were adequately covered by other legislation.

(iv) A Deposit Protection Fund was established. Each bank or LDT contributes to the fund (minimum £5,000, maximum £300,000). In the event of an institution becoming insolvent, depositors are guaranteed 75% of their deposits, up to a maximum of £10,000.

The Banking Act 1987

In 1984 the Johnson Matthey Bank collapsed and had to be rescued by the Bank of England. This led to a review of the Bank's supervisory position and the subsequent introduction of the Banking Act of 1987. This Act effectively replaced the Act of 1979. The main provisions in the legislation are that

- all deposit-taking institutions must be authorised by the Bank of England
- use of the title 'bank' is limited to those institutions with a paid-up capital of at least £5 million.
- any company or person planning to take control of an authorised institution incorporated in the UK must notify the Bank in advance. The Bank can object to such a move.
- a limit of 15% on individual stakes in deposit-taking institutions unless approved by the Bank
- the Board of Banking Supervision within the Bank of England is a statutory body which will oversee the implementation of the Act and will advise the Bank on supervisory matters
- the Bank must be notified of any loans to a single customer which are more than 10% of the bank's capital and any loan greater than 25% of the bank's capital
- auditors of approved institutions are required by law to disclose relevant information to the Bank

The Act therefore established a one class system with authorised institutions being subject to the same rules whether or not they are called banks. The main changes it brought about were

- the distinction between banks and licensed deposit takers was abolished and both are now regulated in the same way
- banks have to notify the Bank of England of any large loan commitment
- limit on individual stakes (15%) in deposit-taking institutions
- passing false or misleading information to the Bank is a criminal offence

The Deposit Protection Fund established in the 1979 Act continues under the 1987 Act. All authorised institutions contribute to the fund based on the size of their deposit base. This fund is used to repay 75% of the protected deposits of depositors of a failed institution. The limit of protected deposits is £20,000, which means that there is a maximum of £15,000 that can be paid to each depositor per institution.

One immediate result of the Act was that Marks & Spencer achieved a deposit-taking licence for its St Michael Financial Services unit. Other department stores which have financial services subsidiaries, such as Debenhams and Harrods, could also apply for a similar licence and bank status provided they have capital and reserves of £5 million.

This is a further example of how high street stores are becoming closely tied with financial institutions and could play a bigger role in the financial services revolution. Already Marks & Spencer is offering personal loans to its Chargecard customers, and the Next organisation has moved into the provision of a unit trust service.

Functions of the Bank

(a) Note issue
Ever since 1928 the Bank of England has been the sole issuer of English banknotes. The Bank produces approximately 7.5m new notes every day at its printing works and destroys about the same number. There are nearly £11 billion worth of banknotes in use. The notes are no longer backed by gold or silver. The note issue is, therefore, a fiduciary one, the notes being backed by government securities.

(b) Bankers' bank
The Bank of England acts as banker to the main banks and discount houses who themselves have accounts at the Bank. The relationship between the Bank and the Discount Houses will be discussed later. The main clearing banks have accounts at the Bank known as 'Bankers' Deposits'. They need these accounts for two main purposes:

Operational balances to settle the debts each bank owes the others after the day's clearing has taken place. The banks merely settle their debts with each other by paying with cheques drawn on their Bank of England accounts.

Non-operational balances. Since 1981 the banks have had to keep ½ % of their total liquid liabilites (call money, treasury bills, commercial bills) in accounts with the Bank. These accounts earn no interest; they are designed to control the credit-creating abilities of the banks. This is part of the government's monetary policy discussed later in this section.

Finally the bank offers highly valued advice to other banks at regular meetings and in regular articles (e.g. the Bank of England *Quarterly Bulletin*). The Bank keeps the clearing banks informed over its intentions, and the clearers let the Bank know of any potential problems.

(c) Government's bank
The Bank has always had a very intimate relationship with the government. It offers advice on a wide range of issues and acts as the government's bank in a number of ways:

Government Accounts. The main account of the government, the Exchequer, is kept at the Bank as are the accounts of many departments such as the Inland Revenue and the National Loans Fund. They appear under the heading "Public Deposits". On occasion these accounts require temporary loans which the Bank arranges under the title "Ways and Means Advances".

Management of National Debt. The main method of funding government spending is by taxation. However, it is always popular to keep taxation low (especially at election times!). This means that, to spend money on all the things it wishes to, the government has to borrow. Its total borrowing is known as the National Debt — the amount it has borrowed from its citizens and from abroad over many years to finance its expenditure. It borrows both short and long-term. It borrows short-term by issuing three-month Treasury Bills each week, which the banks and Discount Houses buy. For long-term needs it sells gilt-edged stock directly to the public or through the Stock Exchange.

The Bank of England oversees the management of this debt. It arranges the issue and redemption of stock and bills, acts as registrar by recording who owns the stock (for purposes of paying interest) and makes regular payments when due. We can begin to see how complex this is when we realise that the size of government stocks is roughly £60 billion. It is held by more than 2 million account holders, with the total National Debt standing at over £100 billion.

(d) Lender of the last resort

The Bank of England manages the weekly sale of Treasury Bills. The demand for these bills by the banks and other financial institutions depends upon their own balance sheets and the state of the economy. The government *could* be faced with a situation where it was left with many Treasury Bills unsold; it could not then raise money to spend on its programmes (health, education, defence).

The ideal situation for the government would be if there could be some guarantee that all the Treasury Bills *would* be bought each week. This is the role of the Discount Houses. They buy (or discount) bills at less than the amount stated on the bill (face value), hold them until the maturity or redemption date, and obtain the full face value. The 'discount' is their profit. Alternatively they can sell them to someone else before maturity, for a smaller profit. Very simply, the Discount Houses guarantee to purchase any Treasury Bills not bought by the banks.

In return for this service the Bank guarantees to act as 'lender of the last resort': should the Discount Houses need cash very quickly (e.g. to pay back the 'call' money lent by the bank) the Bank will lend to the Discount Houses by buying some of their Treasury Bills. For many years this relationship was used as a part of the government's monetary policy (see below).

(e) Supervisor of the banking system

The 1979 and 1987 Banking Acts formally require the Bank of England to act as supervisor of the financial system. It does this through its Banking Supervision Department. It only recognises and licenses those institutions (approximately 600) who are suitable and responsibly run institutions. The Deposit Protection Fund helps safeguard depositors by providing help to compensate depositors in the event of insolvency.

The Bank also has used 'suggestion and request' to supervise the system. For many years before the 1979 Banking Act it was often enough for the Bank merely to 'suggest' a course of action for banks to comply. The Bank always favoured this informal method (often called 'moral suasion') to using its statutory powers of direction. Indeed, it has never resorted to 'directing' a bank by force of law to follow a certain course of action.

(f) Management of gold and foreign currency reserves

Britain's gold and foreign currency reserves are held in the Exchange Equalisation Account and are managed by the Bank.

The pound is bought on the foreign currency markets by foreigners who wish to purchase British goods and by speculators who believe its value will rise. British importers will demand foreign currency to pay for the goods and services they import. Since this demand for British currency does not always equal supply the price of the pound can at times vary. Look at a quality daily newspaper over a short period of time to see how the pound varies in value, for example, in terms of the American dollar.

In order to prevent violent swings in its value the Bank constantly monitors the value of the pound. It steps into the foreign exchange market and buys pounds with gold and foreign currency when its value is falling, and sells pounds when its value is rising too quickly. Because we import so many of our goods and services it is important for business that the value of the pound is kept reasonably stable.

(g) Relations with other central banks and international institutions

More international trade takes place than ever before. Financial systems are far more complex than ever before. What happens at the other side of the world can, because of efficient telecommunications and travel, affect us here in a very short period of time. For these reasons the Bank of England maintains regular contact with other central banks throughout the world, meeting regularly to discuss matters of world importance and possible solutions.

The Bank also has a special relationship with Commonwealth countries. Several of these countries' gold and foreign currency reserves are safeguarded and managed by the Bank.

The Bank also plays an important role with several major international institutions. For example, the Bank works closely with the Chancellor of the Exchequer in his role as a member of the International Monetary Fund (IMF), and is a member of the Bank for International Settlements (BIS).

(h) Executor of monetary policy

The government tries to achieve certain economic policy objectives:

- full employment
- price stability (low rate of inflation)
- economic growth
- balance of payments stability

It has two major means at its disposal to try and bring about these objectives — fiscal policy and monetary policy.

Fiscal policy involves varying the government's income (taxation) and expenditure; monetary policy involves the control and availability of money in the economy. A government can use either of these policies, but usually it uses a combination of both.

The Bank of England helps implement the government's monetary policy. These are some of the instruments used in recent years:

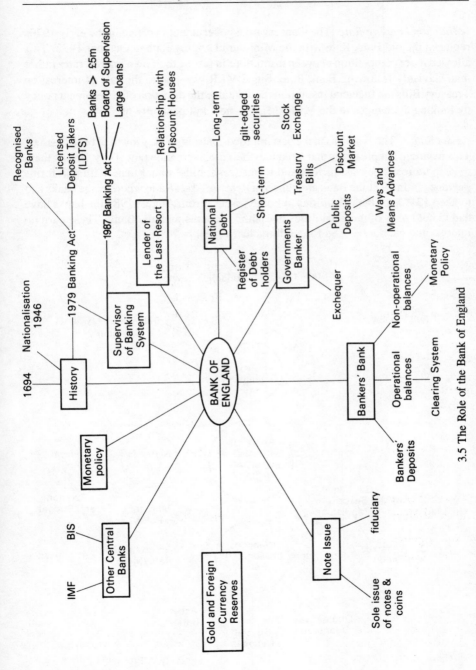

3.5 The Role of the Bank of England

Minimum Lending Rate. The Conservative government in office in the early 1970s replaced the old Bank Rate with the Minimum Lending Rate in October 1972. This allowed more competition between institutions in setting their own interest rates rather than slavishly following Bank Rate. Since MLR was tied to the rate of interest on Treasury Bills the financial institutions could judge the direction of government policy by looking at changes in the MLR. MLR is now not generally used.

Asset Ratios. The Bank has in the past imposed controls on the growth of banks' assets. This means in simple terms that it reduces their credit creation powers by forcing them to keep more of their assets in liquid forms (cash, bills) rather than in illiquid forms (advances). In 1971 the Bank announced a Reserve Asset Ratio whereby the banks had to keep 12½ % of their liabilities in liquid assets. From August 1981 the banks have had to hold ½ % of their liabilities in cash in accounts with the Bank. These earn no interest and cannot be used for settling clearing debts.

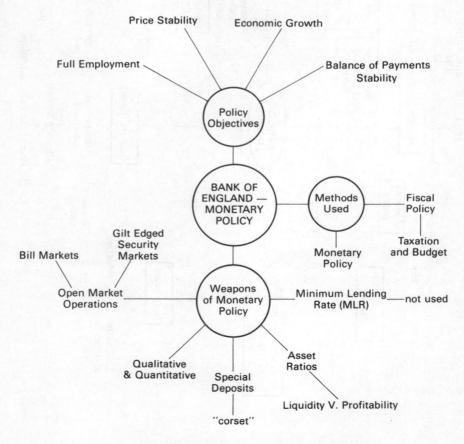

3.6 The Bank of England and Monetary Policy

Special Deposits. The Bank of England can call on the banks to make Special Deposits with it. This reduces the amount they can lend. Between 1973-80 it operated a Supplementary Special Deposit Scheme, known as the 'corset', to check the growth of the money supply.

Quantitative/Qualitative Controls. The Bank can issue instructions concerning the amounts (quantitive controls) banks can lend and the types of people (qualitative controls) to whom they can lend.

Open Market Operations (OMO). This has been a favoured method of the Bank. Basically, it involves selling government securities (Treasury Bills) when the government wants to soak up surplus money in the markets; this reduces the banks' ability to lend. Alternatively, it can purchase bills and thus supply the banks with cash when it wishes to expand lending.

OTHER BANKS

In this final section we will briefly examine the role of the remaining types of banks, namely

> merchant banks
> discount houses
> foreign banks
> overseas banks
> consortium banks

Merchant Banks

As their name suggests, merchant banks originated from rich merchants, especially in the 18th century. These merchants had a substantial network of contacts throughout the world because of the goods they exported and imported. They soon found they could earn more money by using their contacts and financing trade for others, rather than by trading themselves.

The major problem of foreign trade in the 18th and 19th centuries was that the firms involved often knew very little about each other's financial standing. However, the merchant banks had banking contacts in most major cities, especially in Europe, and they could (for a fee) arrange the exchange of currencies and payment for goods and services. The traders were happy because the payment of money and delivery of goods was guaranteed for them by the merchant bank. In this way the merchant banks helped international trade expand.

The method of payment used was the Bill of Exchange. The merchant banks would sign the bill to 'accept' it, in other words guarantee payment. A firm would be happy to receive a bill with, for example, the name of Rothschild on it as a guarantee. Those banks which 'accepted' bills became known as Accepting Houses, and 16 of the most reputable merchant banks became members of the Accepting Houses Committee. Some of the more famous merchant banks included:

Morgan Grenfell
Kleinwort Benson
S.G. Warburg
Baring Brothers
Lazard Brothers
J. Henry Schroder Wagg

Over the past few years competition in the business of merchant banking has increased, assisted by the Big Bang and growing internationalism in securities markets. Companies who traditionally had dealt with only one merchant bank for all their financial needs are now shopping around to find the merchant bank which can best meet their specific present need.

The clearing banks have become more involved with merchant banking business, either through setting up their own bank, for example NatWest developed its merchant banking arm through County Bank whilst Lloyds set up the Lloyds Merchant Bank, or through takeover or amalgamation, e.g. the TSB's takeover of Hill Samuel.

The main functions of these banks today include finance, advice, and dealing.

(a) Finance

A major part of the work of merchant banks centres upon their accepting business, and direct lending to large companies and governments. They also engage in the work of issuing. This involves issuing new stocks and shares on behalf of companies and local government. The merchant banks who carry out this form of activity comprise the Issuing Houses Association.

The merchant banks have been very active in the last few years advising on, and arranging for, the flotation of nationalised corporations and large companies on the Stock Exchange. Some of the better-known flotations have been British Telecom, British Gas, Rolls Royce, British Airways and TSB.

There are also moves by the merchant banks into retail finance. For example, the banks have offered unit trusts to the public and have introduced high interest bank accounts and mortgages, plus personal pensions. Some also issue high interest cheque accounts using a clearing bank to act as their clearing agent. Some are also planning to enter the ATM scene by joining one of the established networks, e.g. Morgan Grenfell is involved with Link, to which the Abbey National, Nationwide-Anglia and Girobank also belong.

Many of the merchant banks engage in factoring and leasing. Factoring basically entails the merchant bank taking over the debts owed by a firm's customers for a fee or discount. This provides much needed capital for the firm. Leasing occurs where the merchant bank buys equipment needed by a firm and hires it to the company for as long as they need it. The firm does not have to find large amounts of capital to buy equipment — but only the money to hire it.

(b) Advice

Merchant banks provide a great deal of advice on many aspects of finance. This includes general financial advice on the running of a business; advising on mergers and takeovers; and portfolio management (managing individuals' and companies' stocks and shares).

(c) Dealing

Many of the merchant banks are directly involved in dealing (buying and selling) in the commodity markets (the markets for raw materials such as tea, coffee, tin, zinc) as well as the financial markets (foreign exchange, gold bullion).

Discount Houses

The Discount Houses have played a special role in the British banking system for 200 years. They are peculiar to Britain; no other country has a similar group of institutions.

The Bill of Exchange developed as a method of payment because of the difficulties of travel and communiction in the 18th century. Very often merchants who accepted these bills (or promised to pay at a future date) could not wait for payment. Instead they took them to brokers who discounted them, in other words exchanged them for the face value of the bill less a discount or fee for providing the service. The broker (or discount house, as they came to be known), would then keep the bill until it was due for payment. The profit would be the difference between the face value of the bill and the amount the broker paid for it.

As trade grew in the 19th century these brokers began discounting international bills; by the end of the century they became involved in the purchase and sale of government bills, especially the Treasury Bill. The London Discount Market Association comprises the discount houses, among them Alexanders Discount plc, King and Shaxson plc, and Union Discount Company of London plc. They have a key role to play in the British financial system. They act as a buffer between the Bank of England and the banking sector.

We have seen that when the government needs money, it can issue Treasury Bills through the Bank of England. By increasing the number of Treasury Bills in the economy the government reduces the amount of liquidity and thus the volume of lending in the banking system, and vice versa. The discount houses play a major role in guaranteeing the sale of the Treasury Bills for the government. Any remaining unsold to the banks will be bought by the discount houses.

In return for this the Bank of England acts as lender of the last resort to the discount houses, it will help ease any liquidity problems experienced by the discount houses by buying Treasury Bills from them when they are short of cash.

Why should the discount houses ever need this support? Discount houses engage in a very precarious activity — borrowing short and lending long. For example, they purchase Treasury Bills from the Bank of England for a period of three months and pay for them by borrowing money from the banks for periods which vary between overnight ('at call') and up to 14 days ('short notice'). Every day the agents of the discount houses must visit the banks to renew existing overnight loans and to arrange new loans to make sure their books balance by 2.30 p.m., the latest time they can approach the Bank of England for assistance if required.

If the banks are unwilling or unable to lend the discount houses enough money, the discount houses are faced with two choices. They can either sell some of their Treasury Bills on the open market, or go to the Bank of England as lender of the last resort. If the market is depressed (prices are falling) it may be too costly for them to sell their Treasury Bills, so they may prefer to go to the Bank of England for help.

The discount market is important. It

- underwrites or guarantees the weekly sale of the government's Treasury Bills through the Bank of England;
- provides a useful interest-bearing home for commercial banks to place their surplus cash for very short periods; and
- provides short-term finance for business by discounting bills of exchange.

Although the discount houses are unique UK institutions they, like the merchant banks, have been faced over the last few years with having to operate in a much more competitive marketplace. By 1986 the number of discount houses had dropped to eight through merger or takeover by larger financial groups, and of the eight only four were independent

      — Gerrard & National
      — Union Discount
      — Cater Allen
      — King & Shaxson

with the other four being part of a larger grouping

      — Alexanders part of Mercantile House
      — Clive Discount part of Prudential Bache
      — Seccombe Marshall & Campion part of Citicorp
      — Quin Cope part of Banque Belge

The reduction in the number of discount houses was again partly a result of the Big Bang, which changed the way the Government dealt in Government Stock. We saw on page 35 that dealing in these stocks is now through market makers which could affect the historic roles of the discount houses. These roles are

- to act as dealers in the money markets, trading in bills and other short term paper
- to provide liquidity for the banking system
- to be a link between the Bank of England and the UK banking system.

Discount Market Balance Sheet (March 1988)

Liabilities (£m)		Assets (£m)	
Sterling	11,900	Bills	6,500
Other Currencies	200	Funds Lent	4,800
		Investments	600
		Other Currencies	200
	12,100		**12,100**

(Bank of England Quarterly Bulletin)

Foreign banks

Being a major financial centre, London has attracted many foreign banks. Indeed, from just 70-odd such banks in 1960 there are now over 450 foreign banks in London.

They originally established themselves in London to cater for customers who had business or private interests in Britain. However, because of the growth of the euro-currency markets, of which London is a major centre, many more foreign banks have come to London.

The major foreign banks in London are the American and Japanese banks though other nations are represented too, for example by Dresdner Bank AG or Banco of Bilbao. At present the American and Japanese banks form over 60% of the market:

Foreign Banks Balance Sheet (March 1988)

	American Banks	Japanese Banks	Other Banks
Liabilities (£m)			
Sterling Deposits	16,000	20,000	60,000
Other Currency Deposits	74,000	205,000	179,000
	90,000	225,000	239,000
Assets (£m)			
Loans	5,600	10,000	28,000
Bills	50	13	400
Advances	11,000	7,500	31,000
Investments	1,000	2,500	4,000
Other Currency Loans	69,000	191,000	169,000
Other Assets	2,000	15,000	12,000
	88,650	226,013	244,400

(Bank of England Quarterly Bulletin)

Overseas banks

This category of bank refers to British banks who have their head offices here in Britain but who operate mainly abroad, such as Barclays Bank International and Standard Chartered Bank. They were originally established to cater for British traders and colonies abroad. Since the Second World War the numbers of these have declined due, partly, to nationalisation by former colonies who have been granted independence, and partly to a number of recent mergers.

Consortium banks

The 1960s saw two major developments in banking; the growth of multi-national companies and the need to provide special facilities for them and the development of the eurocurrency markets. Loans to these new companies were long-term. Because they involved the laws and regulations of more than one country, they were very complicated to put together. Therefore, banks began to join together to form consortia to provide these loans, raised mainly on the eurocurrency markets. A consortium would involve banks from different countries and very often they would specialise in a particular area of activity such as oil.

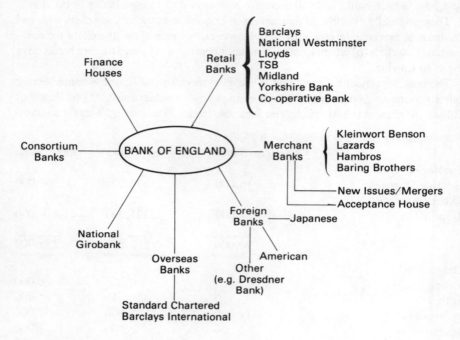

3.7 The Bank of England and Financial Institutions

SUMMARY

Banking System
- The City is a complicated network of financial institutions providing a wide range of services.

Financial Institutions
- All financial institutions provide a link between borrowers and lenders. (financial intermediation).
- The banks' profit comes from charging a higher rate of interest to borrowers than they pay to depositors.
- Banks are divided into:

    (i) Bank Financial Intermediaries
Commercial Banks
TSB
National Girobank

(ii) Non-Bank Financial Intermediaries
National Savings Banks
Building Societies
Finance Houses
Insurance Companies
Pension Funds
Unit Trust Companies
Investment Trust Companies

- Under the terms of the 1979 Banking Act institutions fall into one of the following categories:

  — Recognised Banks
  — Licensed Deposit Takers (LDTs)
  — Exempt

- The 1987 Banking Act effectively replaced the 1979 Act and

  — introduced a system with no distinction between banks and Licensed Deposit Takers
  — all deposit-taking institutions must be authorised by the Bank
  — title of 'bank' limited to institutions with capital of £5m or more.

Money Markets
- The money markets carry out the same function of any other market, i.e. they bring together buyers and sellers to transact business.

- Short-term money markets comprise the following:

  — Discount Markets (the Discount Houses)
  — Parallel Markets — these provide short-term funds for the financial intermediaries. There are several of these markets — euromarkets, inter-bank markets, the Local Authority market, Finance House market, inter-company market, and Certificate of Deposit market.
  — Foreign Exchange Markets
  — London International Financial Futures Exchange (LIFFE).

- Long-term capital markets. Capital is raised principally through the Stock Exchange.

Retail Banks
- All retail banks offer the following services:

  — payments
  — deposit facilities
  — lending facilities

- They have extensive high street branch networks (12,000 branches in England and Wales), over 30m customers, more than 330,000 employees, and deposits of over £140 billion.

- Early in their history the banks realised that they could use deposits to lend to other customers.
- This process is called credit creation.
- As the banks grew there came an increasing call for their activities to be regulated.
- A series of Acts were passed:

  — Bank Act 1826
  — Bank Charter Act 1833
  — Bank Charter Act 1844
  — Companies Act 1862
  — Bills of Exchange Act 1882

- Throughout the 19th century the private banks declined whilst the joint-stock banks grew in size and numbers.
- By the turn of the century the joint-stock banks had begun amalgamating. In 1900 there were 77, by 1914 only 16, and by 1920 only 11.
- The inter-war years saw the banks develop their branch networks.
- Since the 1960s the banks have been extending their product range.
- The banks' balance sheet shows a spread of assets. This is to take account of the dilemma between the need for liquidity and the need for profitability.

Bank of England

- The Bank has always played a special role in British banking.
- It was founded in 1694 to provide finance for William III and has continued to provide finance for the government ever since; this remains one of its prime functions.
- It was nationalised in 1946 but this merely formalised its position as a central bank.
- By the terms of the 1987 Banking Act the Bank has to supervise banking in Britain by licensing institutions who wish to provide banking services.
- The Bank carries out many functions:

  — note issue
  — bank to the retail banks
  — the government's banker
  — manages the National Debt
  — acts as lender of last resort
  — supervises the banking system
  — manages the nation's gold and foreign currency reserves
  — meets with other central banks
  — carries out the government's monetary policy.

Other Banks

- Several other types of bank exist who perform more specialised functions than the retail banks. These include:

  — Merchant Banks
  — Discount Houses
  — Foreign Banks
  — Overseas Banks
  — Consortium Banks

CHECK OUT QUESTIONS

1. What function is common to all financial institutions?
2. What is a financial intermediary?
3. Give two reasons why it is preferable to borrow from a financial intermediary rather than from an acquaintance.
4. What do the terms BFI and NFBI mean?
5. What is the essential difference between the two?
6. Give two examples of BFIs.
7. Give three examples of NBFIs.
8. What was the difference between a recognised bank and a Licensed Deposit Taker?
9. Name two institutions which were exempt from the 1979 Banking Act.
10. List three of the short-term money markets apart from the parallel markets.
11. List three of the parallel markets.
12. What do the initials LIFFE stand for?
13. What is LIFFE's main function?
14. What is the chief source of long-term capital?
15. List three financial instruments used by financial intermediaries.
16. Summarise the main services provided by the retail banks.
17. Approximately how many customers do the retail banks have and what is the size of their deposits?
18. Explain with the aid of a table the process of credit creation.
19. What hindered the growth of the joint-stock banks in the 19th century?
20. Outline the main provisions of each of the following:
     Bank Act 1826
     Bank Charter Act 1833
     Bank Charter Act 1844
     Companies Act 1862
     Bills of Exchange Act 1882
21. List the main assets and liabilities of the retail banks.
22. What do you understand by the phrase 'liquidity versus profitability' in reference to the retail banks?
23. When was the Bank of England founded, and why?
24. What does the phrase 'lender of the last resort' mean?
25. When was the Bank of England nationalised?
26. List the main provisions of the 1979 and 1987 Banking Acts.
27. Why is the Bank of England called 'the bankers' bank'?
28. What are 'ways and means' advances?
29. How does the Bank of England manage the National Debt?
30. What is the Exchange Equalisation Account?
31. How does the Bank of England carry out the Government's monetary policy?
32. What does the 'acceptance' of a bill of exchange involve?
33. Name three of the most famous merchant banks.
34. List two functions of the merchant banks.

35. What is the main function of the discount houses?
36. Name two discount houses.
37. What is the major difference between Foreign and Overseas banks?

4

The Banker/Customer Relationship

On completion of this chapter you will know the

— characteristics of a banker and a customer
— basic banker/customer relationship
— other relationships which affect the banker and customer
— special relationship that exists
— rights and duties of a banker
— case law which relates to the above.

In previous chapters we have looked at the development of banking over the years, and looked at the kind of institutions that make up the banking sector. We also now know what individuals and organisations make up the banks' customer base.

In this chapter we need to look at how the two relate to each other, to make the business of 'banking' work for both the customer and the bank. When we remember that the clearing banks in the UK deal with millions of personal customers alone it is obvious that without sound banking practice, working within a legal framework, both parties could soon end up in chaos.

In order to get the benefits of the legal framework and agreed banking practice the parties need to fit within the definition of what is a banker and what is a customer.

WHAT IS A BANKER?

The **Banking Act 1979** laid down the facts that the Bank of England would consider before allowing a financial institution to trade under the title of Bank. These were that the institution should
— have a high reputation and standing in the financial community
— provide a wide range of banking services which must include current or deposit accounts and overdraft and loan facilities.

In addition, the 'bank' must carry on its business with integrity and prudence and have net assets of at least £5 million.

The **1987 Banking Act** confirmed the 1979 Act in its 'definition' and added that before an institution can be authorised to accept deposits the Bank of England will ensure that
— the institution's directors, controllers and managers are fit and proper persons to hold office
— business is conducted properly in that there is adequate

- capital
- liquidity
- provision for bad and doubtful debt
- accounting records
- internal controls

— the business is carried out with integrity
— the title of bank can only relate to institutions with paid-up capital of more than £5m and for deposit taking it must have net assets of not less than £1m.

The **Bills of Exchange Act 1882** also defined a bank as 'a body of persons whether incorporated or not who carry on the business of banking'. Unfortunately for our definition the Banking Act does not specify the roles and behaviours that could allow us to identify the banker.

However there are three chief characteristics of a banker which have been identified by case law. These are that a banker
— will credit money accepted from its customers and from cheques collected on their behalf;
— will debit customers' accounts by paying cheques and orders drawn on them by the customer;
— will keep accounts (current or similar) against which credits and debits can be made.

These characteristics of a banker were laid down in the case of

United Dominions Trust (UDT) v. Kirkwood (1966)

In this case UDT, which was basically a Finance House providing loans to its customers, sued Kirkwood to recover a commercial loan. Kirkwood argued that UDT was an unlicensed moneylender and not a bank, and that therefore the loan contract was void.

The Court of Appeal however held that since UDT provided the above services it was in fact a recognised bank.

Another interesting aspect of the UDT case was that the Court also took into account the reputation of the organisation with other bankers to help determine whether, for legal purposes, it could be held to be a bank.

In the above case UDT — which was not a bank in the general public's definition — was nevertheless held to be a bank under both of the above criteria. However, since this definition is not laid down by statute it is liable to some variation depending upon current practice.

A banker is someone who

- credits money and cheques

- debits accounts
- keeps accounts.

WHO IS A CUSTOMER?

In order to carry out business, a banker obviously needs customers; these can be defined as 'persons' who have a current account or some similar relationship with the bank.

The account does not need to have been opened for any stated length of time, but to be a customer a person must have entered a contract to open an account in his name. This fact was established in the cases of

Ladbroke & Co v. Todd (1914) and
Commissioners of Taxation v. English, Scottish & Australian Bank (1920)

Here it was laid down that continuous dealing was not the key factor, but that the customer relationship starts when the application to open an account has been accepted, or when money has been taken on the understanding that cheques will be honoured. Duration of the account is not a consideration.

However, even where no contract has been completed to open an account bankers still have to take care when dealing with the public. For example in

Woods v. Martins Bank (1959)

the manager who gave investment advice to a potential customer was held to owe the same contractual duty of care that a customer would be entitled to.

A customer is someone who

- has a current account or other relationship
- has entered a contract to open accounts and
  no particular time period is involved.

BANKER/CUSTOMER RELATIONSHIP

In order that the bankers and the customers can carry out their business they need to be able to transact business within a legal contractual relationship. Three main contractual relationships exist:

— debtor/creditor
— principal/agent
— bailor/bailee

Debtor/Creditor relationship

This is the *basic* banker/customer relationship. It arises out of the fact that the bank holds money which belongs to the customer. The money has to be repaid at some time, and therefore

— the banker is the debtor, and
— the customer is the creditor.

When, however, the customer borrows money from the bank the position is reversed.

Here,

— the customer is the debtor, and
— the banker is the creditor.

This basic debtor/creditor relationship was established long ago in the case of

Foley v. Hill (1848)

This case also decided that when money is placed in a bank it is placed under the *control* of the banker, and he can then deal with it as his own. However, this money must be repaid when demanded by the customer.

In the case of

Joachimson v. Swiss Bank Corporation (1921)

this relationship was confirmed; it was laid down that
— the bank (debtor) borrows the proceeds and undertakes to repay them (to creditor), and
— the bank is not liable until the customer demands payment from the bank (at the branch at which the account is held and during banking hours).

This case also set down other terms for the banker/customer relationship, namely
— the bank undertakes to receive money and collect bills for its customer's account
— the bank will not cease to do business with the customer except upon reasonable notice
— the customer must exercise reasonable care in executing his written order so as not to mislead the bank or make forgery easy
— repayment instructions must be in writing.

An interesting point about the debtor/creditor relationship is that it is not the debtor's (i.e. the bank's) job to seek to repay the debt, but the creditor (i.e. the customer) has the responsibility to ask for the money back. This is the opposite position to the normal debtor/creditor situation.

Principal/Agent

Although not the main contractual agreement, banks and customers often operate in the relationship of principal/agent.

An Agent is someone employed to work for a principal and to make contracts on his behalf.

A Principal is the person who informs the agent what he wants him to do on his behalf. As long as the agent stays within the powers given to him by the principal he will not be contractually liable. For example, when someone (the principal) sells a house, he often asks an estate (agent) to make the sale and negotiate a price on his behalf.

A bank, when dealing with its customer direct, has a debtor/creditor relationship. But where a third party is involved the relationship becomes one of principal/agent. For example, when the bank collects a cheque drawn by a third party, or when the customer draws a cheque payable to someone else, the bank becomes an agent.

Other examples are when the bank arranges insurance, buys stocks and shares, sends money abroad and so on — all on behalf of a customer.

Bailor/Bailee

One of the bank's services is to receive valuables and documents to hold on behalf of its customer. When the bank holds these valuables in safe custody he has to take 'reasonable' care of the property, and has a bailor/bailee relationship with that customer.

A Bailor is the depositor of the property. This deposit is made on the understanding that the goods will be returned by the bailee, or dealt with in accordance with the bailor's instructions.

A Bailee receives the property and must look after it in a careful/professional manner. In law there are two forms of bailee:

Bailee for reward where the bailee is paid to carry out the duties; he must look after the 'deposit' not just as a careful person would, but to the highest possible standards.

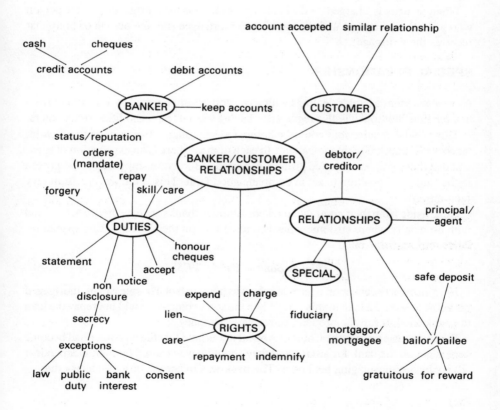

4.1 The Banker/Customer Relationship

The second is the **Gratuitous Bailee;** here the bailee gets no reward and is only expected to act as a careful person would.

A bank can act as either type of bailee when dealing with safe deposit facilities. For example a bank may hold a deposit in safe custody without making a specific charge (gratuitous bailee) whilst it may also provide a safe deposit service and charge a fee for it (bailee for reward).

In theory, the bank can act either as a gratuitous bailee or a bailee for reward, but in practice the banker always provides similar high standards and is therefore usually regarded as a bailee for reward.

Mortgagor/Mortgagee

Aside from the first three relationships the bank and customer can enter into a mortgagor/mortgagee relationship. This happens when a bank takes a mortgage (charge) over securities when granting an advance.

When security is 'charged' to the bank the customer is the mortgagor (i.e. the person who *gives* the mortgage) and the bank is the mortgagee (i.e. the person or body that *receives* the mortgage).

SPECIAL RELATIONSHIP

As we have seen, a bank's dealings with its customers are covered by various contractual relationships, but it is also regarded as having special responsibilities to customers.

This special relationship could be compared with that between parent and child, teacher and pupil, doctor and patient. In each of these there is an expectation of trust, and that there will be no undue influence exerted. All relationships expect the person in the 'superior' position to act in complete good faith. This is known as a **fiduciary** relationship.

Quite aside from their contractual responsibilities, banks are expected to act in good faith especially where customers have come to rely on their advice. This special relationship was illustrated in

Lloyds Bank v. Bundy (1975)

Here an elderly customer, a farmer, who was not much of a businessman, mortgaged his home to secure a loan for his son. When the son's company could not repay the loan the bank tried to sell the property to recover its money.

When the case went to the Court of Appeal it was held that the customer had become dependent on the bank for advice and they should have ensured he took independent advice before mortgaging his home. The bank was in breach of its fiduciary duty.

BANKERS' RIGHTS AND DUTIES

From the various banker/customer relationships there arise a number of legal rights and duties which underlie the practical operation of banking.

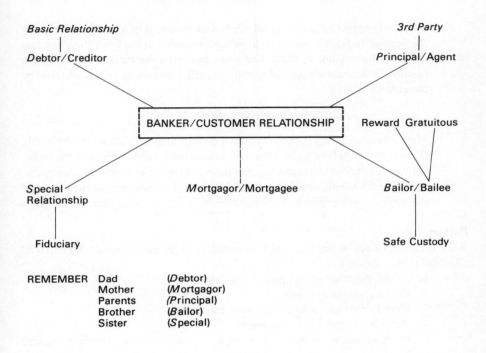

REMEMBER Dad (*D*ebtor)
Mother (*M*ortgagor)
Parents (*P*rincipal)
Brother (*B*ailor)
Sister (*S*pecial)

4.2 Our Relations

Rights

A right is the performance of actions within accepted standards or moral or legal behaviour. A bank has the right to

(i)   charge a reasonable commission for its services and interest on loans and overdrafts;

(ii)   be indemnified for losses incurred when acting for a customer;

(iii)   repayment on demand of any overdrawn balance. (Note that in

Williams and Glyn's Bank v. Barnes (1980)

it was held that reasonable notice must be given where this is implied in the contract.)

(iv)   exercise a **lien** over customer's securities in the bank's possession. For example bills or cheques deposited for collection or promissory notes can be retained against the debt. N.B. This does not include deposits within safe custody. (A lien is the right to keep possession of the goods as payment in lieu of the debt.)

(v)   use the customer's money in any way provided it honours the customer's cheques;

(vi)   expect the customer to use reasonable care in drawing cheques. In the cases of

London Joint Stock Bank v. MacMillan & Arthur (1918)

a clerk altered a cheque for £2 which had been signed by a partner when only the amount in figures was shown. When presented to the bank the clerk had changed the amount to £120. The court held that the bank could debit the customer's account for the full amount as sufficient care had not been taken by the customer; and

Greenwood v. Martins Bank Ltd (1932)

Mrs Greenwood forged cheques drawn on her husband's account. When Mr Greenwood found out he told his wife to stop but he did not inform the bank. When his wife died Greenwood sued the bank for the amount of the cheques.

The bank won the case because of Greenwood's delay in informing them of the forgery, thus preventing the bank from taking action against the forger.

Duties

A duty is a task or action that a person is bound to perform for moral or legal reasons. The banker has the duty

(i)   to honour the customer's cheques provided
   — they are properly drawn
   — a credit balance or approved overdraft exists
   — there is no legal bar to payment
   — the bank has no knowledge of death, bankruptcy proceedings, or mental incapacity regarding the customer
   — there is no notice of a winding-up procedure or receiving order being made
(ii)   to abide by any express mandate from the customer such as a standing order; the bank is required to pay a standing order if there is sufficient balance in the account

Whitehead v. National Westminster Bank Ltd (1982)

Here a customer's account fluctuated, which meant that on many occasions there was enough money to pay the mortgage standing order whilst on others there was not. When no money was in the account the mortgage was not paid. The bank did, however, agree sometimes to make the last payment when the balance of the account rose sufficiently to allow the payment. Eventually the mortgage arrears rose to the extent that the building society took possession and sold the house.

Mrs Whitehead brought an action claiming that the bank had the duty to pay the standing order on the same date or at the earliest date that the account balance allowed. She lost the case as it was ruled that the bank's duty was to comply with the payment of the standing order on the due date and if there was in-sufficient funds available at that time it had no further obligations regarding the payment.

(iii)   not to disclose its customer's affairs unless
   — compelled to do so by law. This does not include disclosure to police or tax

officers unless there is compulsion by law. For example; disclosure can come about when a court order is served on the bank and when the Inland Revenue asks for a return of interest paid to customers.
— there is a duty to the public to do so, for example if the customer were trading with the enemy or there was a danger to the state. This situation is difficult to assess and great care is needed.
— it is in the interests of the bank such as when issuing a writ to demand repayment of a loan.
— the customer has expressly or impliedly consented.
These four justifications for disclosure were established in

Tournier v. National Provincial Bank (1924)

Tournier overdrew his account without prior agreement and then failed to keep up with the agreed repayments. The branch telephoned his place of work; being unable to speak to Tournier they advised his employer of the situation and of his gambling.

Tournier, who was employed on a three month contract, lost his job when the company did not renew the contract at the end of the period. Tournier sued the bank for slander and breach of contract by disclosing the state of his account and transactions.

In this case none of the above reasons for acceptable disclosure was present and the bank was held liable for breach of contract.

Today there is also cooperation between the banks and law enforcement officers where there is cause to suspect that drug monies are deposited in the bank. This cooperation was a result of the Drug Trafficking Offences Act 1986. Under this Act a judge may make an order compelling a bank (or any other person) who may have information to produce it to the police. Such orders are made when there are 'reasonable grounds for suspecting that a specified person has carried on or has benefited from drug trafficking.'

The Criminal Justices Act 1988 extends this cooperation to include information on funds which are suspected of being acquired through illegal acts.

Secrecy is a key duty for all bank staff and they must be careful not to divulge information on customers' business even when done innocently. *Bank staff must not therefore*
— talk amongst themselves about customers' business outside the bank.
— talk to friends and relations about customers and their financial position.
— give customers information over the counter in such a way that it can be overheard by other customers.
(iv) to give reasonable notice of closure of an account in order to enable the customer to make alternative arrangements and that the bank may avoid having to return cheques that have already been issued
(v) to provide a statement of account within a reasonable time or provide details of the balance on request.

The banker should keep an accurate record of the customer's account. The customer, however, does not have an obligation to check the bank statements or advise the bank of errors, though he can, subsequently, challenge their accuracy.

This means the banker needs to be careful to avoid errors when recording transactions on an account.

For example, if the bank credited an amount to a customer's account, in error, the excess credit may not be recoverable. However, if the money is to be retained the customer must prove that
— the bank misrepresented the state of the account to the customer
— the customer was misled by the inaccurate information and he used the funds as a result
— as his position had been changed, it would be unfair for the customer to have to repay the money.

In the case of

United Overseas Bank v. Jiwani (1976)

the bank credited the customer's Swiss bank account by telex with an amount of $11,000 giving a total account balance of $21,000. The customer then issued a cheque for $20,000. Confirmation of the telex was then received by the bank who took it as a further instruction to credit another $11,000 and advised the customer that it had done so. The customer then issued another cheque towards the purchase of a hotel.

The bank claimed the overcredited amount, and was allowed the claim by the court on the grounds that, although the first two factors stated above were present, the final one was not. This was because the customer had other funds which he could have used towards the purchase of the hotel. It was not therefore inequitable to require the customer to pay.

Should a banker incorrectly debit an account there is less confusion. He has no authority to have debited the money and therefore the amount must be repaid.

A banker should take care to avoid an incorrect debit because if, as a result of such a mistake he dishonours a cheque, he would be liable to compensate the customer for any loss to his credit or reputation following such an action.

(vi)   to receive the customer's money and cheques for collection and credit the amounts to the customer's account

(vii)   to repay money on demand
— at the customer's *written* request
— during banking hours
— at the parent branch or another agreed branch.

(viii) to advise the customer immediately if/when the forgery of a customer's signature is brought to the bank's attention. For example in

Brown v. Westminster Bank Ltd (1964)

the bank admitted that it had paid over 100 cheques which were forged. However, because it had queried the signatures with the customer on several occasions, and he had informed them that they were genuine, the customer was prevented from making a successful claim against the bank.

(ix) to exercise proper care and skill. This is particularly important in practice with regard to the payment and collection of cheques if the bank wishes to enjoy the protection of the Bills of Exchange Act 1882 and the Cheques Act 1957.

SUMMARY

- A banker is someone who accepts money and collects cheques for payment to an account, pays the customer's cheques and keeps accounts.
- A customer is a person who has a current account or some similar relationship with a bank.
- The basic banker/customer relationship is a debtor/creditor relationship and the roles can be reversed.
- Other contractual agreements
  — principal/agent
  — bailor/bailee
  — mortgagor/mortgagee.

BANKERS RIGHTS	BANKERS DUTIES
C harge commission and interest	**H** onour cheques
I ndemnified for losses	**A** ccept money and cheques
R epayment on demand	**N** otice of closure
C ustomer care	**D** isclosure non
L ien over securities	**S** tatement of account
E xpend money as wishes	**F** orgery
	O rder (mandate) action
REMEMBER	**R** epay monies
Rights lead to a CIRCLE	**S** kill and care
	REMEMBER
	HANDS FOR S (SALE) (SERVICE)

4.3 Do Your Duty Right

- The bank has a special relationship with its customers to act in good faith and not apply undue influence (a fiduciary relationship).
- The banker has several *rights*. These include:
  - payment for service
  - indemnification against loss
  - repayment on demand of overdrawn accounts
  - lien over securities
  - to use customers' money how it sees fit
  - to expect customers to use reasonable care.
- The banker also has several *duties* towards his customer. These include to
  - honour his cheques where appropriate
  - obey his mandates and orders
  - maintain secrecy
  - give notice of closure
  - provide a statement of account
  - receive money and cheques for credit
  - repay money on demand
  - advise customer of forgery
  - exercise proper care and skill.

CHECK OUT QUESTIONS

Now that you have read this chapter, try answering the following questions to make sure you understand it:

1. What Acts define the factors determining which organisations can trade under the title of bank?
2. What two important facts did the 1979 Act lay down?
3. What was the definition of a banker given by the Bills of Exchange Act 1882?
4. What are the three characteristics of a banker that have been identified by case law?
5. How would you define a customer?
6. How long does an account have to be opened for someone to become a customer?
7. Can you be defined as a customer without having an account?
8. Name three main banker/customer relationships.
9. What is the basic relationship?
10. What terms were laid down in the case of *Joachimson v. Swiss Bank Corporation* (1921)?
11. When does the relationship become one of principal/agent?
12. What is a bailor and bailee, and when does their relationship come about?
13. Name the two types of bailee.
14. What is the special relationship called and what is it?
15. How would you define a right and a duty?
16. List the banker's rights and duties.
17. What is meant by a lien?
18. Under what conditions must a customer's cheques be honoured?

19. Under what circumstances can a bank disclose its customer's affairs?
20. What were the main case law points of the following cases?
    United Dominions Trust v. Kirkwood (1966)
    Ladbroke & Co v. Todd (1914)
    Woods v. Martins Bank (1959)
    Foley v. Hill (1848)
    Lloyds Bank v. Bundy (1975)
    Williams & Glyn's Bank v. Barnes (1980)
    London Joint Stock Bank v. MacMillan & Arthur (1918)
    Greenwood v. Martins Bank (1932)
    Tournier v. National Provincial Bank (1924)
    United Overseas Bank v. Jiwani (1976)
    Brown v. Westminster Bank (1964)

5

Bank Customers

On completion of this chapter you will know

— the types of personal and business customers
— the importance of obtaining customer information and references
— the advantages and disadvantages of the type of business
— the main characteristics of the

sole trader
partnership
company

— the importance of the Memorandum and Articles of Association
— the types of shares issued by limited companies
— some factors to be considered when opening a business account
— some of the other types of bank customers

clubs/societies
executors and administrators

Banks and bank staff have to deal with several types of customers, and each type brings its own problems, demands and opportunities.

The competition for personal customers is today very hot indeed. Banks are no longer the only organisations that provide the savings and investment services, loans and money transmission services these customers require. Building societies in particular have entered the market with a vengeance; together with insurance companies, finance houses, the National Savings Bank and the National Girobank amongst others, all are seeking to satisfy the needs of the personal sector (figure 5.1). The way in which these institutions compete is dealt with in more detail in Chapter 8.

In obtaining the money which gives rise to this financial competition these personal customers earn income from a variety of sources. These would include wages and salaries from working for a large or small company, fees from 'professional' practice such as solicitors or accountants, or perhaps even profits from working for themselves.

No matter who provides the money, one thing is certain; all these customers need some kind of bank account. This group will form the banks' business customer base (figure 5.2).

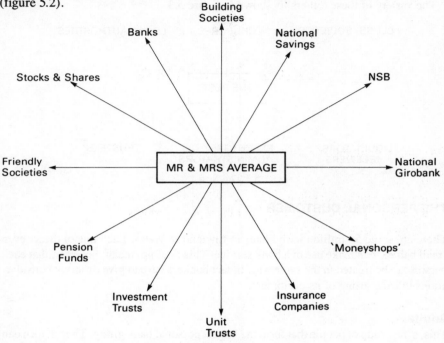

5.1 The Personal Market

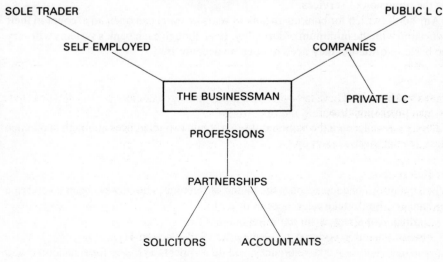

5.2 The Money Makers

Not only do banks have to deal with individuals and the places where they earn their money, but also with a wide variety of groups who have one thing in common — the need for an organisation that deals with 'money' — a bank.

The variety of these 'others' is shown in figure 5.3.

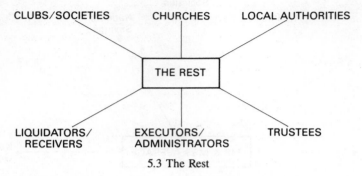

CLUBS/SOCIETIES   CHURCHES   LOCAL AUTHORITIES

THE REST

LIQUIDATORS/   EXECUTORS/   TRUSTEES
RECEIVERS   ADMINISTRATORS

5.3 The Rest

THE PERSONAL CUSTOMER

There are some 50 million individuals in England & Wales. Each one of these, even small babies, can make use of a bank service. This does not mean, however, that each person can be treated in the same way. In fact bankers have to give different considerations to each group of its customers.

Adults
This is the group of people that form the largest personal bank group. They in turn can be broken up into smaller groups, such as students, young marrieds, and senior citizens, for the provision of services.

Any adult (which for banking means 18 years or over) can open an account in their own name with the minimum of formality. Even though each bank's systems will vary the basic information they need to open an account is:
— name
— address
— occupation
— specimen signature.

For a current account the bank should also obtain two references although in practice these are not always taken up.

(a) References
When opening a cheque account the taking of references has always been a key issue for bankers. Banks take references in order to
— confirm that a new customer is reputable
— obtain protection under the Cheques Act 1957 (Section 4)

If the bank does not take references, and then collects a cheque for a customer who had no entitlement to it, it would have acted negligently. It could not then obtain pro-

tection under the Cheques Act. In such a case the bank would be liable for **conversion**.
Conversion occurs where a person deals with property belonging to someone else in such a way that it denies the owner's title and right to possess the property. The main danger areas for conversion are in

— collecting a cheque on behalf of a customer who has no right to it. Because it is very difficult for a banker to know whether the presenter has a good title he needs the protection obtained under the Cheques Act 1957 s. 4. To obtain this protection the banks must act in *good faith and without negligence.*
— safe custody deposits where conversion can be committed in several ways

  ● by wrongfully taking possession of goods
  ● by wrongfully damaging or destroying them
  ● by wrongfully disposing of them
  ● by wrongfully refusing to part with them.

Although references are probably not required by law, where a potential customer is
— known to the bank as suitable, or
— introduced by a person of 'repute'
references should in practice be taken up to avoid any charges of negligence.

The taking up of references would remove such a charge as it would be evidence of having made reasonable enquiries when the account was opened.

The importance of taking references for a customer who was not known to the bank was shown in the case of

Ladbroke & Co v. Todd (1914)

Ladbroke, a firm of bookmakers, issued a cheque to a client. The cheque was then stolen and paid into the bank by the thief who had endorsed it. The bank lost its statutory protection because it had not taken references. In later cases, however, the importance of always taking written references has been lessened.

In

Marfani & Co v. Midland Bank (1968)

a Pakistani (Kureshi) got his employer (Marfani) to sign a cheque for £3,000 in favour of 'Eliaszade'. He had introduced himself to a restaurateur as Eliaszade and he gave the restaurateur's name to the Midland Bank as one of two referees. An acount was opened and Kureshi, as Eliaszade, deposited £80 and then the cheque for £3,000.

The bank asked the restaurateur for a reference and he replied verbally saying that he had known the person for some time and believed he was about to open a restaurant.

The bank then issued Eliaszade with a cheque book and, having specially cleared the cheque, allowed him to spend most of the balance.

Marfani sued the bank for conversion but the court accepted *normal banking practice* as the standards against which a banker should operate.

This 'normal banking practice' included the taking of a verbal reference couched in general terms. This reference was of more significance than normal as the restaurateur was well known to the bank and had introduced several satisfactory customers previously.

Nor was failing to take a second reference considered to be negligent in this case and the bank was not guilty of conversion.

Banks were not only expected to check their potential customers through references; where the referees were not well known to the bank they were also expected to check the authenticity of the reference. This was demonstrated in

Lumsden & Co v. London Trustee Savings Bank (1971)

A man named Blake, who was an accountant for a firm of stockbrokers, opened a deposit account in the name of Brown. He said he was a self-employed chemist who had recently arrived from Australia.

He gave as reference the name of Dr Blake, who was also said to have recently arrived from Australia. The reference received was excellent — hardly surprising as Mr Blake, Brown and Dr Blake were all the same person.

Blake then paid in cheques worth thousands of pounds signed by his employers payable to Brown. When the fraud was discovered the bank was sued and found guilty of negligence, although they claimed protection under the Cheques Act 1957.

The reason for being found guilty was in part due to not following up the reference of Dr Blake, who although giving a first class reference, did not give the name and address of his bankers. This, it was felt, should have been done, especially as Dr Blake had only recently arrived in the country.

An interesting point about this case is that it was considered that banking practice changes over time and therefore what is required of the careful banker will also vary. Some banks have today decided not to take references in all cases of new customers.

(b) Customer's employer

Apart from building up a picture of the customer to establish his 'repute', and to provide marketing information, banks have taken the name of the customer's employer, again to avoid the dangers of conversion.

The dangers of failing to obtain the employer's name was shown in

Lloyds Bank Ltd v. E B Savory & Co (1932)

In this case the importance of obtaining the name of the *spouse's* employer was also shown. This could cause the bank some difficulties when opening an account for a married woman, as we will see later.

Here, one of two dishonest stockbroker's clerks stole bearer cheques belonging to their employer and drawn in favour of a third party.

One of the clerks paid some of the cheques into his wife's account. It was held that when opening the account the bank should have found out her husband's occupation and employer. This would have enabled the bank to spot the problem and prevent the fraud.

In the case of the other clerk, who paid cheques into his own account, the bank was held to be negligent because although it knew its customer was a stockbroker's clerk it had not ascertained the name of his employer.

Minors

For banking purposes a 'minor' is anyone under 18 years of age. People under this age cannot be bound by contract, and so the operation of these accounts should be usually on a credit basis. Repayment for money lent to minors used not to be legally enforced (Infants Relief Act 1874) although banks would sometimes lend where
— the minor had a known income and would repay
— a parent was well known to the bank.

The law relating to minors was reviewed by the Law Commission in 1984 and recommendations were made to revise the Infants Relief Act 1874. The main recommendations were that
— the age of 18 should remain for contractual purposes
— where 'infants' obtain luxury goods on credit by, say, misstating their age, these goods can be recovered (through the court) even though the contract is unenforceable
— previously unenforceable contracts can be ratified by the customer when they reach the age of 18
— any guarantee given for example by parents for a loan or a bank account is enforceable against the guarantor.

These recommendations were incorporated in the Minor Contracts Act 1987, which in effect abolished the Infants Relief Act. This Act
— established that contracts for the repayment of money are now subject to the rules of common law, the principle behind which is that an infant is of immature intelligence and discretion and therefore infants' contracts are generally voidable.
— minors, upon reaching the age of majority, can ratify contracts entered into when they were minors. This applies to contracts entered into after 9th June 1987.
— if a minor's debt is guaranteed and the minor is not liable, 'the guarantee shall not for that reason alone be unenforceable against the guarantor.'
— the court can order a defendant to transfer any property acquired by the defendant under a contract, or any property representing it, even if the contract had been with a minor and therefore unenforceable, provided it is 'just and equitable to do so.' Previously this could only be done if the minor had induced by fraud the other party to enter the contract.

Married women

Married women must be treated in exactly the same way as any other adult customer (Sex Discrimination Act 1975). We did, however, see earlier that banks were expected to obtain the name of the spouse's employers. This can cause problems for the bank if it is not their normal practice to ask for the wife's employer's name when opening an account for a married man.

To avoid the customer relations problems (as well as any accusations of sex discrimination) most banks have decided to accept the slight risks attached to not asking this question.

In one instance, however, banks *are* expected to treat their married women customers differently: they should advise a customer to seek independent advice from a solicitor when that customer is proposing to deposit a security on the behalf of a third party, usually the husband.

This is done to avoid any future arguments that the wife was unduly influenced by the third party (the husband) or even possibly by the bank.

Joint accounts

Joint accounts are usually opened by husband and wife, although it is not uncommon for other people to open such accounts. Any number of people can join together to open such an account, although in practice the number is usually two or three.

To open a joint account, all parties must sign a form known as a **mandate.** This will establish who is to sign cheques and withdrawals (e.g. all to sign, both to sign, anyone to sign, or either to sign) or who can sign for the release of documentation in safe custody.

Another important part of this mandate is that the parties agreed to **joint and several liability** for any overdraft on the account.

Joint and several liability

The importance of this 'clause' for banks is that if an overdraft was granted on a joint account, and it is not repaid, the bank can take legal action against *all* parties to the account.

For example, suppose there is a joint account of Mr X and Mr Y, with an overdraft of £1,000. The bank could take action against

     Mr X or

     Mr Y or

     Mr X *and* Mr Y.

This means that if Mr Y could not repay his share (£500) but Mr X could, then the full debt can be recovered from him.

Other important benefits of 'joint and several' are

— the ability to use private account credit balances of one customer against the debit balance of the joint account. This is clearly of benefit to the bank.

— on the death of one party the other(s) still have access to a source of money. This is of particular benefit to a wife on the death of her husband.

One obvious problem for the bank when managing a joint account is if the parties to the account fall out. This is probably most common with husband and wife joint accounts, although care must be taken with *all* accounts when any such dispute comes to the notice of the bank.

If the original mandate was for *either* party to sign then there is the danger that all the funds could be withdrawn by *one* of them. Whilst the bank would not be legally liable in such an event this would create bad customer relations which could be detrimental to the bank's present and future business.

To avoid such a situation, the bank — on finding out about such a dispute — should advise both parties that it will not act upon one signature, and that for all future transactions both parties must sign.

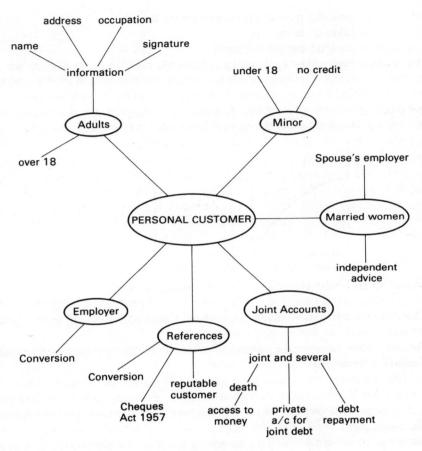

5.4 Personal Customers

BUSINESS CUSTOMERS

Although business customers are fewer in number than personal customers, they provide the banks with a greater potential for making profits (and losses).

There are three main types of business customers:

— sole traders
— partnerships
— limited companies.

We will look at each in turn.

Sole traders

You will be aware of this type of businessman. They are in business on their own, running a variety of businesses including shops, small factories, garages, farms, and so on.

These businesses are usually quite small. The owner

— provides most of the finance for the business
— takes all of the risk
— receives the income/profit.

The account operated by a sole trader is much like that of a personal customer. In fact, if the individual is trading under his own name the account will appear to be the same as a personal customer account. Closer scrutiny of the account will, however, show that the transaction throughput of a sole trader and a personal customer account vary. For a personal customer the normal flow is shown below in figure 5.5

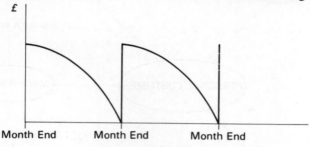

5.5 Typical Movement of a Personal Account

This personal account shows regular input of income once a month, and a regular pattern of expenditure during the month.

For sole traders, however, the pattern is much more variable over the month and also the year (see figure 5.6).

This fluctuation occurs because no regular monthly salary cheque is being paid in. The sole trader is dependent for cash upon his customers paying his bills. As most sole traders also have their own bills to pay, care has to be taken to try and match the income to the outgoings.

Because of these fluctuations it is common for sole traders to slip into the 'overdraft' situation. Because the bank is often their only source of borrowing, such accounts need to be regularly looked at to make sure the customer is not running into financial problems.

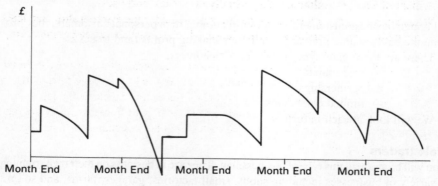

5.6 The Ins and Outs of the Sole Trader

CUSTOMER – ADVANTAGES	CUSTOMER – DISADVANTAGES
Independence	Total liability for debt
Control of the business	Expansion difficult (plough back profits)
Personal service	Long hours
Personal supervision of work and employees	Profit/loss of business when ill or on holiday
Business easy to set up	
Income /profit to owner	
BANK — ADVANTAGES	**BANK — DISADVANTAGES**
Large numbers	Irregular income & expenditure
Borrowing required (profit)	High risks
Could grow into larger company	Amount of monitoring needed

5.7 Advantages and Disadvantages of the Sole Trader

Partnerships

Quite often, when a sole trader wishes to expand his business, he will take on a partner. When operating as a sole trader there were few special legal requirements placed on his operation — for example, there is no need for a sole trader to even produce an annual statement of accounts (although they usually do for tax purposes).

When a partnership is formed the partners come under the **Partnership Act 1890.** This act defines a partnership as 'The relation which subsists between persons carrying on business in common with a view to profit'.

Obviously there have to be at least two partners but the maximum is normally limited to twenty. Partnerships greater than twenty are usually only allowable for practising solicitors or accountants, or for business carried out on the Stock Exchange.

Examples of partnerships can be found in most areas of business, but they are particularly common in the 'professional' areas such as solicitors, accountants, estate agents, architects, doctors, and dentists.

Unlike the sole trader who can operate his account much like a personal customer, it is important for the bank to know the names of all the individuals involved in the partnership as each one can materially affect the running of the account.

ADVANTAGES	DISADVANTAGES
Increased capital available	Each partner fully liable for all the debts
Specialisation possible	Decision-making could be slower (may be improved with more involvement)
Cover for sickness and holidays	Danger of disagreement between partners
	Death/retirement may affect the business because of capital or special business skills
	Finance limited by maximum of 20 partners
	One partner can bind all the other partners
	No changes in partnership can be effected without the consent of *all* the partners

5.8 Advantages and Disadvantages of Partnerships

In fact partnerships are required by law (**Companies Act 1981**) to print the names of all the partners on their letterheads and other business documents and also to display them at the firm's premises. There is however no legal requirement for the partnership to be established in writing. An oral or implied agreement is all that the law requires.

These are two important rules that affect the bank's dealings with its partnership customers.

RULE 1   Any partner can bind the firm by his actions done in the normal course of the firm's business. For example, a partner in a driving school can sign for the purchase of ten new cars. All the partners are then bound by that signature.

Although banking arrangements are outside the normal course of the firm's business, banks when opening a partnership account get the partners to agree that any act carried out in dealing with the bank is part of the firm's normal course of business. Therefore any partner can obtain an advance and bind the firm by that action.

RULE 2   All partners are all fully liable in law for the debts of the firm. When opening the account all partners should sign to establish the joint and several liability of all partners for any monies lent.

It is possible to establish a *limited* liability partnership where some partners have *limited* liability for the partnership debts, provided that at least one of the partners remains *unlimited*.

In addition to these two 'rules' the bank needs to establish, on opening an account, who is to sign cheques and other bank documents (SO/DD) on behalf of the firm.

Companies

Although sole traders and partnerships form an important part of the country's economy it is the company sector that carries out most UK business. Limited companies are therefore extremely important to the banks.

We have already seen that, as business moves from sole trader to partnership, additional legal requirements are added. The same is true in the move to limited company status. These organisations are controlled by various Acts of Parliament, the most relevant of these being the various Companies Acts.

There are two main forms of company:
— private companies
— public companies.

Before dealing with these individually, let us look at certain factors which apply to both types.

(i)   Both types of company have their *own legal identity*; both have rights and responsibilities which are separate from the individual shareholders. This is an important difference from sole traders and partnerships who are individuals and means that the bank must give special treatment, particularly when granting a loan or taking a security from a company.

The separate legal entity was laid down in the case of

Salomon v. Salomon & Co Ltd (1897)

Here, Salomon, who was the managing director and major shareholder of the company, lent the company money and took a debenture which gave him security for the loan. When the company failed he claimed priority over the ordinary creditors and this claim was upheld in court on the grounds that he was a separate legal entity to the company which bore his name.

(ii)   Most companies are 'limited liability'. This means that the shareholders' liability for any debt is limited to the amount of shares they hold. The personal assets of the shareholders cannot be taken to settle a company debt.

(iii) Each year, companies must send a statement of their accounts and Director's Report to the Registrar of Companies. These documents are then available for public scrutiny.

(iv)   Two key documents must be registered at the very beginning with the Registrar. These are the
— Memorandum of Association

— Articles of Assocation.

(v)   A Certificate of Incorporation is then issued by the Registrar when he is satisfied
       with the documents filed. In addition a public company will be issued with a
       Trading Certificate. Without these certificate(s) the company cannot start trading.

(vi)   Both types of company issue shares.

(a) Memorandum of Association

This is a key document for both the company and the bank. It sets out the relationship
the company will have with the general public. There are six areas covered by the
Memorandum:

(i)   the name of the company followed by 'public limited company' (PLC/plc) or the
       word 'Limited' if a private company

(ii)   whether the registered office is to be situated in England and Wales or Scotland.
       This determines to which country's law the company shall be subject

(iii) the objects of the company, i.e. the reasons for its formation and what business
       activities it proposes to carry out

(iv)   a statement that the liability of members is limited to the amount which they have
       contracted to pay for their share in the company

(v)   details of the share capital and how it is divided up e.g. £100,000 divided into 10,000
       £1 6% preference shares, plus 90,000 £1 ordinary shares. There can be all kinds
       of combinations

(vi)   the 'association' clause. This is a declaration signed by the founder members
       stating the number of shares they agree to take.

The section on the objects of the company is of great importance to the banker. This
part of the memorandum will tell the banker

— the powers of the company when borrowing money

— the purposes of the company.

Should a banker lend outside the objects clause this would be **ultra vires** (beyond
the powers); the bank may not then be able to recover its loan. For example, suppose
a company was set up with the object of printing books, but then borrowed money from
a bank to buy a string of racehorses. This would be *ultra vires* and the loan could be
declared void.

In the case of

Introductions Ltd v. National Provincial Bank Ltd (1970)

the company's main object was to provide entertainment and services for overseas
visitors. The bank who had seen the memorandum of deposit lent money for the purpose
of pig breeding. As this activity was not mentioned in the memorandum the loan and
the security provided for it was declared void.

(b) Articles of Association

This document sets out the regulations for the internal management of the company.
It covers such aspects as

(i)   method of appointment of the directors

(ii)   duties of the directors and secretary
(iii) directors' borrowing powers
(iv)   procedure to be followed at general meetings and the notice needed to call them
(v)   details of shareholders' rights, share issues, limitations on the transfer and forfeiture of shares provision as to audits and accounts.

For companies formed before 1st July 1985 the most important of these sections for bankers is the one relating to the directors' borrowing powers. Once again, if these powers are exceeded the loan may be voidable even though the loan was within the 'objects' of the company. The Companies Act 1985 changed the situation for companies formed on or after 1st July 1985 in that the amount directors can borrow is now only restricted by any limitations specifically placed in the Memorandum or Articles of Association.

(c) Types of shares

The Memorandum of Association states the proposed share capital of the company and how this capital will be split between the types of shares. This figure gives the company's *authorised share capital,* in other words the amount it could raise.

In most cases, however, the company does not *issue* all its 'authorised' shares. It issues enough to raise sufficient capital to run the business, and keeps back some for future plans.

Thus a company may be *able* to issue:
200 million shares at £1 = £200,000,000 (authorised capital).
In *fact* it may issue:
150 million shares at £1 = £150,000,000 (issued capital).

This leaves a further 50 million shares to be issued at some future date without having to seek a resolution from the company shareholders.

The authorised and issued share capital is usually made up of
— preference shares
— ordinary shares.

  Preference Shares are shares which
— pay a *fixed* dividend e.g. 7% out of the company's profits (non-cumulative preference shares)
— are paid in *advance* of ordinary share dividends
— are often *cumulative* i.e. if no dividend is paid in one year it is carried forward and added to the next year's dividend (cumulative preference shares)
— are given *preference* on the repayment of capital on the company being wound up
— may also *participate* in an additional dividend if the ordinary shareholders are paid more than a certain percentage (participating preference shares).

  Ordinary Shares are the most commonly issued shares.
— They receive a *dividend* in accordance with profits made. If there are no profits, no dividend is paid
— they are *last* to receive repayment should the company be wound up
— they carry the major *voting* rights.

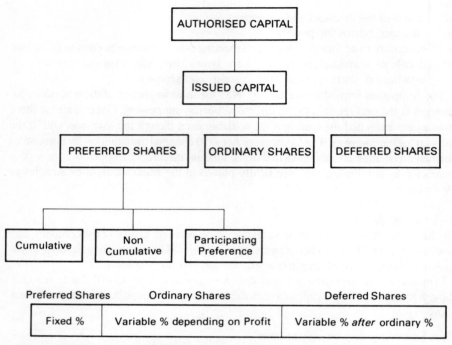

Preferred Shares	Ordinary Shares	Deferred Shares
Fixed %	Variable % depending on Profit	Variable % *after* ordinary %

N.B. Not all Profit has to be distributed — some is usually placed in Reserves.

5.9 Your Share of the Company

In addition to these two main types there are also Deferred (or Founders') Shares which are often held by the founders or promoters of the company. They are not common today. They receive dividends only after the ordinary shares have received a stated fixed dividend.

The private limited company

This type of company is the logical extension of business from

       sole trader $\longrightarrow$ partnership $\longrightarrow$ private limited company

Private Limited Companies are usually formed to

— provide more capital for expansion

— obtain the benefits of limited liability.

By setting up a private company, capital can be raised through the issue of shares although they cannot be advertised to the general public.

     Prior to 1980 private companies were subject to certain other restrictions:

          — the right to transfer shares was restricted

          — the maximum number of members was 50 (plus employees).

These have, however, now been removed by the **1980 Companies Act.**

	PRIVATE COMPANY	PUBLIC COMPANY
Name	.... Ltd	.... plc
No. of members	Minimum 2	Minimum 2
Buying and selling shares	Private dealing	Public dealing
Share capital	No minimum	£50,000 minimum

5.10 Private v. Public

Public Limited Company

This is the largest form of business. PLCs are usually formed to obtain access to the large sources of capital to be obtained by selling shares to the general public. This fact together with their size of operation is the key difference between a public and private company.

To obtain these funds the company issues a **prospectus** which invites any member of the public to subscribe for shares. This prospectus is often incorporated into a very big newspaper advertisement, for example in the *Financial Times*. It gives details of the company's past trading activities (if any), its future aims and the reasons for the new share issue. Normally the prospectus contains a form of application for shares; interested persons or companies can then complete and return this form as directed.

In this way the public can buy shares which are easily marketable at any time, for example on the London Stock Exchange.

A public limited company is defined as having
— a Memorandum of Association stating it to be a public limited company
— a minimum of 2 members
— a share capital of £50,000 (or more)
— a name ending in 'public limited company' or 'plc'.
Companies which do not meet this definition are private companies.

Other types of company

Although private and public limited companies dominate the company scene there are two other forms of company which are bank customers.

(a) Companies limited by guarantee

These companies are usually *non-trading* organisations such as a chamber of commerce, research organisation, club or society formed to look after the interests of their members. They are not mainly concerned with profit.

BOB—G

ADVANTAGES	DISADVANTAGES
Limited Liability (limited risk to shareholders)	Greater statutory control is imposed
Owners (shareholders) can sell their interests easily	The rules of the company (in its Memorandum and Articles) are more formal than for other businesses
Actual control is delegated to experts	The company must pay expenses on formation
A controlling interest can be obtained in a company without 100% ownership. E.g. 51% would give control	Accounts must be filed each year with the Registrar (thus open to public inspection)
A larger membership is permitted than for any other type of business, thus allowing a larger capital to be built up	

5.11 The Company — Advantages and Disadvantages

Unlike the previous companies, where shares are bought when the company is set up, members are only liable to 'pay up' when the company is wound up; the amount each has to pay is then limited to the amount they have each guaranteed.

(b) Unlimited companies
Here the members have unlimited liability for the debts of the company. Because of the potential risk of loss these companies are today very rare!

The only advantage of such a company is that it does not (with a few exceptions) have to lodge a statement of its accounts with the Registrar of Companies.

THE BANKER AND BUSINESS CUSTOMERS

Because of the many business and legal risks involved in dealing with business customers, bankers have to take a good deal of care when opening and operating business accounts.

Opening a business account
In order to open a business account the bank will usually need to see the
— Certificate of Incorporation
— Trading Certificate (for plcs)

ITEM	PARTNERSHIP	COMPANY
1. Liability of Members	Unlimited	Limited
2. Membership	Not over 20 (with certain exceptions)	Normally no maximum
3. Management	By partners, who all have right to take part in management	Delegated by shareholders to directors
4. Regulations	Contained in formal or informal (sometimes unwritten) agreement	Defined in the stamped and registered Memorandum and Articles
5. Main Legislation	Loose control by Partnership Act 1890, and Limited Partnerships Act 1907	Close control by modern Companies Acts
6. Capital	Easily varied. It fluctuates, since profits, drawings, etc. are often adjusted in capital accounts	Fixed by Memorandum. Strict regulations on variations
7. Status	No identity separate from partners	Separate legal entity – a corporate 'person'

5.12 The Company and the Partnership

— Memorandum of Association
— Articles of Association
The bank should also obtain
— a certified copy of the resolution appointing the first Directors (it should also be kept up to date with changes)
— a bank mandate signed by the Chairman and the Secretary which confirms that the mandate contents have been approved by the Board of Directors
— the signature(s) of persons empowered to run the account (on the mandate).

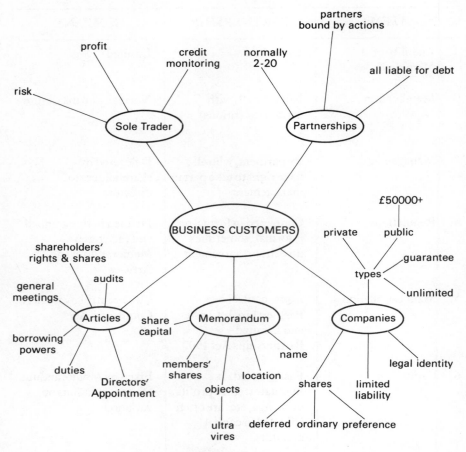

5.13 Business Customers

Operating a business account

There is no need at this stage to go into all the factors involved in operating a business account. Let us simply highlight a couple of points that arise from the areas covered by this chapter. When operating the account the banker must ensure that

— Bills of Exchange (which include cheques) are signed by those authorised to do so
— these cheques are signed 'for and on behalf of the company' or 'per pro'. The name of the company must be shown in full. Without the company name the person signing the 'bill' is responsible for it and could be personally liable to pay it. Even the omission of 'Ltd' has been held to make the individual liable
— the 'person's capacity' (e.g. Secretary) is shown
— money can only be drawn out of the account after the Certificate of Incorporation has been seen
— money lent to the company is in line with the Memorandum and Articles of Association (company objects and borrowing authority of Directors).

OTHER CUSTOMERS

Although personal and business customers are the most important ones for the bank there are other types of customer who will open accounts and transact business. The variety of these customers are shown in figure 5.3 but for our purposes we will deal with only these:

Clubs/Societies

These accounts are usually opened by social or sports clubs and societies. They are needed to deal with the club's income from subscriptions, bar or fund-raising events, and to pay the expenditures involved in running the club or society.

To open an account the members (or the committee) have to pass a resolution to do so, and this fact is stated in the mandate. The mandate will also show who is to sign (with specimen signatures) on behalf of the club/society.

Because the officials of clubs and societies change regularly the bank must be kept up to date about new appointments, especially of those who will sign on behalf of the club or society.

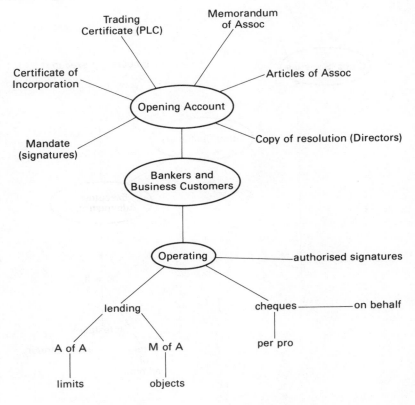

5.14 Bankers and Business Customers

One important fact about such customers is that the club or society cannot be sued for any money it has borrowed. Before any loan is made therefore the bank will want one of the individuals involved to take personal responsibility for the debt, and give a **guarantee** of its repayment.

Executors and Administrators

When someone dies, there is a need to appoint someone to manage the financial affairs of the deceased's **estate.** For example, to collect money owed, pay debts or tax, and distribute the estate. If a Will has been left the people will be named and known as **executors.**

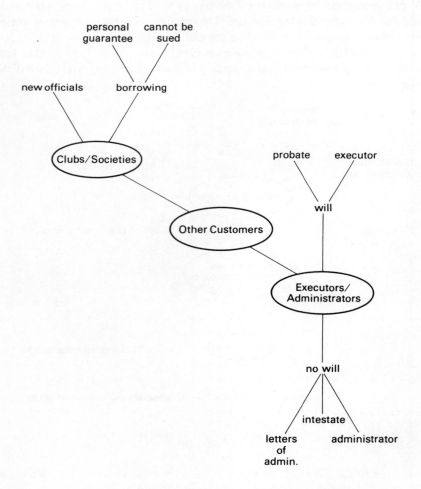

5.15 Other Customers

If no will has been left, or if the executor does not wish to act, these people will be appointed in accordance with a set of rules laid down by law. These appointed individuals are known as **administrators**. Where someone dies without leaving a Will he is said to have died **intestate.**

Before a bank can allow the accounts of the dead person to be dealt with it must receive proof that the executor or administrator is entitled to deal with the affairs. This proof is given by

— **Probate.** This is the approval for executors and is given when the Will has been proved in court. The executor receives a 'probate copy' of the Will and a certificate stating that the Will has been proven.

— **Letters of Administration.** This is the document given to administrators by the court giving them power to deal with the estate.

The 'personal representatives', as they are called, deal with the account until it is settled or wound up.

SUMMARY

● When opening a personal account certain information is needed, for example name, address, occupation, and specimen signature.

● References are needed to confirm the 'respectability' of a new customer and to obtain protection under the Cheques Act 1957.

● Conversion is a worry for bankers; conversion is the transfer of property to someone who is not the true owner.

● Banking practice changes over time, and what is required of the careful banker may alter over the years.

● Knowing the employer's name can be useful to the bank.

● A minor is anyone aged less than 18. Care must be taken regarding the provision of credit (cannot be legally enforced against minors although can be against a guarantor).

● Married women must receive the same treatment as any other adult customer. (Except that they may be advised to seek legal advice).

● Joint and several liability is a key factor in a joint account.

● Joint and several liability allows the bank to recover debt from one or all parties.

● There are three main types of business customer — sole traders, partnerships, and limited companies.

● Sole traders operate bank accounts much like personal customers.

● Partnerships have more legal considerations, for example under the Partnership Act 1890.

● Most partnerships have between 2 and 20 members.

● Any partner can bind a firm of partners.

● All partners are fully liable as individuals for the debts of the whole partnership.

● There are two main types of company - private and public.

● The main advantage of the company is limited liability.

- The Memorandum of Association and the Articles of Association are key company documents for the banker.
- The objects clause (Memorandum) limits the purposes for which lending can be made to the company (some lending can be *ultra vires*).
- There are three main types of shares — preference, ordinary and deferred.
- Banks also deal with other organisations and individuals e.g. clubs, executors and administrators.

CHECK OUT QUESTIONS

1. What basic information is needed when a customer wishes to open a personal account?
2. Give two reasons why references are needed.
3. How would you define conversion?
4. What is the importance of finding out the person's employer?
5. Below what age is a person a minor?
6. When should a married woman be treated differently to other adults?
7. What is meant by joint and several liability?
8. What benefits are there for the bank of joint and several liability?
9. Give three advantages of doing business as a sole trader.
10. What is the 'normal' size of a partnership?
11. State the two Rules that affect the bank's dealings with a partnership.
12. What are meant by the Memorandum of Association and Articles of Association?
13. What is *ultra vires* lending?
14. What are the differences between ordinary and preference shares?
15. What are authorised and issued capital?
16. What is the meaning of limited liability?
17. What is the minimum share capital of a plc?
18. What is the main difference between private and public limited company shares?
19. What documents will a bank want to see when opening a business account?
20. Can a club/society be sued for money it has borrowed?
21. What are executors and administrators?
22. A person is said to have died [   ] when no Will is left.
23. What are probate and letters of administration?
24. What key points were brought out in the following cases:
    Ladbroke & Co v. Todd (1914)
    Marfani & Co v. Midland Bank (1968)
    Lumsden & Co v. London Trustee Savings Bank (1971)
    Lloyds Bank Ltd v. E.B. Savory & Co (1932)
    Introductions Ltd v. National Provincial Bank Ltd (1970)
    Salomon v. Salomon & Co Ltd (1897)

6

Payments Systems and Funds Transfer

On completion of this chapter you will know the:

— various methods of payment and funds transfer
— definition of a cheque
— key items on a standard cheque form
— key cheque card instructions
— use of a banker's draft
— use and advantages of cheque cards
— differences between a credit card and a charge card
— working of Bank giro, standing orders and direct debits
— various cheque clearing systems including general, town and credit clearing
— importance and main considerations for both collecting and paying banker
— automated clearing systems of BACS and CHAPS
— main aspects of EFTPOS, National Giro and Homebanking.

In Chapter 2 we found out about the use of money today, and some of the means by which debts can be settled. However, in today's complex personal and business world there is a need to make payments in an increasingly sophisticated way.

For centuries payments systems have been based on metal or paper, and these items have been handled directly by the parties concerned or by their agents. The passing of 'paper' around the banking system has become a massive job. An estimated 8 million cheques are processed each working day and this is becoming a very expensive method of dealing with payments. Therefore banks and their customers have sought to use the benefits of automation to allow them to deal with increased business at an economical cost.

In this Chapter we will consider the existing payment methods including:
- cash
- cheques
- banker's drafts
- standing orders and direct debits
- credits and charge cards
- bank giro credits

together with their advantages and disadvantages and then find out how these payments are handled within the system.

PAYMENT METHODS

Cash (notes and coins)

Cash is still the basic form of payment today, although its use is being restricted to the 'cheaper' transactions. To see the decline of cash as a method of payment you need only go into a supermarket where there are now special tills for people wanting to pay by cash. Most of these customers are spending less than those customers who go through the other tills.

For a variety of reasons including:
- security
- bulk carrying
- cost of goods and services
- high costs of dealing with cash

banks, businesses and customers have moved away from cash as a means of payment for the more expensive goods and services.

Cheques

The cheque is the most important method of payment and of transferring funds. Cheques are today a widely accepted form of payment despite the fact that they are not legal tender. Their acceptability has increased since the introduction of the cheque guarantee card in 1965 which guaranteed the payment of a cheque up to a stated amount.

(a) Definition

A cheque is defined as an unconditional order in writing drawn on a banker signed by the drawer, requiring a banker to pay on demand a sum certain in money to the order of a named person or to the bearer.

The meaning of the different parts of the definition are:

1. *Unconditional*   Payment cannot hinge on certain conditions being met, for example 'pay Mr J Jones £50 provided my salary cheque has been paid into my account'.

2. *Writing*   Must be in writing. Pen, biro, print, even pencil can be used although the latter is not recommended because details can easily be altered.

Cash

The most widely used way of making payments. Almost 90% of all payments are still settled with cash.

Cheque

Can be used to purchase goods and services or to obtain cash from a bank account.

Credit Cards

Card holders can obtain goods and services from those shops, garages and other organisations which accept the cards. Can also be used to obtain cash from banks at home and abroad.

Regular Payments

Standing Order

Used by customers who want the bank to make payments for them on a regular basis, such as rent; hire purchase instalments; insurance premiums; club subscriptions. It saves people having to remember each time.

Direct Debit

A variation on a standing order. Used mainly by organisations which receive vast numbers of regular payments. The companies draw on the customers' bank accounts by computer.

Cash Dispenser + Card

Enable customers to obtain cash from a machine. In some cases even when the bank is closed. You can also order a statement or a cheque book.

Cheque Cards

Will guarantee payment of a cheque up to a sum of £50. A big help when you are shopping.

Travelling Abroad

Travel cheques are a safe and convenient way of carrying money for holidays. Banks also supply foreign bank notes.

Bank Giro Credit

A convenient way of paying bills through the banking system. You can also pay money into your own account when you are away from home.

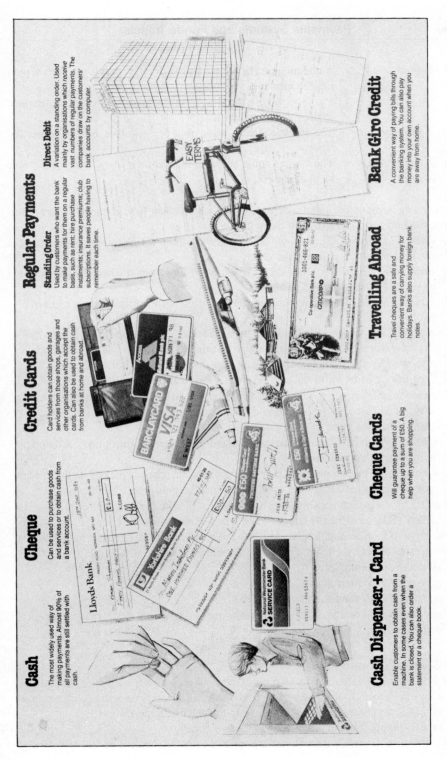

6.1 Banks and Payments (courtesy of Banking Information Service)

3. Signed	A cheque must be signed by the drawer, that is the person paying the money.
4. On demand	It is expected that the cheque will be paid as soon as it is presented to the other bank.
5. A sum certain	The amount of the cheque must be definitive, both in words and figures.
6. Named person or bearer	The cheque must be payable to someone by name or payable to 'the bearer'.

The key items on the standard cheque form which allow the cheque to be an acceptable method for the transfer of money:

1. *Bank and Branch.* This shows the branch on which the cheque is drawn (that is the branch which will pay the cheque).
2. *Branch Sorting Code.* This six figure number identifies the branch and is used to simplify the 'clearing' process.
3. *Payee's Name.* This identifies the 'person' to whom the amount should be paid.
4. *Name of the Account.* This identifies the account which should be debited.
5. *Account Number.* This not only identifies the account to be debited but it is also used by the branch and the computer systems to debit the money.
6. *Signature.* To be valid the cheque must be signed by the customer.
7. *Amount in Words.* ⎫ These two give the sum to be transferred and obviously
8. *Amount in Figures.* ⎭ they should be the same amount.
9. *Date.* Cheques must show a date.
10. *Cheque Number.* Cheques are issued usually in books of thirty and each cheque is numbered consecutively.
11. *Crossings.* The two parallel lines drawn across the cheque mean that the cheque cannot be cashed across the counter. It must be paid into a bank account.

Items *2, 5, 10,* which are shown on the bottom of the cheque, are printed in magnetic characters. These enable the cheque to be 'read' electronically. There is also a space to the right of the account number to allow the cheque amount to be put in (encoded).

When writing out a cheque customers should ensure that:
— all details are completed
— cheques are written in ink
— no space is left for fraudulent additions
— any corrections or changes are signed although in practice initials may be accepted
— words and figures agree.

(b) Cheque guarantee cards

The introduction of these cards has increased the acceptability and use of cheques as a means of payment to the extent that most 'business' operations will accept a cheque which is supported by a guarantee card (up to the cheque card limit).

The acceptance of the cards is based on two contracts:

(i) *The banker and the customer* where the customer agrees to use the card in

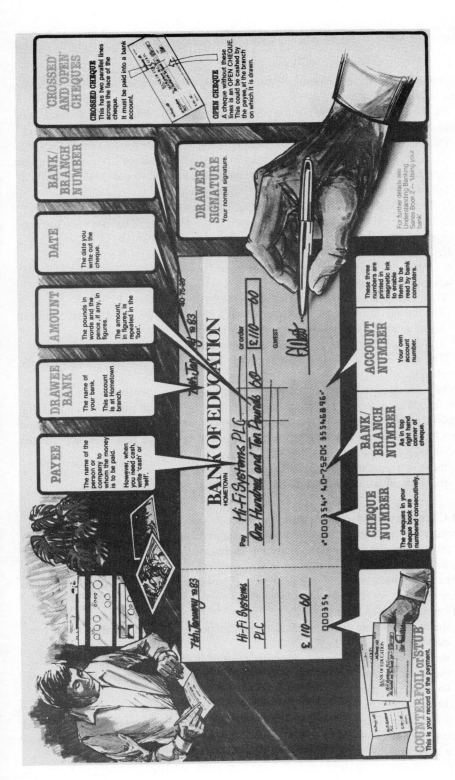

6.2 Understanding Your Cheque (courtesy of Banking Information Service)

accordance with the conditions of issue and accepts that the cheques cannot be 'stopped' from payment.

(ii) *The banker and the payee* (the receiver of the cheque) where the bank guarantees payment provided the instructions on the reverse of the card are followed.

The instructions which must be followed are shown on the back of the card. They are:

'_____ Bank guarantees in any single transaction the payment of one cheque taken from one of its own cheque books for up to £50 provided the cheque is not drawn on the account of a Limited Company and

1. The cheque bears the same name and code number as the card.
2. It is signed before the expiry of the card in the presence of the payee by the person whose signature appears on the card.
3. The card number is written on the back of the cheque by the payee.
4. The card has not been altered or defaced.'

It is important to note that

— The card number should be written on the back of the cheque.
— The cheque limit is £50. This means that a cheque can be countermanded if it is for an amount in excess of the stated limit.
— The signatures on the card and the cheque should be the same.
— The card is within the date and bears the same bank/branch code number as the cheque.

Only *one* cheque is guaranteed. If therefore two cheques are issued for a £90 bill, one for £50 and one for £40 the guarantee covers only one of them. It could also be argued that the conditions have not been followed when two cheques are issued and therefore neither is guaranteed. In practice, however, banks will guarantee such cheques and only question their use when:

— there is irregular or unauthorised use of the cards
— there are insufficient funds to pay the cheques.

(c) Cheque guarantee cards and fraud

Because they virtually guarantee acceptance of a cheque as payment, the combination of cheque and cheque guarantee card has increased the potential for fraud either by the bank's customer or by a third party gaining access to the cheque book and card. In the mid 1980s some 300 fraudulent cheques were being issued every hour that shops were open.

In order to try to limit losses:

— the bank restricts the issue of cheque guarantee cards to established and proven customers;
— the card remains the bank's property (part of the terms of issue);
— the customer cannot use the card to overdraw the account without prior agreement;
— the card and cheque book should be carried separately.

Three parties are involved in a cheque guarantee transaction:

(i) *The Payee*. Provided the signature on the card and cheque are compared and found to be acceptable, and the other conditions of acceptance are followed, the payee's position is secure.

(ii) The Customer. Where a card has been used fraudulently by a third party the customer's position is also secure provided he has not been negligent. Where negligence has taken place, for example in the care taken with the card and cheque book, the bank would have a claim against him for cheques that it had to honour.

Where, however, the cheque card is used by the customer to obtain an unauthorised overdraft this is an offence under the Theft Act 1968.

This was brought out in the cases of:

Regina v. Kovacs (1974)

In this case the bank wrote to the customer whose account was already overdrawn asking that no more cheques be issued. This was followed by a request to return the cheque book and cheque card. The customer claimed that she no longer had either of them. Two months later, however, two further cheques were issued. The court found that she was guilty of deception in her dealings.

Metropolitan Police Commissioner v. Charles (1976)

In this case the customer, who had an overdraft limit of £100, wrote out 25 cheques of £30 each (old cheque card limit) in a single evening at a gambling club. The bank had to honour all the cheques and as the customer had no authority to use the card beyond his limit he had committed an offence. The customer was found guilty of theft by deception.

(iii) The Bank. Bankers attempt to reduce their potential loss by the rules and conditions that surround the issue and use of cheque cards.

They are particularly vulnerable when a cheque book and card are stolen and they are continually seeking methods of preventing thieves from tampering with and forging the cards. Banks have now introduced cheque cards with holograms which are more difficult to alter or copy. It is for this reason also that banks are reluctant to increase the amount guaranteed by each cheque even though today's limit is felt to be too low for many transactions.

Where a customer has deliberately issued cheques supported by a cheque card which increase his indebtedness beyond an agreed amount, the bank will certainly initiate proceedings to recover the amount.

Banker's drafts

A banker's draft is similar to a cheque but it is drawn by the customer's branch on the bank's Head Office rather than being drawn by the customer on his branch. The result of this is that 'guaranteed' payment is ensured and, after cash, a draft is the next best thing to receive in payment for goods or services.

Banker's drafts are used therefore when a bank customer has to provide a guaranteed payment before he can receive the service, for example solicitors acting on behalf of a house seller quite often ask for a banker's draft in payment before handing over the deeds of a house if there is any danger of a cheque being 'bounced', that is not paid.

Drafts are also commonly used in payment for a car.

The benefits of using a draft are:

— there is no need to carry large amounts of cash
— there is no need to wait for a personal cheque to be cleared (the purchaser can take receipt of goods and services immediately)
— a seller is guaranteed payment.

Credit cards

The use of credit cards has increased dramatically over the last five years. The original credit card companies, VISA (Barclaycard, Trustcard) and Mastercard (Access) have now been joined by credit cards which are issued by retail outlets for use in their own stores such as Marks & Spencer, Debenhams, or by groups of stores such as the Sears card. Credit cards can be used as a means of payment in their own right. Some (such as Barclaycard, Trustcard) can also be used as a cheque guarantee card.

Credit card customers are given a credit limit on the credit card account and can buy goods and services up to this amount. The credit account is totally separate from any bank account that is held.

Goods and services can be bought at any retail outlet which displays the credit card signs and most retailers will accept payment by one of several cards.

When the card is used for purchasing, the customer must sign the sales voucher and the signature is then compared to the signature on the card. Copies of the vouchers have the details of the card embossed upon them by a special machine and they also show the details and amount of the sale.

A copy of the sales voucher is given by the retailer to the customer and a copy is sent to the credit card company through the local bank branch from which the retailer receives payment. Increasing numbers of retail outlets are now using terminals for such transactions, where information held on the magnetic strip on the back of the card is read by the terminal. This information is sent to the credit card company by electronic means thereby eliminating the need for vouchers (*see also* page 131).

Each month the cardholder receives a statement from the credit card company which details all his purchases in the month, together with the total amount outstanding and any minimum amount that needs to be paid.

When he receives the statement the customer can:
— pay the full amount of the balance;
— spread the payments over a period of months.
These payments can be made:
— by post;
— through a bank account using a giro credit slip;
— by regular monthly Direct Debit.

When the full balance is not settled each month, the customer is charged interest on the outstanding balance and this provides the card company with a main source of income. The company also receives an income from the retailers who make use of its cards. Every time a card is used the retailer has to pay a percentage of the sale, between 1% and 5% to the credit card company.

The advantages of using credit cards to pay for goods and services are as follows:

(a) Advantages to the customer:
— no need to carry cash (convenience and security);
— immediate delivery of goods;
— payments can be spread;
— free credit is given. There is no need to pay until the account statement is received which could be up to a month after purchase. The customer then has a further 25 days to make his payment which gives almost 2 months' free credit;
— permanent access to credit (as soon as the customer repays some of his borrowing he has that amount of credit available again to make purchases. This is known as revolving credit);
— for travellers who pay by credit card there is automatic accident insurance.

(b) Advantages to the retailer:
— receives immediate payment when the vouchers are 'paid in' to the bank;
— provides some security as the retailer contacts the credit card company to check the account when large amounts are involved;
— increased sales.

(c) Advantages to the banks (operating a credit card company):
— cost effective way of granting credit (no need for continuous loan or overdraft approval);
— credit limit control is carried out by a credit card operations unit (by computer);
— banks can provide credit to non customers (for example 25% of Barclaycard customers are not Barclays' customers);
— banks who provide credit for in-store cards gain access to a wider customer base.

	CHARGE CARD	CREDIT CARD
COST	Enrolment fee Annual membership fee	Free
PAYMENT	Full amount paid monthly	Monthly or by instalments
CREDIT PERIOD	Amount paid immediately on receipt of account No credit period allowed for payment	25 days further credit after account statement

6.3 Charge Cards and Credit Cards

Charge cards

Charge cards such as American Express, Diners Club or 'Gold' cards are very similar to credit cards as a means of payment; the customer uses the card to pay for goods and services and then receives a monthly account of purchases.

Outlets are charged a commission (up to 5%) on sales. The main differences between the two cards are shown in Figure 6.3.

Bank giro credits

Frequently, customers wish to pay money into someone else's bank account and this can be done by means of a Bank giro credit (or credit transfer as it is also known).

Bank giro credits enable the transfer of money to any bank in the country. The system is commonly used for the payment of bills such as electricity, gas, credit cards, telephone, rates. In fact, many organisations who are due a regular payment issue books of giro credits for use by their customers.

The Bank giro system is also used by employers to pay wages and salaries to their staff. Here a credit transfer slip is made out for each employee and passed to the bank with one payment to cover the total salary bill. The branch then credits the bank account detailed on the slip. And it is used by the banks themselves for making standing order payments such as mortgage payments. As we will see later, in both of the above cases computer crediting through BACS is replacing the paper system.

Standing orders/direct debits

These systems are used for regular payments such as insurance, loans, annual subscriptions and involve the customer authorising the bank to make payments on his behalf.

(a) Standing orders

With this system the customer advises the bank to make payments on a certain date for a fixed amount; it is then the bank's job to make the payments. If the amount or date on which the payments are made are changed then the customer simply advises the bank of the changes.

(b) Direct debits

This payment system is also used for regular monthly payments. But instead of the customer telling the bank the amounts and when to pay them, the company is authorised to tell the bank what to pay and when. Obviously, before it will make the payments, the bank will require the customer's authority to do so.

For this reason direct debits can deal with variable payments more easily than standing orders, as it is the receiver who produces the document demanding payment and the customer does not continually have to tell the branch of changes.

The use of direct debits is not confined solely to personal customers. Today business customers (such as breweries/public houses, oil companies/garages) use the system when regular supplies are provided and regular payments need to be collected.

Because the company is required to make correct charges at the right time there are certain safeguards to protect the banks and their customers.

These are:
— their use is restricted to approved organisations
— direct debits must be made in line with the customer's instructions
— any changes in amount or date must be given to the customer in advance
— the bank and the customer must be reimbursed by the organisation in cases of incorrect direct debit claims.

	Advantages	Disadvantages
CASH	Acceptable Used for small purchases	Bulky to carry large amounts Security
CHEQUES	Ease of payment (with cheque card) Acceptable method No need for cash	Possible fraud if stolen Need to keep record of account Large amounts may require cheque to be cleared before goods supplied
PLASTIC CARDS e.g. Trustcard Barclaycard Access	Convenience and security Immediate delivery of goods Payments can be spread Free credit possible Revolving credit	Higher rates of interest May encourage overspending
SO/DDs	Payments made automatically Variable amounts easy via DD	Need to remember payments made
DRAFTS	No need to carry large amounts of cash Guaranteed payment (for receiver) No delay in waiting for cheque to be cleared	Cannot be stopped unless lost or stolen

6.4 Customer Advantages and Disadvantages

FUNDS TRANSFER

In the previous section the various methods of transferring money were highlighted. We now need to consider the process by which money is moved from bank to bank or from the customer to the organisation.

The system for transferring cash always involves the handing over of notes or coins, a situation in which both payer and receiver are present.

Today, however, it is more common for funds to be transferred between banks and bank accounts using either paper or automated systems which only 'reveal' themselves when the sender and receiver are sent a statement of their bank account.

Clearing cheques
To obtain payment for its customers for cheques that are paid into the branch from customers of other branches the bank needs a system of sending these items from one to another. This process is known as cheque 'clearing'. In its simplest form this would consist of

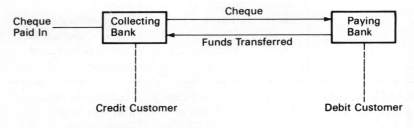

6.5 Cheque Clearing

This very simple system identifies two key roles that branches have to play in the cheque clearing system. These are the roles of collecting banker and paying banker.

(a) The collecting banker
When a customer pays a cheque into his branch which is drawn on another branch or bank, he is asking his branch to obtain payment on his behalf and to have his account credited. The bank is here acting as a collecting banker.

The term collecting banker is applied to the banker who accepts a cheque for credit into an account. The duty of a collecting banker is to credit the customer's account with the value of cheques deposited and to collect the money from the bank on which the cheque is drawn. It must ensure that the cheque is being credited to the account for which it is intended.

To carry out the role of collecting banker it is important that all the cheques accepted for deposit are carefully scrutinised. The easiest and quickest way is to start from the top of the cheque and work downwards:

Date. There are three things to be considered when examining the date of a cheque. They are as follows:

Out of date. A cheque is valid for six months from the date of issue, unless a shorter period is written on the face of the cheque. For example, if a cheque dated 1st March 1988 was presented on the 5th September 1988 it would be out of date.

Post-Dated. This means that the cheque is dated later than the day on which it is presented. In the above example, if the cheque was presented on any date before 1st March 1988 it would be 'post-dated'.

Undated. If a cheque is presented undated the payee can insert a date and should be asked to do so by the cashier. If any undated cheques are mistakenly accepted, the date stamp can be used to insert it. However, once a date is entered on a cheque it cannot be altered by the payee.

Payee. The payee's name should be the same as the one shown on the account that the cheque is being paid into. If the name is different then an endorsement is required (endorsements are covered later). If a cheque is presented with no payee's name entered then it cannot be accepted and it cannot be written in by the customer or by a cashier. Care should be taken should the payee's name be mis-spelt.

Words and figures. Both words and figures should be written and should agree. If they disagree then the cheque should be returned to the drawer for amendment or for a new cheque to be issued.

Signature. The cheque must be examined to see if it is signed. Presence of a signature is sufficient for the purposes of a collecting banker.

Crossings. When a cheque is crossed it must be paid into a bank account and cannot be cashed over the counter. More detail on crossings is given in the section on the paying banker.

Endorsements. There are occasions when the person to whom a cheque is made payable (that is the payee) wishes to transfer the cheque to a third party. In order to do this, the payee signs the cheque on the back. This signature is called an endorsement. For example:

1. A cheque payable to a Mr A Jones can be paid into an account in a different name if Mr A Jones has signed the back of the cheque.

2. A cheque payable to *joint* names, Mr A & Mrs D Jones, is presented for deposit to the sole account of one of the payees Mrs D Jones. The cheque must be endorsed by the other payee(s). In this example Mr A Jones must sign the cheque on the back.

   The endorsement signature must, as far as possible, accurately reflect the name of the payee. The endorsement should be the normal signature of the payee. Courtesy titles such as Mr, Mrs, Captain must not be included as a prefix to the signature (but may be included as a suffix):

Payee	*How endorsed*
Dr J Brown	James Brown Dr or MD
Capt M Philips	M Philips Capt

A married woman must endorse with her normal signature and may add her courtesy title as a suffix:

Payee	How Endorsed
Mrs Alice Jones	A Jones
	Alice Jones
	A Jones Mrs
	Alice Jones Mrs

If, however, the cheque is payable to her husband's Christian name or initials the endorsement must include such words as 'wife of . . .'

Actual Name	Payee	Endorsed
Mrs Alice Jones	Mrs Jack Jones	Alice Jones wife of Jack Jones

There are three types of endorsements, blank, specific and restrictive:

(i) Blank. A blank endorsement or general endorsement is a signature of the payee on the back of a cheque. The effect is to make the cheque payable to the bearer. For example payee J Smith endorsed 'James Smith'.

(ii) Specific. A specific endorsement consists of the payee's signature on the back of a cheque, together with the name of the person to whom the cheque is being transferred, for example payee J Smith endorsed 'James Smith pay to L Green or order'.

(iii) Restrictive. A restrictive endorsement is one which consists of a specific endorsement with a restrictive wording added. The additional wording prevents further transfer of the cheque, for example payee J Smith endorsed 'James Smith pay to L Green only'.

Banks usually ask for endorsements in the following circumstances:
— when cheques in favour of joint payees are credited to a sole account;
— when cheques are cashed over the counter (not usually for customers' own cheques);
— when R (receipt) is printed on the cheque, for example a cheque issued by an insurance company to a policyholder who is receiving the benefits of the policy;
— if the cheques are payable overseas;
— if cheques have been negotiated, ie cheques which have been transferred (a very small percentage of all cheques).
Endorsements are not required when
— a cheque is paid into the payee's account;
— cheques in favour of a sole payee are credited to a joint account.

(b) Paying banker

When a cheque has been passed through the 'clearing' system it will reach the paying banker whose role is to debit the cheque to the customer's account. However, before a cheque is debited the paying banker has a duty to ensure that the cheque is correctly completed, and that it is paid in accordance with the account mandate or returned within the legally recognised time limits.

It is important to consider:
(i) legal obligations of the paying banker;
(ii) identifying the paying banker and the time limits for dishonouring cheques;
(iii)scrutinising the cheques and the drawer's account;
(iv)risks and protection;
(v) returning cheques — reasons and replies.

(i) Legal obligations of the paying banker
The paying banker has a legal obligation to honour his/her customer's cheques provided that:
— there is sufficient cleared credit balance or an available overdraft limit;
— the cheque has been completed correctly and has no defects;
— there is no legal bar to payment such as death, bankruptcy.
   The bank MUST NOT PAY the cheque if:
— it has notice of defect in the presenter's title that is where the bank has received notice that the cheque is lost or stolen and it is then presented for payment;
— the drawer's signature is forged.
   The banks must always honour a cheque guaranteed against a cheque card issued in accordance with the cheque card regulations.

(ii) Identifying the paying banker and the time limits for dishonouring cheques
A bank is acting as a paying banker when it is presented with a cheque to be debited from an account held at that branch.

Ways in which a cheque may be presented	*Time limits for dishonouring*
An uncrossed cheque may be presented for payment over the counter at the paying bank for encashment by the holder.	The cheque must be paid or dishonoured immediately.
Special presentation by another banker through the post.	The cheque is paid, or dishonoured on the day of presentation by telephone.
Through the Clearing House.	The cheque is usually paid or dishonoured on the same day.

(iii) Scrutinising the cheque and the account mandate
Before debiting a cheque from the customer's account the following details must be checked:

— date
— payee
— endorsements
— crossings
— alterations
— drawer's signature
— mutilation
— stopped cheque
— legal bars to payment
— payment in accordance with the Account Mandate.

Date
All cheques must have a date on them. If the cheque is:
— Undated — the correct date may be inserted
— Postdated — that is a date in the future, the cheque must be returned
— Out of date — that is after 6 months or as otherwise stated on the cheque, the cheque must be returned.

Payee
The payee's name must be present on the cheque.

Endorsements
The paying banker should ensure that any endorsement on the cheque is consistent with the payee's name.

Crossings
A crossing is a direction to the paying bank and it appears as two parrallel lines drawn across the face of the cheque reasonably near the centre.

A crossing may be pre-printed or hand written. It means that the cheque must be paid into a bank account. It is a means of minimising the chances of someone fraudulently obtaining payment of a cheque. Uncrossed cheques do not have to be paid into a bank account and payment can be made over the counter.

General Crossings
A general crossing consists of two parallel lines drawn across the face of the cheque with or without the words: 'and Co', 'and Company' or 'not negotiable'.

A crossing is an instruction which must always be obeyed.

All four crossings are treated in exactly the same way. The most common form is

&Co   and Company   not negotiable

just the two parallel lines, with 'and Co' or 'and Company' being less frequent. Of the four the only one that means anything different from the rest is 'not negotiable'.

Not Negotiable

Unless the words 'not negotiable' appear on the face of a cheque, the cheque may be assumed negotiable. In general terms this means that a person who accepts the cheque, in good faith, and gives some value has a perfect legal right to that cheque. The words 'not negotiable' alter the position to the effect that if the cheque was stolen, the person who receives the cheque does not have any better legal right to the cheque than that of the thief, that is no right at all.

If the cheque had not been crossed 'not negotiable' anyone dealing with the cheque after the thief would have a valid title provided that they took the cheque in good faith and for value and had no notice of the theft.

In the case of

Great Western Railway v. London & County Bank (1901)

the bank had previously cashed cheques for a Poor Law overseer. When this overseer fraudulently obtained a cheque for the poor rate from the railway company crossed 'not negotiable', the bank cashed it for him. The bank was sued for reimbursement when the fraud came to light. The House of Lords held that because of the 'not negotiable' crossing the bank had no better claim to the cheque than the overseer, ie none.

The use of 'not negotiable' on a crossed cheque is therefore beneficial to the drawer of the cheque, protecting him in the event of the cheque being stolen. It does not, however, in any way restrict the cheque's transferability.

Special Crossings

A 'special crossing' consists of the name of a bank (possibly including the branch) across the face of a cheque, with or without parallel lines. The cheque must be paid into the bank to which it has been crossed. The paying banker must only pay a specially crossed cheque to the bank/branch specified in the crossing. If a crossing stamp is not consistent with the bank named in the crossing then the cheque must be returned.

Barclays Bank PLC | TSB England & Wales | Lloyds Bank PLC Shrewsbury Branch

Other Instructions

An instruction to the collecting banker that is often found on a cheque are the words 'account payee only' (or 'account J Smith' or 'account payee'). This instruction is in addition to the crossing but is not strictly part of the crossing.

It is an instruction to the collecting banker and means that the cheque in question must be paid into the account of the named payee only. Even an endorsement does not override this instruction. The collecting banker would be quite justified in questioning an 'account payee only' cheque if it is not being deposited to the account of the named payee.

If a satisfactory answer is not given and the cheque is credited to another account the bank could be liable for conversion.

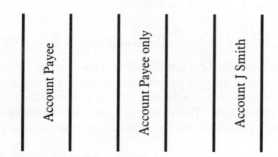

Alterations

Any alteration on the cheque must be authorised by the drawer. This is done by signing any alteration.

Drawer's Signature

The Drawer's signature must be present and correct.

Mutilations

A mutilated cheque is one that is torn or is in more than one piece, even though it may have been stuck together, and it is considered invalid.

Where the cheque has been mutilated by the collecting banker an explanation and the collecting bank stamp should appear on the reverse of the cheque.

Stopped Cheques

A customer has the right to stop a cheque until the moment the banker pays it.

When giving notice of a stopped cheque the customer (drawer) must provide the bank, in writing, with clear and precise details which identify the cheque without ambiguity: the payee's name, the amount of the cheque and its number.

When a cheque is stopped by telephone, written confirmation should follow. The banker can however postpone payment or dishonour, pending the drawer's written confirmation.

It is the customer's duty to quote the correct cheque number. If the wrong number is provided the bank will not be liable for paying the cheque that it was intended to stop. In the case of

Westminster Bank Ltd v. Hilton (1926)

Hilton placed a stop on a cheque but gave the bank the wrong cheque number. When the bank received a cheque which had the details of the original cheque but was a different number the bank tried to contact Hilton but were unable to do so. The bank paid the cheque, assuming it to be a duplicate. Hilton sued the bank for disobeying his instructions and for subsequently returning other cheques for lack of funds.

It was held that the bank had done all it could to protect Hilton and was justified in returning the cheques as, although cheques can have the same details, they can only have one number.

Notice may be given by telephone but the bank should ensure written confirmation is obtained and signed in accordance with the account mandate. It is permissible for one signatory to confirm the stop. To become effective the stop must be actually delivered to and read by the paying banker. In

Curtice v. London City & Midland Bank Ltd (1908)

Curtice telegrammed the branch, stopping payment but the telegram was not delivered until after the branch closed and so it was placed in the letter box. The telegram was overlooked the next day when the box was cleared. It was held that the cheque was not stopped as the notice did not come into the bank's hands and Curtice lost the case.

Where a customer maintains accounts at different branches he need only advise one branch that he wishes to stop a cheque. That branch should then notify the others. In

Burnett v. Westminster Bank Ltd (1966)

the customer, Burnett, had two accounts at the Borough and Bromley branches.

Burnett issued a cheque from his Borough cheque book but altered the address to Bromley. He did not alter the computer print at the bottom which meant that the cheque would be returned to Borough.

Burnett advised Bromley to stop the cheque, but Borough paid it as they had not been advised and they did not notice the alteration.

Burnett won his case despite that fact that the bank said there was a notice in the front of each cheque book which said that cheques would be applied to the account for which they had been prepared.

Where an account is transferred to another branch any stop instruction should be transferred also.

If a payee has a cheque stolen or it is lost he may contact the drawer's bank to advise them. The bank must always attempt to contact the drawer to obtain his authority to stop the cheque. Where the drawer cannot be contacted the banker in law may disregard the payee's instructions. However, great care would need to be taken in case the cheque was subsequently presented.

Legal Bars to Payment
Where the bank has notification of such events as death, bankruptcy, court order, the
cheque should be returned with the appropriate reply.

Payment of the Cheque in Accordance with the Account Mandate
It must be confirmed that all necessary signatures are present and correct.

(iv) Risks and protection
Provided the paying banker carries out his duties correctly there is little risk of legal
action being taken against the bank by the customer. The main risks that the paying
banker incurs are:

- liability for damages for cheques wrongly debited to the customer's account
- wrongful dishonouring of cheques leading to:
  - Breach of contract, the bank is not fulfilling its duties to pay its customers'
    cheques;
  - Libel, depending upon the reply given on the returned cheques, the customer
    may consider that his character has been adversely affected;
  - Conversion, allowing someone who is not the rightful owner to have the funds.

Figure 6.7 shows the practical dangers of failing to scrutinise cheques or accounts
properly, leading to incorrectly drawn or stopped cheques being honoured.

The rules and regulations regarding the acceptance and payment of cheques are determined by the:

- Bills of Exchange Act 1882;
- Cheques Act 1957;
- Case Law.

In addition the statutes and case law offer a form of legal protection to the banker
who abides by the regulations. The main sections are:

- Bills of Exchange Act 1882:
  Section 60 — Protects the paying banker if there is a forged or unauthorised endorsement, provided that the cheque is paid in good faith and in the ordinary course of
  business.
     Section 80 — Protects the paying banker if the collecting bank's customer has
  no title, or a defective title, provided that the cheque:
  - is taken in good faith;
  - is taken without negligence;
  - is paid in accordance with the crossing.

- Cheques Act 1957:
  Section 1 — Protects the paying banker if it pays a cheque bearing an irregular
  endorsement or an unendorsed cheque provided that the cheque is paid:
  - in good faith;
  - in the ordinary course of business.

- Case Law:

Greenwood v Martins Bank Ltd (1932)

The plaintiff's failure to inform the bank promptly of forgeries precluded him from successfully suing the bank.

HONOUR OF	PRACTICAL DANGERS	POSSIBLE LEGAL ACTION AGAINST THE BANK	PROTECTION
Post-Dated Cheque	Wrongful dishonour of correctly dated cheques Non payment of standing orders, direct debits, personal loans Customer may request to stop cheque prior to due date Death/bankruptcy	Libel Breach of contract	None
Cheque containing unauthorised alteration (apparent or non apparent)	Customer's account may be debited with an incorrect amount leading to: ● wrongful dishonour of correctly drawn cheques ● non payment of standing orders, direct debits, personal loans	Libel Breach of contract Damages for any excess amount	None NOTE: If the customer had contributed to the alteration by careless completion of the cheque then the damages may be reduced
Stopped cheque	As above Duplicate cheque may have been issued	Libel Breach of contract	None
Cheques containing forged drawer's signature	Wrongful payment	Breach of contract	None NOTE: The customer may be stopped from bringing an action against the bank if he was aware of the forgery and did not inform the bank
Cheques containing irregular or no endorsements	Wrongful payment	Conversion	Bills of Exchange Act 1880 S60, S80; Cheques Act 1957 S1

6.7 Some Practical Dangers

London Joint Stock Bank v. MacMillan & Arthur (1918)

The customer did not exercise reasonable care in drawing his cheque, and so facilitated an alteration of the amount.

Davidson v. Barclays Bank Ltd (1940)

The bank wrongfully dishonoured a cheque. The words 'Not Sufficient' were found by the Courts to be libellous.

(v) Returning cheques: reasons and replies
When a cheque is to be returned unpaid to the collecting bank, the reason for the return is stated on the top left corner of the face of the cheque. The following points must be noted:
— care must be exercised in the wording of the reply in order to protect the bank from possible claims of damages for libel;
— all reasons for dishonour should be clearly written on the top left hand corner of the cheque.

The following table shows some reasons that will be given for return of the cheque:

REASON FOR RETURN	REPLY
Cheque not signed	Drawer's signature required
Additional signature required	Another signature required
Signature invalid	Signature requires drawer's confirmation
Insufficient funds	Refer to drawer, please represent/refer to drawer
Cheque stopped but not yet confirmed in writing	Orders not to pay – awaiting written confirmation
Cheques stopped by writing instruction	Orders not to pay
Account holder deceased	Drawer deceased
Account in dispute	Refer to drawer

The two most common phrases used when returning cheques are
— refer to drawer
— refer to drawer, please represent.
Refer to drawer implies that the bank will not pay the cheque, whilst **refer to drawer, please represent** means that although there are not enough funds at present if the cheque is represented in the future there could be enough money in the account to pay the cheque.

Care must be taken as using the wrong phrase could lead the bank into a claim for defamation. Any statement which lowers 'a person in the estimation of right-thinking members of society generally' is held to be defamatory. In the case of

Davidson v. Barclays Bank Ltd (1940)

the bank returned a cheque for £2.15.8d (£2.78) marked 'not sufficient', meaning that the balance in the account was less than the cheque. The bank had, however, paid a cheque which had previously been stopped by Davidson and had they not done so there would have been enough money left to pay the cheque which was returned. The words were held to be libellous (defamatory) and Davidson was awarded damages.

In a New Zealand case of

Baker v. Australia & New Zealand Bank (1958)

Mrs Baker had three cheques wrongfully returned stating 'present again'. Nominal damages of £2 per cheque were paid plus £100 for the libel.

In 1972 the Post Office paid damages to settle a libel case involving five National Giro cheques wrongfuly returned 'refer to drawer'.

The clearings
There are several clearing systems in operation, ie systems which allow accounts to be debited and credited by banks through the transmission of paper. Almost every payment that is not made by cash passes through one of these systems.

The first clearing system was for clearing cheques and was set up in the 18th century. Since that time systems for clearing large amounts (Town Clearing), automated transfers of large amounts (CHAPS), credit transfers, and standing orders/direct debits and wages (BACS) have been established.

The management of these clearings has recently been brought under the control of the Association for Payment Clearing Systems (APACS), the fourteen founder members of which were

Bank of England	Girobank
Bank of Scotland	Lloyds Bank
Barclays Bank	Midland Bank
Citibank	National Westminster Bank
Clydesdale Bank	The Royal Bank of Scotland
Co-operative Bank	Standard Chartered Bank
Coutts & Co	TSB (England & Wales)

In addition to this structure change the rules for entry into the clearings were also changed, so that institutions other than clearing banks were allowed entry to the systems. The first such new outside members were the Abbey National, which joined the cheque clearing in 1988, and the Abbey National and Halifax Building Societies, which joined BACS in 1987. The Yorkshire Bank also joined BACS, and Citibank and Standard Chartered Bank joined CHAPS and Town Clearings in 1987.

Through APACS the clearings are divided into three groups, according to type, with each group to be owned and operated by a separate company. These groups are

— bulk paper clearings, to be run by the Cheque & Credit Clearing Co Ltd
— high value clearings, to be run by the CHAPS & Town Clearing Co Ltd
— bulk electronic clearings, to be run by BACS Ltd

In addition to managing the clearings, APACS will also oversee EFTPOS development and currency clearings (fig.6.8).

6.8 APACS and its Associated Companies/Operational Groupings

Cheque and credit clearing (bulk clearings)

(a) General cheque clearing

While the use of cheques was uncommon, the cheques could be sent directly between the branches concerned. This was originally done by clerks walking round the banks handing over cheques and receiving payments. As the use of cheques as a means of payment grew the clerks began to meet at a central point in order to exchange cheques and reach a settlement. The first meeting place (clearing house) was started in 1773 in a London Coffee house. Although the operation has grown in size and complexity over the years the basic principles of the 'clearing' are still present.

The membership of the Clearing House was restricted for many years to the main clearing banks (Barclays, Lloyds, Midland, National Westminster and Williams & Glyns), but over the past ten years membership has expanded to take account of the increasing number of banks involved with 'cheque account' banking. Today's membership includes:

Bank of England
Barclays
Co-op
Lloyds
Midland
National Girobank
National Westminster (incl. Coutts)
Royal Bank of Scotland (formerly Williams and Glyns)
TSB

A significant widening of the membership happened in 1988 when the Abbey National became the first building society to become a member.

Most of the cheques moving around the banking system are those paid in at branches which are drawn on other banks. These cheques are dealt with through the *General Clearing*.

The way in which the system works is shown in Figure 6.9.

Day 1

During the day the branch (e.g. Bootle Branch TSB) will have received on behalf of its customers cheques drawn on

— other clearing banks;
— branches of its own bank.

At the end of the day these cheques are

— sorted into banks;
— stamped with details of branch/bank (Bootle TSB);
— encoded on the bottom of the cheque with the amount.

The cheques are then sent by courier to the bank's own clearing department (in our example TSB Clearing Department).

Day 2

The Bank Clearing Department (TSB) receives 'bundles' of cheques from all its branches. It has to

— check each bundle and amalgamate them into a total for each bank;
— take the other bank's cheques (e.g. Barclays) to the Central Clearing House;
— retain the cheques drawn on its own branches (i.e. TSB). These cheques are sent to the bank's own branches without going to the clearing house (Interbranch Clearing).

The Central Clearing House arranges for all banks involved in the clearing to attend to 'swap' cheques and arrange for any difference in amount to be settled. For example, TSB may have cheques drawn on Barclays Bank customers amounting to £20 million whilst Barclays Bank may have cheques drawn on TSB for £15 million. In this case Barclays owes TSB £5 million and this amount will be paid to TSB on the following day. When the cheques have been swapped they are returned to their own bank's clearing department.

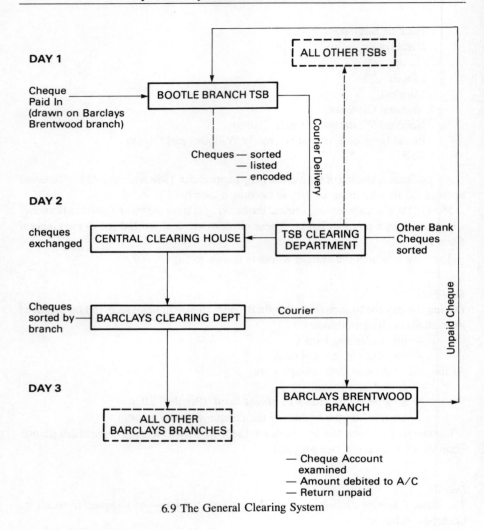

6.9 The General Clearing System

Clearing Department (Barclays) receives its own cheques from the clearing. It then
— lists and sorts them into branch order by scanning the information printed on the
   bottom of the cheque;
— records cheque information into the bank computer (to debit the customers'
   accounts);
— sends the cheques to the branches.

Day 3
The branches, e.g. Barclays Branch Brentwood, will receive cheques drawn by their
customers. The branch has to check it is in order and to return any cheques that cannot
be paid. Any 'unpaid' cheques are sent by first class post on day 3 to the branch that
collected them (shown by the stamp placed on the cheque on day 1).

6.10 The Life Story of a Cheque (courtesy of Banking Information Service)

(b) Credit clearing (Bank Giro)

The outline of the Bank Giro credits was covered earlier. The Credit Clearing, which is much like the General Cheque Clearing System, allows for the transfer of these funds.

As with the cheque clearing, the Giro credits are sorted and listed by the branches and sent by courier along with the cheques to the bank's clearing department. The clearing department takes out the bank's own credits and sends the other banks' credits to the banker's clearing house. Distribution to the branches then follows as in the cheque clearing system.

Because of the number of credit transfers that have to be handled by the banks there are attempts to increase the automation of credit transfers. Vouchers are now encoded rather like cheques; this allows them to be processed via computers as for the cheque (debit) clearing.

CHAPS and Town Clearing (high value clearings)

(a) CHAPS (Clearing House Automated Payments System)

This system was set up in 1984 to provide a fully automated transfer system between accounts in different banks. CHAPS links twelve English and Scottish Clearing Banks (known as settlement banks) and deals with remittances of £10,000 and over. Other banks and corporate customers can use the system but they must pass their messages through a 'CHAPS gateway', in other words one of the settlement banks. The advantages of CHAPS are that
— transfers are made on the same day
— funds are treated as cleared
— funds can therefore be drawn immediately.

As awareness and use of CHAPS grows the system will develop into an alternative to the Town Clearing. The Bank CHAPS are:

Barclays	Royal Bank of Scotland	Bank of England
Lloyds	Bank of Scotland	TSB
Midland	Clydesdale	Co-operative Bank
National Westminster	Citibank	Standard Chartered

(b) Town Clearing

This is a speedy system of clearing cheques for bank branches which are within walking distance of the Clearing House in Lombard Street in the City of London. The reason for this system is that there are many insurance companies, shipping companies and financial institutions and the Stock Exchange within the City, all of which deal in large sums of money and need their cheques to be cleared as quickly as possible. The Town Clearing provides such a service, but deals only with cheques of £10,000 or more.

The system works in a similar way to the General Clearing. But in Town Clearing a large cheque paid into a City branch is walked to the Clearing House where it must arrive before 3.45 p.m. After this they are taken to the branches on which they are drawn. Any cheques that cannot be paid have to be returned to the bank that 'presented' them by 4.30 p.m.

The great benefit of this same day settlement is that large funds can earn interest immediately; they do not lose three days' interest should the cheque go through the General Clearing. Alternatively the money could be used to reduce or eliminate any overdraft, and so reduce interest charges.

Because of the size of the cheques involved in the Town Clearing the sums saved can be very significant. For example, on a cheque of £500,000 there could be a gain of £350 in interest earned over a cheque that took the normal time to clear.

Although the volume of cheques handled by the Town Clearing is much less than that of the General Clearing, in money terms the Town Clearing is more important. In fact, the cheques they deal with average more than £1 million each.

BACS (Bankers Automated Clearing Services) (bulk electronic clearing)

This service was set up in 1968. Its aim was to move towards the electronic transfer of funds, and to remove the need for sending vast amounts of paper around the system. It was formed by the clearing banks to carry out the role that the Bankers' Clearing House carries out manually, in other words the movement of funds from one bank branch to another. BACS is part of the clearing system. It is used for

— standing order payments
— direct debits
— salary credits
— bank giro credits.

The BACS System

The BACS system has certainly proved very successful. Some 900 million transactions were processed in 1985. The figure is expected to grow to 1900 million transactions by 1990.

The system operates through the user. This can be either a bank (or a company which has been sponsored by a bank) producing data in the form of magnetic tape, diskette, or disc. This data is then sent to the BACS computer centre for processing.

Alternatively information can now be sent directly to BACS via a telephone line. This system is known as BACSTEL; data can be sent down the line by the user either at specific transmission times or on an 'on demand' basis.

The input information is then processed by BACS and tapes are produced for each participating bank of the debits and credits to be made to their customers' accounts. These tapes are processed by the banks' computer centres and the appropriate funds are transferred to and from accounts on the same day. This whole process takes three days and is illustrated in Figures 6.11 and 6.12.

Advantages of BACS

There are several advantages for both the bank and sponsored companies in using BACS. These are shown in Figure 6.13.

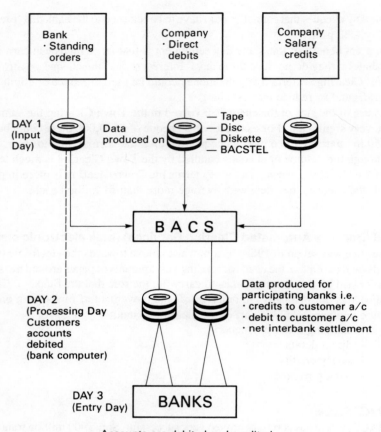

6.11 Bankers Automated Clearing Services (BACS)

Other clearings
Although the General Clearing system deals with the majority of cheques there are other methods of clearing cheques. These are:

(a) Interbranch clearing
This clearing has already been mentioned. It is the clearing of a bank's own cheques through its own Clearing Department.

(b) Special collections
Should a customer wish to clear a cheque immediately he can arrange for it to be specially presented to the paying bank. Here the cheque will be *taken* by a member of the collecting bank staff to the paying bank, or *sent direct by first class post*. A telephone call will then confirm clearance.

DAY 1 (Input Day)	DAY 2 (Processing Day)	DAY 3 (Entry Day)
9.00 p.m. CREDIT APPLICATION — PAYROLL Magnetic tape or diskette payroll information reaches BACS by hand, post, Datapost, courier or via a telephone line in the case of BACSTEL. Despatch of input reports, by 1st class post.	**6.00 a.m.** BACS validate and process overnight submissions received and pass information relating to customers to Banks for internal processing. Receipt of input reports.	**9.30 a.m.** Employer account debited with total payroll amount. Individual employee accounts credited.
DEBIT APPLICATION — DIRECT DEBIT Magnetic tape or diskette direct debit information reaches BACS by hand, post, Datapost, courier or via a telephone line in the case of BACSTEL. Despatch of input reports, by 1st class post.	BACS validate and process overnight submissions received and pass information relating to customers to Banks for internal processing. Receipt of input reports.	Originator's account credited with total of all direct debit input collected. Payers' accounts debited with individual direct debits.

6.12 The BACS 3 Day Processing Cycle

BANK	CUSTOMERS
Decreased costs of clearing	Reduced clerical costs
Reduced use of stationery such as cheque books	Lower bank charges, since BACS transmission charges are lower than using cash, cheques or giro credits
Decreased workload on staff e.g. clearing	Increased security since the need for cash dealings such as wages payments is eliminated
	Improved cash flow with the certainty of payment, and with debits and credits usually taking place simultaneously
	Savings on interest. With bank giro, customers have to pay in several days before the payment date, but with the BACS simultaneous credit and debit interest is saved. This is very significant for large payroll accounts.

6.13 Advantages of BACS

(c) Cheques for non-clearing house members
The General and Town Clearing systems cater for the clearance of cheques drawn on clearing banks who are members of the Clearing House.

There are, however, other financial organisations who issue 'cheques' which are passed over branch counters and which need to be cleared in the same way. Such cheque issuing bodies would include those shown in Figure 6.14.

— A clearing bank may act as an agent; cheques are then cleared in the normal way through the Clearing House. This would be the case for Building Society cheque accounts where their cheques, although issued by the Society, are drawn on a clearing bank.

— Walks clearing is applied to other cheques where the clearing department of an organisation arranges for the cheques to be walked to the banks or offices concerned. Here they will be exchanged for a payment of a banker's draft or a cheque drawn on a clearing bank.

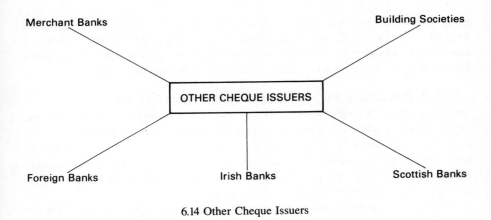

6.14 Other Cheque Issuers

— Scottish and Irish Banks who are not members of the Clearing House can get their cheques cleared by having them sent to their London Office (using the walks as above) or direct to their Head Office.

(d) Truncation
This is a system which is already used between branches of the same bank. Their cheque (and bank giro credit) details are sent over the bank's computer network for the appropriate credits and debits to be made. If the banks' computer systems are developed to allow them to 'speak' to each other the use of truncation — the stopping of the paper before it enters the system — should increase on an interbank basis and so further reduce the need for the 'paper' clearing systems.

(e) National Giro(bank)
The previous systems have been largely the province of the clearing banks. The National Giro was introduced in 1968 as an attempt to provide a cheap and efficient money transfer system for people who did not have a bank account, and it was run originally by the Post Office. It is a national computerised system for account holders, enabling payments to be transferred quickly and cheaply.

The system is extremely simple and allows money to be transferred easily between giro account holders. As all these accounts are held on a central computer (at Bootle, Merseyside) there is no need for a clearing system as used by the clearing banks.

The potential of this simple system has not been realised, however, partly because the threat of the Giro competition pushed the clearing banks to modernise their own money transmission services. Certainly Giro was a major reason for the introduction of BACS.

If an account holder wishes to transfer money he uses a transfer/deposit form. These forms are used where payments are made to another account holder. Each account holder is supplied with a stock of these forms. In addition large organisations like the Gas and Electricity Boards and British Telecom print a National Giro Transfer form at the foot of their bills with their account number on it. Payments can then be made to them by post to the Girocentre at Bootle on Merseyside. Alternatively payments can be made through any Post Office. Account holders can also make regular payments by standing order and receive credit transfers direct to their accounts.

EFTPOS (Electronic Funds Transfer at the Point Of Sale)

For many years it has been anticipated that the use of computer terminals in stores and supermarkets would allow goods to be paid for by an automated transfer from the customer's account to that of the shop. The system would operate by using a plastic card (cheque or credit card). This would be encoded with the bank account details in a magnetic strip on the reverse of the card. It would allow data to be transmitted via a telephone line to the appropriate bank computer.

But despite the great advances in computer and terminal technology EFTPOS has had only a relatively low-key impact to date. The early schemes were of limited scope and included:

Counterplus, which was run by the Clydesdale Bank. It was introduced in 1983 in conjunction with BP for use in some 26 filling stations in north and west Scotland. In 1984 the system was introduced into an Aberdeen supermarket.

On Line Card Service, which was set up by Access, Visa, American Express and Diners Club to allow immediate checking and verification of the transaction.

Rail Tickets. Customers could write their own rail tickets and pay by credit card (Barclaycard) at various British Rail stations.

Anglia Building Society introduced an EFTPOS system into retail outlets in Northampton. The fact that a building society is in the forefront of this development is an example of the competition the banks are facing today in the financial area.

The use of EFTPOS has to some degree been limited by the conservative approach taken by banks to national EFTPOS schemes, although since the setting up of APACS there has been some movement towards a bank-driven national system. At present there are three levels of EFTPOS activity:
— national EFTPOS, which is run through EFTPOS UK
— Barclaycard/Access
— individual systems

(a) National EFTPOS

An inaugural scheme is operating on 2,000 terminals in Edinburgh, Leeds and Southampton, whereby goods and services can be bought using a plastic card and without the need for vouchers or cheques. Where transactions are approved payment to the retailer is automatic and guaranteed. The system will accept bank debit and credit cards, and the retailers' own cards. The EFTPOS services within the nationwide EFTPOS UK are provided by

● founder members of the company

- other members, such as building societies
- existing schemes which can be linked, e.g. Counterplus

(b) Barclaycard/Access
The two credit card companies had installed payment terminals in retail outlets, mainly shops, petrol stations and railway stations, with both systems — Barclaycard's PDQ and Access' ACCEPT — using identical technology. A tie-up was arranged in 1987 to allow cardholders to use either machine, and with American Express also becoming involved some 5,000 terminals were in use at the end of 1987.

(c) Individual systems
Midland Bank has installed terminals at retail outlets and petrol stations in Milton Keynes. Here the system will accept the ATM cards of Midland and National Westminster Banks and Access credit cards.

National Westminster Bank has also installed terminals in petrol stations which will accept the same cards.

Lloyds Cardpoint has been operating in Peterborough since 1987.

Funds Transfer Sharing Ltd (FTS), the company behind the Link network of ATMs, has 23 BP garages close to the M25 motorway using Link terminals to allow Link cardholders to buy petrol, goods and to withdraw cash.

After a slow start it now seems that EFTPOS is becoming a more popular method of payment and funds transfer. Increased use of such systems will bring the following benefits
- greater efficiency with less time taken in writing out cheques or vouchers
- savings in cash handling
- increased security (less cash)
- reduction in queueing time
- guaranteeing of accepted transactions (retailer benefit)
- possible reduction in bank charges (retailer benefit)

Homebanking
For several years there has been talk of transacting 'banking' business from home, but despite the potential for such a service until recently there was little demand.

One of the first schemes was run by the Nottingham Building Society in conjunction with the Bank of Scotland; a second system was run by the Bank of Scotland itself. Both systems were based on Prestel and required a television screen, personal computer and special adaptor to give access to the bank's computer. This made the transacting of business relatively expensive and complicated. The services provided by these early systems were
- payment of bills up to 30 days in advance
- the switching of funds to interest-earning accounts
- a viewing facility via TV of account transactions
- cheque book and statement ordering

— a cash management module for small businesses.

In 1987/8 more advanced homebanking services were introduced. The first of these was TSB Speedlink, which operates on a real time computer system thereby allowing immediate funds transfer, the updating of accounts and account balances. The system operates over the normal Telecom telephone (although a tone pad about the size of a TV remote control unit may be needed) and allows customers to

- obtain account balances
- transfer funds between accounts
- pay bills immediately or up to 30 days in advance

The Speedlink service is available to sole traders and partnerships as well as personal account holders.

The Nationwide Anglia Building Society has a system similar to TSB Speedlink where instructions are keyed in through the telephone to be processed by the computer which talks customers through the transaction and provides appropriate information.

Lloyds Bank is experimenting with its Homebank service which also uses the telephone to contact the computer. Unlike Speedlink, which used a PIN (Personal Identification Number) to gain access to the computer, the Lloyds system involves a fairly bulky keyboard about the size of a telephone which is plugged into the handset. The customer has to pass a Cashpoint card through the keyboard before use and all messages are encoded before being sent down the line. Lloyds believe this gives their system greater security. The services available on the system are

— balance enquiries
— payment of bills
— requests for cheque books and statements
— orders for travellers cheques and currency
— amendment of standing orders and direct debits.

The Royal Bank of Scotland are also testing their Phoneline system, giving the first three services provided by the Lloyds system but operating in a more advanced manner than the others. The system is based on a voice recognition computer and therefore, to use the service, Phoneline customers need only to speak normally into the telephone and remember the codeword.

In addition, Barclays and NatWest are planning similar voice response services.

Despite these important advances, Homebanking is still in its infancy due in part to
— the fact that banks still have large branch networks
— public indifference or lack of need
— possible security problems.

Automated Teller Machines (ATMs)

The availability and use of automated teller machines has increased dramatically over the years since the first cash dispensers were introduced in the 1970s. The early machines were unsophisticated and provided only a cash dispensing service. These machines have now been replaced by the modern automated teller machines which, being linked to a computer, can provide customers with a range of services as well as simple cash dispensing. The services provided by these machines are covered elsewhere in the book.

A major development in the ATM system is the move to allow customers to use the machines of *several* organisations rather than just those provided by the card issuing organisation. These are shown in Figure 6.15.

Many ATMs installed by the Visa and Access banks will now let customers use their cards to withdraw cash from their accounts.

Royal Bank of Scotland
Lloyds
Barclays
Bank of Scotland

Midland
NatWest
TSB
Clydesdale

Link
Abbey National
Nationwide
Co-op Bank
Girobank
American Express
Diners Club
Allied Dunbar
Britannia
+18 others

Halifax (Cashcard)

Matrix
Alliance & Leicester
Nationwide Anglia
Bradford & Bingley
Bristol & West
Leeds Permanent
National & Provincial
Woolwich

6.15 Cash Machine Connections

Smart cards

These cards, which are the same size and thickness as credit cards, can hold far more information than the magnetic strip on present plastic cards, and are felt to be the next electronic answer to funds transfer. Up to two typed pages of information can be held including

— details of the customer's account(s)
— credit limits
— previous purchases
— security numbers.

The card incorporates a microprocessor which is able to prove the holder's identity and credit availability without the necessity of access to a central computer.

One use is to credit the card with 'electronic money' which can then be debited with the holder's transactions. Using the card this way saves the need to carry cheques or cash. The cards can also be used to obtain cash from an ATM or to make purchases using an EFTPOS terminal.

Although the cards have the benefits of

- security
- speed
- independence from on-line computers
- reduction in paper

the banks are still not convinced that the additional cost of the card (£2 compared with 11p for a credit card) is justified and, although there are 16 million such cards in circulation in France, use in the UK domestic market is limited to trial schemes.

SUMMARY
METHODS OF PAYMENT
Cash remains important for low value transactions.
Cheques
- The acceptability of cheques has increased since the introduction of the cheque guarantee card.
- A cheque is
  — an unconditional order
  — drawn on a banker
  — signed by the drawer
  — requiring a banker to pay on demand
  — to the order of a specified person
  — or to bearer.
- When writing cheques customers should ensure that
  — all the details are completed
  — cheques are written in ink
  — no space is left for fraudulent additions
  — any corrections or changes are signed
  — words and figures agree.
- Cheque guarantee cards guarantee payment of a cheque to a stated figure provided that the
  — customer uses card as per conditions
  — payee must follow instructions on back of card.
- The instructions are that
  — the card number is to be written on the reverse of cheque
  — only one cheque is guaranteed
  — the cheque limit is £50
  — the signatures on card and cheque are same
  — the card is within date and has same branch/bank code number as the cheque.
- Cheques supported by cheque card cannot be stopped.
- To prevent the possibility of loss (through stolen cards or fraud) the
  — bank restricts card issue to known customers
  — account should not be overdrawn without consent
  — cheque book and card should be carried separately
  — card remains the bank's property.

- *Bankers' Drafts*
- Similar to a cheque but drawn on the bank's Head Office.
- Drafts cannot be stopped.

Credit Cards
- Two main card issuers in UK — Visa and Access (Mastercard).
- Cards also issued by retail stores.
- Customers given a credit limit and this gives revolving credit as debt is paid off.
- Debt can be paid off over time with interest charged on debt.
- Free credit of nearly two months can be obtained.

Charge Cards
- Similar to credit cards as means of payment but
  — enrolment fee and annual membership
  — full account paid off monthly
  — no credit period allowed for payment.

Bank Giro
- Used to pay into account held at another bank
- Payment of bills.

Standing Orders/Direct Debits
- For regular payments.
- With standing orders the customer has to advise the bank of amount and any changes.
- Direct Debits are 'raised' by the person receiving the payment.
- Direct Debits are better for variable payments.

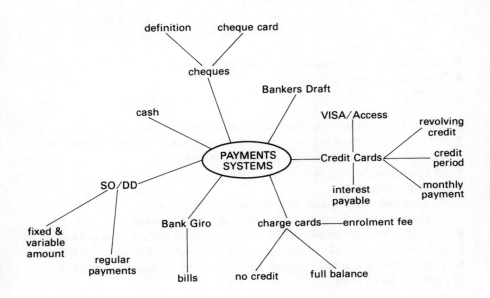

6.16 Payments Systems

FUNDS TRANSFER
Collecting Banker
- The collecting banker receives the cheques in the branches for credit to an account.
- Collecting banker must
  - credit customer's account with the amount
  - collect money from the bank on which the cheque is drawn
  - ensure the cheque is credited to the account for which it is intended.
- Collecting banker must 'scrutinise' the cheques for
  - date   — signature
  - payee   — crossings
  - words and figures   — endorsements
- A crossing establishes that a cheque should be paid into a bank account.
- An endorsement transfers the cheque to a third party.
- There are three types of endorsement
  - blank — makes cheque payable to bearer
  - specific — transfers cheque to named person
  - restrictive — this prevents further transfer of the cheque.

Paying Banker
- Paying banker has to honour the cheques provided that
  - funds are available (credit or overdraft)
  - the cheque has been completed correctly
  - there are no legal bars to payment.
- Paying banker should scrutinise for
  - date   — crossings   — mutilation
  - payee   — alterations   — stopped cheques
  - endorsements   — drawer's signature   — legal bars
  - account mandate
- Crossings are an instruction to the paying banker
- Two types of crossings
  - general
  - special
- The term 'not negotiable' does *not* mean cheques cannot be passed on.
- 'Not negotiable' means that the person taking the cheque does not receive, and cannot give, a better title than the person transferring it.
- Mutilated cheques are considered invalid.
- To stop a cheque
  - clear and unambiguous instructions must be given
  - the instructions must be delivered to the paying banker.
- The rules and regulations regarding the acceptance and payment of cheques are determined by the Bills of Exchange Act 1882 and the Cheques Act 1957.
- When a cheque is returned unpaid the reply should be carefully worded.

CLEARING SYSTEMS
General Cheque & Credit Clearing
- Deals with majority of cheques and bank giro credits; and takes 3 days

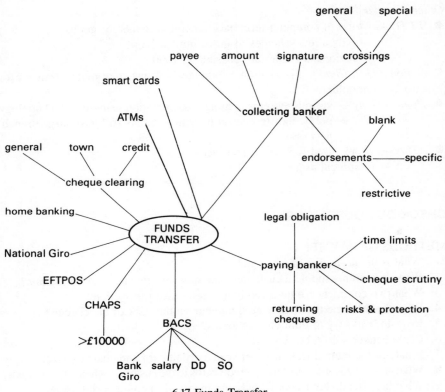

6.17 Funds Transfer

- Is used by all bank branches.

CHAPS & Town Clearing
- *CHAPS* — links 'gateway' banks and deals with remittances of £10,000 or over
  — provides same day transfer and is an alternative to Town Clearing.
- *Town Clearing* — for branches within walking distance of Clearing House.
  — deals with cheques of more than £10,000.
  — provides same day settlement.

BACS
- Is an electronic funds transfer system
- Clearing is used for SO, DDs, salary and bank giro credits
- Used by banks and sponsored companies
- Data sent via computer tapes, discs or BACSTEL.

Other Clearings
- *Interbranch* — is the clearing of a bank's own cheques.
- *Special Collections* — are cheques which are presented to the paying banker.
- *Non Clearing House Members* — cheques are cleared via an agent, or by 'walking' or through the London or Head Offices.
- *Truncation* — computer credit and debit of cheques.

Other Transfer Systems
- *EFTPOS* — use of computer terminals to debit accounts for goods
  - only a few schemes so far of limited scope
  - national schemes are possible in 1990.
- *National Giro (Bank)* — is a national computerised system of money transfer for giro account holders.
- *Homebanking* — various systems coming into operation using latest technology
  - public indifference at present as banks still have large branch networks.
- *ATMs* — widely used for range of services
  - reciprocal usage.

CHECK OUT QUESTIONS

METHODS OF PAYMENT
1. What is the definition of a cheque?
2. What five points should a customer remember when writing out a cheque?
3. What two contracts are involved in a cheque card transaction?
4. Who should write the cheque card number on the back of the cheque?
5. How do banks try to limit cheque losses?
6. Can a banker's draft be stopped?
7. What are the main differences between a credit card and charge chard?
8. What are five advantages of using credit cards to the customer when buying goods?
9. What benefits do banks get from being involved in credit card business ?
10. What are bank giro credits used for?
11. What is the main difference between a standing order and direct debit?
12. What are the safeguards to prevent companies misusing the direct debit system?

FUNDS TRANSFER
1. What are the duties of a collecting banker?
2. What three things need to be considered concerning the date on a cheque?
3. What is the significance of a crossing on a cheque?
4. What does an endorsement do?
5. What are the three types of endorsement?
6. If R appears on a cheque what does this mean?
7. What is the role of the paying banker?
8. Bankers must honour a customer's cheque if three factors are present — what are these factors?
9. If a cheque is specially presented by another banker through the post, how long does the paying banker have to pay or dishonour?
10. If there is no date on the cheque can the paying banker insert one?
11. What types of crossing are there?
12. What does 'not negotiable' mean?

13. What does 'Account Payee' mean?
14. What details must be given to stop a cheque and how should they be given?
15. What are the main Acts that protect the paying banker?
16. What reply would you give when returning cheques for
    — cheque not signed
    — insufficient funds
    — cheques stopped in writing?
17. What does the Central Clearing House do?
18. What is the Town Clearing?
19. What is a special collection?
20. What is meant by truncation?
21. What does BACS stand for?
22. How does BACS operate?
23. What is CHAPS?
24. How does EFTPOS transfer funds?
25. What is the non-bank national funds transfer system called?

7

Bank Accounts and Services

On completion of this chapter you will know:

— the main functions of the retail banks
— which accounts offer immediate access
— which accounts provide interest on deposits
— why people save
— the features and benefits of the main types of bank account
— which accounts are suitable for the following:

- regular savers
- young savers
- large amounts of money

— the principal method of money transfer
— the advantages of using overdraft facilities
— why 'free' banking came about
— the difference between Standing Orders and Direct Debits
— why bank charge cards are a useful temporary form of 'free' credit
— the range of services offered by Automated Teller Machines
— what details are required by a bank for a personal loan
— the principles of lending
— the main benefits of a budget account
— the main objectives of the Consumer Credit Act 1974
— why banks credit-score personal loan applications
— the main types of mortgages available to customers
— the major types of loan available to businesses.

INTRODUCTION

In some of the other chapters of the book we have examined the relationship between the banker and his customers, the banks' main competitors and how payments can be made. In this chapter we are going to look at the basic role and functions of the retail banks — the services they provide for their customers.

Bank customers fall into two main groups:

- personal customers
- business customers

Some of the services provided by the banks are provided for both personal and business customers, such as current account facilities; others are provided for just the one group, for example leasing services for business customers. The distinction between the two will be outlined when we examine each of the banks' services in turn.

All the major retail banks have similar functions. These can be grouped into four broad categories:

Deposit taking

This involves the acceptance of money and deposits from personal business customers for storage and safekeeping. Banks offer a range of accounts to suit the individual needs of customers.

Some customers may wish to have constant and immediate access to funds held in the bank. Other customers do not need access to their deposits for a certain period of time. Banks have increasingly developed the range of accounts available to fit in with the ever changing needs of their customers. Often, more than one account will be necessary to provide the customer with the best service, for example, a cheque account for immediate access plus a deposit account where any long term savings would accrue interest.

Money transfer

A main area of activity for the retail banks is the collection and transfer of money for their customers. This involves not only the encashment of cheques for their own customers, but the transfer of funds from their own customers' accounts to accounts in other branches and other banks. It also includes the collection of monies owed to customers by clients of other banks.

We have seen in an earlier chapter how the banker is legally obliged to make sure these transfers take place quickly, promptly and safely. A vast, highly sophisticated network has been developed involving millions of pounds of expenditure and some of the world's most technologically advanced computers. This network arranges the daily transfer of millions of cheques and debit and credit vouchers through the clearing system. The system ensures that, for example, cheques written by a Barclays customer to customers of Lloyds and the TSB will, within three working days, result in money being debited from the Barclays bank customer's account and credited to the accounts of the Lloyds and TSB's customers. It sounds simple, and in principle it is, but when we realise that the process involves the accounts of 25 million customers and some 2,000 million cheques annually, we can begin to see just what a mammoth process is involved. (We saw in an earlier chapter that the banks keep operational balances with the Bank of England to settle the differences created by the clearing system between the banks.)

Advances

Early banks (the goldsmiths) made a living by simply charging customers for safe-guarding deposits of gold. However, they quickly realised that they could earn higher returns by lending (or advancing) the gold in their vaults to those wishing to borrow, and charging them a rate of interest. Advances or lending to personal and business customers is by far the most profitable of the retail banks' activities.

To meet the changing needs of the customer the range of advances available has grown, especially in the recent past. For example, the banks are now marketing mortgages (just as, in fact, building societies are now offering cheque accounts, personal loans and other facilities).

Other services

The history of the retail banks shows distinct phases. Initially, as the public became attuned to the benefits of banks the number of banks grew. Secondly, a series of amalgamations followed as banks grouped together to gain the advantages of large scale operations. Thirdly, once amalgamated, the banks began to concentrate on expanding their branch networks. They wanted to avoid becoming too localised, and suffering from local unemployment and recession in particular industries and areas. A wide network of branches allowed the banks to iron out these localised problems. Finally, the most recent phase has been to expand the number and quality of services they offer to customers. Today the banks have become "one-stop financial supermarkets" where both personal and business customers can satisfy all their financial needs. For example, banks are already establishing working relationships with building societies and estate agents (e.g. Lloyds Bank owns its own estate agency).

Let us look at each of the main functions in turn and examine the range of services and accounts available to personal and business customers. Each will be described and the benefits to particular customers highlighted.

DEPOSIT TAKING

We have seen the problem of defining exactly what a bank is — retail banks, merchant banks, foreign banks, consortium banks, recognised banks, and so on. However, of all the varied services offered, one links them all — they all accept deposits. Some special-ised banks only accept deposits from a limited range of customers (e.g. the Bank of England only accepts deposits from government departments, the banks, and foreign governments) but they all function by accepting deposits from customers.

These deposits, the liabilities of the banks, enable the banks to lend money to customers. They play the role of financial intermediary — accepting and safeguarding deposits from customers who have funds to spare, and lending to customers who are in need of finance.

Before looking at the facilities offered by the banks it is useful to understand exactly why people save. All income which people receive is either spent on goods and services, or saved. The money *not* spent by individuals, households and, indeed businesses, represents a surplus — money which they do not wish or need to spend immediately.

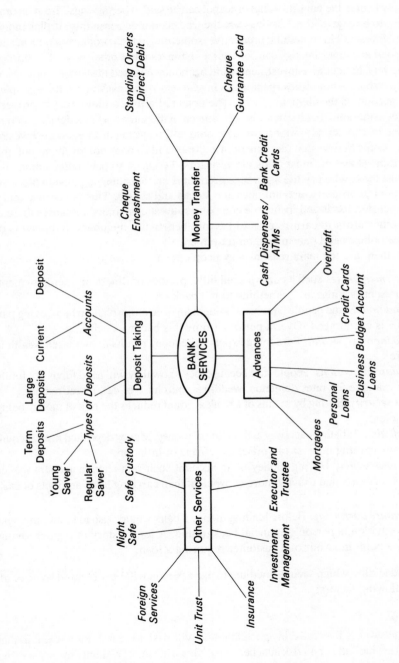

7.1 Bank Services

A distinction should be made here between savings and investment. Money not spent but simply kept in the pocket, wallet or teapot can be said to be "savings" from income. However, to be regarded as "savings" in the true economic sense this surplus money must be "invested" in something productive, something which produces a return, such as a deposit account. Savings can, of course, be invested in other ways, for example speculatively. Speculative investment could be money invested in stamps, antiques, or property. What distinguishes speculative investment from investing in for example a deposit account is the element of risk. The potential return on investing in property *may* be considerable, but it cannot be guaranteed in the same way as a deposit account rate of interest. After all, property values could fall, resulting in a loss to the investor.

Many people believe that investment in antiques and so on is not for them, but only for the rich. However, most of us are investors. People who pay trades union subscriptions, those who pay life assurance premiums or contribute to pension plans are all investors in property, art, antiques and stocks and shares. This is because trades unions, pension funds and insurance companies invest customers' money in these as well as other areas to earn returns to pay out benefits to members, lump sums on insurance policies and pensions upon retirement.

What, then, are the main reasons why people save?

(i) for emergencies such as unexpected bills, periods of illness or unemployment. This represents savings as "something to fall back on".

(ii) tradition. Some people have been brought up in an atmosphere where saving part of income is encouraged. Over a period of time this becomes habit.

(iii) to increase wealth. Foregoing expenditure today results in increased wealth in the future.

(iv) future obligations. People save because they know they will need funds at a future date, for example for rates demands, weddings, purchase of car, or retirement.

(v) for security. Saving by means of a bank account reduces the risk of money being lost or stolen.

(vi) inflation. Inflation eats away at the value of money. Money deposited in an account with a bank earning interest can offset the effects of inflation.

(vii) convenience. Having money in an account such as a cheque account makes payments very easy and usually more convenient than carrying large amounts of cash around.

(viii) future borrowing. Before lending money a bank would wish to know, amongst other information, a person's financial background. A long history of regular saving would be a point in favour of a customer requiring a loan.

When deciding which savings medium to use a person will bear in mind some or all of the following factors:

Security

Unless the saver is interested in speculation he will wish to search for a medium that is secure (i.e. has little or no risk attached to it). This will almost certainly mean choosing some form of interest-bearing account rather than investing in stocks and shares.

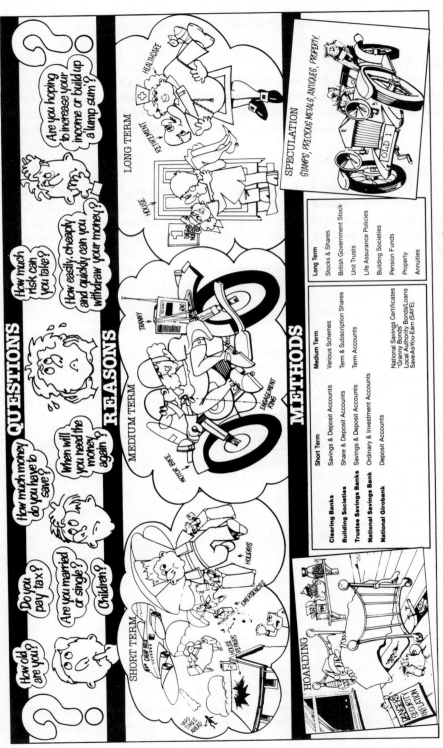

7.2 Managing Money (courtesy Banking Information Service)

Rate of return

The saver will wish to place his savings so that he obtains a high rate of return. Certainly he will wish the rate of return to be greater than the current rate of inflation. Rates of return (interest) in bank deposit accounts vary with length of notice needed and amount saved. The longer the term and the larger the deposit the higher will be the rate of interest paid.

Liquidity

Liquidity can be defined as the ease with which an asset can be converted into cash without significant loss or penalty. Savers often place some of their savings in fairly liquid investments, such as a deposit account or even a current account, whilst placing some savings in longer-term, less liquid investments such as an endowment policy or long-term savings plan.

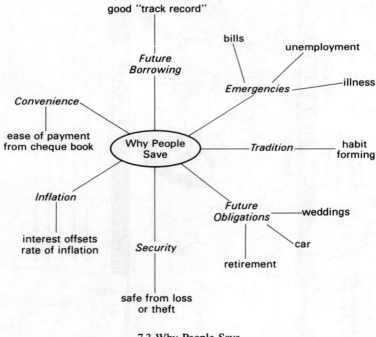

7.3 Why People Save

Let us look at the types of account available.

Current account

The current account (or cheque account) is used by those who want instant access to their money. It is the main method by which a customer can utilise the full money transfer facilities of the bank such as credit transfers, standing orders, and direct debits.

Deposit account

All the banks offer a basic deposit account. Many also offer variations on this basic service (see later in this section).

The salient features and benefits of the deposit account are as follows:

Features	Benefits
Age range unlimited	Can be used by young and old and be operated in single or joint names.
Deposits: no maximum	A customer can invest any amount large or small at any time free of charge.
Passbook/Paying-in Book	A personal record of all transactions.
Statement sent out regularly	A check on transactions over a period of time (yearly, half yearly).
Interest paid usually half-yearly or annually	Paid net of basic rate tax, so no worries about receiving tax bills for most customers.
	Usually calculated on a daily basis so a customer knows his money is working for him every day.
	Can be paid into cheque account for spending or left to accumulate more interest.
Withdrawals — usually at 7 days notice	Can have access to funds quickly (immediate access may result in loss of 7 days' interest).
Easy to open	Uncomplicated procedure — simple form to complete.

Ordinary savers will find this account ideal for their purposes. However, the banks have refined the deposit account to meet the needs of specific types of savers. For example:

(a) Regular savers

Some of the banks offer higher rates of interest for those who save regular fixed amounts. They can do this because they know exactly how much will be coming in each month from these accounts, unlike ordinary deposit accounts where deposits can be for any amount at any time.

(b) Higher rate deposits

The banks have a wide range of accounts to cater for those customers who can retain large balances in a deposit account. The minimum amount is usually £1,000 and should the account balance fall below this amount the interest paid would fall to the normal deposit rate. These accounts pay higher rates of interest than a normal deposit account although varying according to the

— account balance
— period of notice required for withdrawal.

(c) Term deposits

For savers willing to leave their money for fixed periods the banks offer term deposits. These offer higher rates of interest than other accounts because access to the deposit before the term is over is restricted if not excluded. These accounts can be for different terms — 1, 3, 6 and 12 months up to, say, 5 years. Rates of interest on these accounts are often determined by London money market rates and are usually fixed at the time the deposit is made for the term of the deposit.

(d) High interest cheque account

This type of account has been introduced to meet the demands of those customers who want to be able to use some of their funds but would like to earn interest on their account balances. Most of these accounts have a minimum account balance (e.g. £2,500) on which interest is paid and often restrict the number of cheques that can be issued or place a minimum amount for withdrawal by cheque. High interest account holders are usually provided with a 'cashcard' to make withdrawals through the ATM network, together with a cheque or credit card, if appropriate.

(e) Young savers

The banks have specially designed schemes for young savers, aged usually between seven and sixteen, who can receive gifts and incentives to save and budget their money. With a growing awareness of what money can do, increased money in the form of pocket money and birthday gifts, young people comprise a large market for the banks. The banks are keen to attract them because of the potential long-term business they would generate for the banks over their lifetimes. Gifts to young savers include budget kits, calculators, geometry sets, sports bags, record discounts and so on.

(f) Student accounts

When young customers become too old to be members of the young saver schemes the banks offer them student accounts, which are basically cheque accounts. Students are often encouraged to open accounts by the offer of gifts, for example personal organisers (Filofax), cheap travel or book tokens. The accounts will have additional facilities such as

— free banking (whilst in credit)
— overdrafts
— cashcard (ATM)

— cheque card (available to approved customers at age 18)
— preferential treatment for future services, e.g. mortgage

They will have to pay interest on overdrawn amounts.

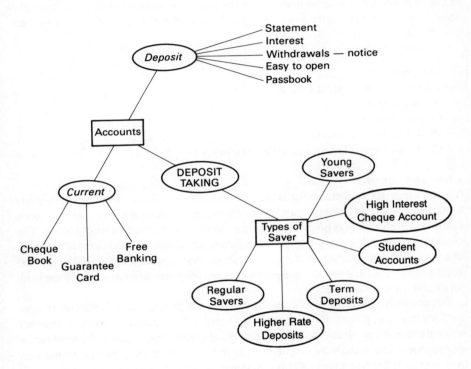

7.4 Bank Deposit Taking

Composite Rate Tax

Since 6th April 1985, interest paid or credited to individuals resident in the UK has been subject to Composite Rate Tax.

This simply means that basic rate tax payable on interest is paid by the banks. The individual paying basic tax thus receives his interest net of tax and does not have to worry about tax bills at the end of the financial year. Only those individual tax-payers who pay *more* than the basic rate of tax will have to pay an extra amount to the Inland Revenue at the end of the year. Special provision is made for companies and non-residents who are paid interest at the gross rate (the rate of interest without any deduction for tax purposes). The reason for this change is that it now brings the banks into line with other institutions, such as the building societies, who had been paying interest net of basic rate tax for many years.

MONEY TRANSFER

A major area of the banks' operations is concerned with the transfer of funds between its own customers and those of other banks. In earlier chapters we examined the rights and duties of the banker and customer with regard to bank accounts and the workings of the money transfer systems in detail. In this section on bank services we will simply identify the principal methods of money transfer and outline the main features and benefits to customers of each one.

We shall be looking at

— Cheque Account
— Standing Orders/Direct Debits
— Cheque Cards
— Charge Cards
— Debit Cards
— Cash Dispensers/Automated Teller Machines (ATMs)

Cheque account

The most popular form of account is the current account or cheque account. The cheque book given with this account enables the customer to make payments and purchases easily and conveniently; he does not have to carry around large sums of money. The cheque book usually comes with a cheque guarantee card (discussed later) to make the cheque an acceptable method of payment; shops, restaurants, garages and so on who accept cheques backed by a cheque guarantee card are guaranteed payment by the bank up to £50 for each cheque.

Statements are issued regularly, usually every month or after a certain number of transactions (e.g. 25). Extra full statements may be ordered at any time, but often a customer will have to wait several days before it is sent. Mini-statements, detailing the most recent transactions, can usually be obtained over the counter or through one of the new Automated Teller Machines (ATMs). Statements not only record all cheques issued but also list all credits to the account as well as details of Standing Orders, Direct Debits and, if applicable, charges levied on the account.

(a) Overdraft facilities

Cheque account customers can make arrangements to overdraw their accounts up to certain limits for specific periods of time. This service is very useful if funds are to be paid into the account in the near future, but the customer needs money now to pay for an unexpected bill or to take advantage of an unexpected bargain in the shops. Interest is charged on the amount overdrawn for the period it is outstanding. Once the overdraft is agreed there is no need to spend the money immediately; interest will only be charged when the account is actually overdrawn. The quicker the overdraft is paid off the lower the interest charges will be.

(b) Bank charges

When we consider the cost of making the cheque system work efficiently it is easy to see why for a long time the banks charged customers who had cheque accounts. The charges were usually based upon a certain amount per cheque issued and cleared on behalf of the customer, or a flat charge for a quarter or half-year (usually credits to cheque accounts were free).

The increased competition between the banks themselves — and new competitors such as building societies — resulted in the introduction of free banking. At first the banks offered free banking to cheque account customers who kept an average minimum in their account during a charging period, usually a quarter. Today the banks offer free banking if the account is kept in credit.

This means that as long as the account is in credit during a charging period, no matter how little is in the account, then all transactions (cheques, standing orders, direct debits, statements, withdrawals from cash dispensers) are free. However, should the account be overdrawn at any time during that period then customers may have to pay for some or all of the transactions during that charging period.

The banks do try to offset these charges. For example, in calculating bank charges for the charging period they will often make a notional allowance for credit items during the period and deduct this from the overall charge. In effect customers are only paying the net difference between the allowance for credits and the charge for debits in this case. Usually, if the amount payable in bank charges falls below a certain level, the charges are waived.

Alternatively, charges could be waived if an average credit balance of, say, £500 were held over the charging period. (The average balance is calculated by adding together each day's credit balance for the charging period — debit balances are counted as zero — and then dividing the total by the number of days.)

Figure 7.5 looks at some of the main features and benefits of a cheque account.

Standing Orders/Direct Debits

Standing Orders and Direct Debits are most commonly used with cheque accounts. They permit the transfer of money from one customer's account to another's. The two customers need not have accounts at the same branch, or even the same bank, for the transfer to take place.

(a) Standing Orders

These are instructions to a customers' bank to make regular payments (usually fixed amounts). All the customer needs to do is sign a Standing Order Mandate which authorises the bank to make the payments.

They are ideal for regular payments such as rates, mortgage, insurance premiums. Standing Orders have several benefits for customers:

- Regular bills paid on time automatically;
- No need to post cheques to make payments;
- Money can be regularly transferred to another account e.g. to Deposit Account to gain interest on surplus cash.

Features	*Benefits*
Cheque Book provided free	Customers can make purchases without risks associated with carrying large amounts of cash
Cheques widely accepted	Purchases can be made easily and safely
Cash available at — own branch — other branches — other banks (often a charge is made)	Customer need not worry about running out of cash at any time
Regular statements	Up-to-date record of account Avoid overspending Check on standing orders and direct debits
Joint Account	Convenient for both parties to draw on the same account
"Free" banking	No cost involved to customer in running the account
Can be sent through post	Less risky than sending money. More convenient than having to buy postal orders
Salary can be paid directly into account	No need to visit branch to pay in
Overdraft facilities	Once agreed gives instant access to short term credit
Access to other services — Standing Orders — Direct Debits — Cash Cards — Cheque Guarantee cards	discussed later in this chapter

7.5 The Cheque Account

Details of Standing Orders appear on regular statements sent to cheque account holders, so a check can be made of payments. Personal loans are usually repaid by Standing Order.

(b) Direct Debits

The main difference between the Standing Order and the Direct Debit is that with the former the customer authorises his bank to make certain payments on specified dates; but with Direct Debits the customer authorises a *third party* to debit his account. Direct Debits are usually preferred to Standing Orders when the amount and date of payment varies or is uncertain.

For both types of payment the main advantage is that once they have been set up they require no further action on behalf of the customer.

Cheque cards

As we saw in an earlier chapter, cheques are not always accepted as a method of payment. Part of the reason is the risk of fraud: when a shopkeeper takes a cheque in payment for goods he has no guarantee the cheque will be honoured or that he will receive his money. However, the cheque guarantee card increases the acceptability of cheques; the bank guarantees payment of cheques up to the value of £50 per cheque so long as the conditions, written on the back of the card, are fulfilled.

Charge cards

We saw earlier that the major types of charge card (or bank credit card) included Visa and Access. The development of such credit cards achieved certain objectives. They were:

— simpler to use than cheques;
— less bulky to carry than cheques or cash;
— a new system of obtaining credit.

The third function was the most important. Customers purchasing goods would simply sign a sales voucher filled in by the shop assistant and be given a copy as a receipt. The shop would then claim the amount from the credit card company who in turn claimed the amount from the cardholder, sending details of purchases on regular monthly statements. The statement contains details of all purchases made within the month together with any amounts outstanding from previous months, and details of the cardholder's present credit limit.

The cardholder can then either pay the *total* amount outstanding or just a *part* of it (usually a minimum of £5 or 5% of the balance) by sending a cheque or using a bank giro credit. Payment is not due for 25 days after the date of the statement, so cardholders can obtain up to 56 days' free credit. Interest is charged on all outstanding balances if the whole balance is not settled.

Depending upon a person's credit limit, this method of payment can be cheaper than obtaining overdraft facilities, because interest on overdrafts is charged from the time the overdraft facility is used.

BOB—K

Further benefits of using a bank's credit card are that it:

- can be used abroad to purchase goods and services;
- can be used to obtain cash;
- can be issued with additional cards (e.g. for spouse);
- some can be used as a cheque guarantee card (e.g. Visa);
- may also be used in cash dispensers, e.g. Midland's Autobanks, TSB's Speedbanks.

Debit cards

These are plastic cards similar in size and shape to credit cards but their use is somewhat different. The debit card is intended to allow customers to buy goods and services using the card and to have their account debited immediately with the cost of the item. The customer gives the card to the seller who swipes the card through an electronic funds transfer terminal (EFTPOS), thereby debiting the customer's account with the amount of the transaction. This type of card was intended to

- cut down on the number of cheques issued by customers
- free customers from the cheque guarantee card limit
- be used in cash dispensers
- allow goods to be bought with a plastic card through a current account and not on credit.

The main advantage for the retailer is the guarantee of immediate payment. If there is not enough cash in the account to pay for the item the retailer would be advised and would not risk the possibility of a cheque being returned for lack of funds.

The first debit card, named Connect, was introduced by Barclays in 1987. Its launch was surrounded by problems, many of which will relate to debit cards in general and which will have to be solved before they become as widely used as Visa and Access. These problems include:

- not all retailers will accept the cards, e.g. Marks and Spencer
- without a terminal the seller cannot know whether there is enough money in the customer's account.

The advantages associated with using a debit card are

- convenience and control — customers get the convenience of using plastic with the control of a current account statement listing the amounts spent and where spent;
- they are less complicated than cheques — the seller completes the sale and the customer merely signs a sales voucher;
- there is no £50 limit, which gives more freedom — purchases can be made up to the amount of money in the account;
- the ability to get cash through a cash dispenser or from a branch in similar fashion to a credit card;
- increased versatility — the card can be used to order goods over the telephone, to pay bills (using a normal Bank Giro form), or to guarantee cheques.

Cash dispensers/ATMs

Increasing use of technology in the banks, and the need to extend service beyond the basic 0930 to 1530 banking hours, led to the development of automated machinery.

Initially this took the form of 'through the wall' cash dispensers. These machines operated on the outside wall of many banks and enabled customers to obtain cash outside normal banking hours. A customer inserted a card into the machine and requested cash in pre-set units such as £5, £10 and £20. The earliest machines retained the customer's card; staff had to collect them and debit the customer's accounts with the correct amount and then send the card back to the customer.

Further research brought two major developments:

- more sophisticated cash dispensing and automatic account updating;
- extension of services.

The new generation of machines were more than just cash dispensers. They were, in fact, automated cashiers, performing many of the cashiers' duties. These Automated Teller Machines or ATMs have been developed by all the banks. Some of them perform a single function, like the fast cash machines, whilst others provide many services. These machines have now appeared not only through the wall but also inside the banking hall in an attempt to reduce queues at tills, and to free cashiers to deal with more individual queries and transactions.

Indeed Lloyds Bank has pioneered the concept of lobby banking by providing fully automated areas (or lobbies) in 1700 of their branches. These are secured locked areas to which a customer gains access outside bank hours (0630 to 2330 hours seven days a week) by inserting a special card into the door. Once inside, the customers can use their Cashpoint card to obtain cash from their Current Account as well as their Deposit Account. They can also use the Creditpoint (at over 1000 branches) to pay into their accounts by filling in a credit slip and placing the deposit and credit slip in a specially provided envelope, and then putting the envelope into the Creditpoint.

With all ATMs, customers are issued with a card and an exclusive PIN (Personal Identification Number). After inserting the card and keying in the PIN the ATM will put a menu on the screen, listing the services provided. This will vary from a simple fast cash machine, where a selection of pre-set amounts of cash will appear, to the very sophisticated ATM where a whole range of services appears:

- cash withdrawal (exact amount to be input by customer);
- deposit facility;
- statement request — mini and full. Sometimes full statements are sent through the post but the newest machines will print out a statement immediately upon request;
- account balances;
- request for new cheque book;
- other services, such as request for product information.

Banks have now developed their systems on a reciprocal basis, allowing customers to use each other's ATMs. Examples of these links are shown in Figure 6.15.

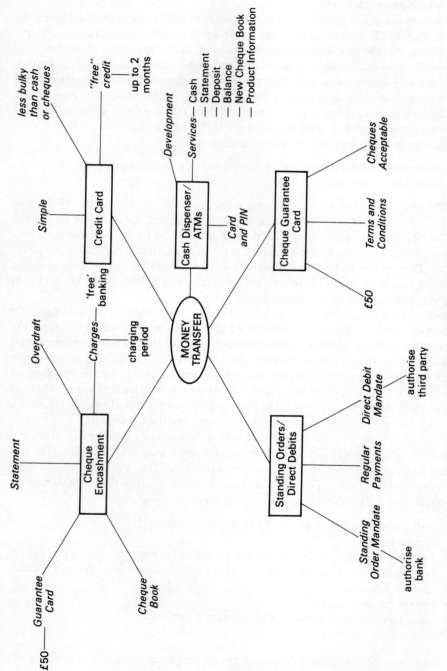

7.6 Money Transfer

One problem with ATMs is that they are now the greatest source of customer complaint, particularly over 'phantom' withdrawals — withdrawals which customers argue were not made by them. Whilst banks would never claim that their machines are infallible they do argue that these withdrawals are usually made by friends or family who have access to the card and PIN. This again emphasises the need to memorise the PIN and not to allow other people to have access to the card. Certainly you should never ask other people to withdraw money for you from an ATM.

ADVANCES

Banks are in business to make profits. The main way they do this is by lending or advancing money to customers.

Banks are willing to lend for most purposes (such as to buy household goods, houses, to start and run a business, develop products, or export) to both personal and business customers. Usually the manager will complete a form such as the one shown in figure 7.7 before deciding whether to grant the loan.

No matter how big or small the loan, no matter whether it is to an individual or to the largest multi-national corporation, all banks follow certain principles of lending. These can be listed and remembered by the mnemonic IPARTS:

I   NTEGRITY
P   URPOSE
A   MOUNT
R   EPAYMENT
T   ERM
S   ECURITY

Integrity. The integrity of the customer is an important factor in determining whether a loan will be repaid or not. There are many examples of customers having enough money to repay a loan but not feeling obliged to honour the debt. In these circumstances the bank often has to spend time and money (perhaps even take legal action) to recover the debt. Certainly there are customers who will stop making repayments to the bank as soon as cash gets a little short. On the other hand there are customers who will cut down on other spending to ensure that a loan is repaid. These customers have the integrity that bankers like to see when granting a loan.

Purpose. What is the loan to be used for? Besides wishing to avoid anything illegal, the bank manager needs to know if there will be any technical problems connected with the loan, e.g. exporting or importing goods and services which may involve delays in payment. Also, at various times the government lays down rules governing loans. For example, loans to importers of manufactured goods may be limited to specific amounts. All these factors need to be taken into consideration.

Amount. Is the amount requested the *right* amount? A good manager will want to make sure his customer has not overestimated his requirements nor, more importantly, underestimated what he needs. This could result in the former case in the customer paying for credit he does not need, and in the latter case not having enough to complete the project.

Bank Manager Decision Sheet

Part 1: Customer Details

Customer's Name.. Age.........................

Customer's Address...

....

Number of years and months customer has had a bank account with you....................

Has the customer's bank account been satisfactory?   YES/NO

If not, state reasons...

....

INCOME (customer's income per month after deductions of tax,
national insurance, etc.)

£

EXPENDITURE (customer's expenditure *per month*):

Board and lodging	£...................	
Other loans/Hire Purchase	£...................	
Other expenses	£...................	

Total Expenditure £

DISPOSABLE INCOME (INCOME minus EXPENDITURE) £

Part 2: Loan Details

Purpose of loan..

Total cost of customer's project £

Amount to be supplied out of customer's personal resources £

Amount customer wishes to borrow £

Length of loan requested | years

Annual Interest Rate % | %

Total interest to be charged £

Total cost of loan (interest plus amount of loan) £

Cost of each monthly repayment £

Does the customer have any security? If so, what (eg house, shares, life insurance)?

....

Part 3: Decision

Loan agreed: YES/NO

Reasons for decision – use the reverse side of the decision sheet to outline the reasons for your decision.

7.7 Bank Manager Decision Sheet

Repayment. What will the repayments be? The manager must ensure that the borrower can and will make the repayments. For personal customers the manager will examine details of his customer's income and expenditure paying particular attention to the *net* figure. After all, it is out of this net figure that the repayments must come. For business customers the manager will wish to see cash flow statements to ensure that enough cash is flowing into the company to make the repayments regularly.

Term. How long is the loan for? The longer the loan the greater the interest payments, and thus profits, accruing to the bank. But long term involves greater risks of something going wrong and of the loan not being repaid. Banks prefer to lend for short periods (up to three years) to minimise these risks.

Security. Although many loans, and particularly personal loans, are unsecured, some form of security should be taken whenever possible as an insurance against the risk of default by the customer. The bank will then always have an asset it can sell to cover the loan if necessary. The bank obviously prefers to take security that does not fluctuate in value and is easy to realise. For example, a bank would prefer to take a life policy as security rather than the house of a married couple with two young children.

Let us now examine some of the lending facilities available to bank customers.

Overdraft

This service is useful for both personal and business customers. Personal customers can use it to pay for emergency expenditure pending receipt of future income. Business customers find this facility very helpful for the day-to-day running of the business. For example, a manufacturing company will need to purchase and pay for its raw materials before the finished goods are produced and sold. The overdraft facility helps to meet this temporary cash shortfall.

Credit cards

We have mentioned the benefits to personal customers of using these cards, and the ability to obtain up to two months' credit. For business customers company credit cards are available. Such cards have two major benefits. First, the statements which are received provide a record of all business expenses incurred by employees; and second, the need to maintain large cash balances to reimburse employees' expenditure on business is eliminated.

Budget account

This service is used to spread the effect of bills which appear irregularly throughout the year. A customer simply estimates what bills will be arriving throughout the year and divides the total amount by 12. This gives the monthly figure to be paid to the bank. For example, if your total bills come to £2400 per annum the monthly payments would be £200. Should several bills arrive in February totalling £500 they could still be paid by the cheque book supplied with the account; the regular £200 per month repayment to the bank would cover that over the whole year. This means that in some months the budget account would be in credit, and in others not. It does mean you can budget ahead for a whole year for those major bills.

7.8 Borrowing (courtesy Banking Information Service)

Payments	Monthly expenditure													Expenditure over the year
Month														
Rent														
General rates and water rates														
Telephone														
Electricity														
Gas														
Fuel (including Oil and Coal)														
Life insurance														
House and contents insurance														
Car insurance														
Car tax														
Television licence														
Clothing														
Car maintenance														
Other expenses														
Total														

Divide the total by 12 = your monthly payment

7.9 Budget Check

With these accounts you usually receive a budget form to work out total payments, like the one shown in figure 7.9.

Personal loans

At various times people need to purchase expensive items, such as a car, furniture, boat, stereo or holiday. All too often bargains may be lost if individuals waited to save up to buy them. The Personal Loan is a way of buying goods when required, and paying back over a period of time.

Lending is governed by the Consumer Credit Act 1974. It regulates institutions lending to individuals, societies, sole traders and partnerships amounts up to £15,000. The Act laid down certain rules, for example the licensing of all bodies who wish to lend to these groups. It ensures that the total charge for credit is shown on all agreements to stop borrowers being faced with hidden charges once they have signed the agreement.

All agreements now have to show details of the *total* charges (e.g. amount of loan, charge for credit, total amount payable and monthly payment as well as the Annual Percentage Rate (APR)).

Although the decision to grant the loan remains with the bank staff member, many banks have introduced computerised credit scoring systems as an aid to decision making. The credit scoring system allocates points to certain personal attributes of the customer which have been proved statistically to identify the stability of a customer and, therefore, the likelihood of the loan being repaid without difficulty. For example, a customer who has remained in the same job for ten years and has lived at the same address for fifteen years will be awarded more stability points than a customer who has had six jobs in five months and never stayed at the same address for longer than four weeks.

After allocating the points to the various attributes, the computer will total the points and make a recommendation on the likelihood of the loan being repaid. Each bank sets a cutoff point, above which acceptance is recommended, and below which rejection is recommended. Although some banks permit staff to overrule the computer, it is likely that a reason for going against the statistical data will have to be given. In the final analysis it is the staff decision that matters.

Once the loan has been granted, a Personal Loan Agreement is completed and signed by the bank and the customer, each keeping a copy.

Often personal loans include free life cover. This ensures that the outstanding loan is repaid automatically in the event of the death of the borrower. This also relieves the surviving relatives of the burden and worry of the loan repayment.

Customers also have the option of taking out accident, sickness, and unemployment cover on payment of a small fee. In the event of the customer falling sick or having an accident the insurance will continue to make the loan repayments until the customer is able to return to work. If the customer loses his job the insurance will go on making the loan repayments until another job is found or for a set period of time such as six months.

The amount that can be borrowed by way of a personal loan varies between banks. An example is a minimum of £300 and a maximum of £10,000. The term over which it can be repaid again varies, although an example would be a minimum of twelve months and a maximum of five years. The interest on some personal loans is eligible for tax relief which has the advantage of reducing the actual cost, for example Home Improvement Loans.

Mortgages

Mortgages are a fairly recent addition to the range of banks' services. They reflect the increasing competition in the financial services industry as a whole. All the major banks offer facilities for customers to purchase properties. Mortgages vary between the banks from as little as £8,000 to over £200,000. Indeed, the banks would consider a request for a mortgage for *any* amount so long as the customer can afford to repay and the property is adequate security to the bank. This service has proved so successful for the banks that they are now taking around 50% of the UK mortgage market.

The size of the mortgage will depend on the following:

(i) Age of the property
(ii) Income of borrowers
(iii) Length of repayment period

Newer properties are usually easier to mortgage than older ones, and the term is usually 25 years. The percentage of the buying price which the bank will advance will vary. For example, for young newly married couples moving into a small new house the bank may advance 90% of the buying price, or even more. But for second time buyers banks only tend to advance 80% of the buying price. This is to encourage borrowers to put more of their own equity (the profit from the sale of their previous house) into the purchase.

There are four basic types of mortgage:

(a) Repayment mortgage
With this type of mortgage the customer is paying both interest and capital (i.e. the sum borrowed) throughout the term of the loan. In the early years repayments mostly consist of interest. Later, as the amount on the mortgage reduces so does the interest element of the repayment. But as the interest element reduces, so does the tax relief (tax relief currently given to basic tax payers up to the first £30,000 of the mortgage). This means that customers (such as a young married couple) would get the most benefit from tax relief when needed most, in the early years of mortgage when they are likely to be financially stretched.

(b) Endowment mortgage
With this mortgage a customer takes out an insurance policy. At the end of the mortgage the policy matures and the sum insured pays off the outstanding mortgage. This means that only interest and not capital is paid during the whole term. This tends to be more expensive because of the insurance policy, but customers do have the advantage of obtaining tax relief throughout the whole term of the mortgage.

(c) Unit linked endowment mortgage
This mortgage is an alternative to the normal endowment mortgage. Here the premiums are invested in one or more funds which operate similarly to unit trusts. The premiums buy units, the price of which is determined by the worth of the fund's investment holdings. As the value rises and falls so does the value of the 'Investor's units'. This kind of mortgage allows the individual to 'play' the Stock Market whilst buying a house. The returns can obviously be much higher than with a straightforward endowment-linked mortgage, but so can the risks.

(d) Pension mortgage
This is similar to (b) above except that interest *only* is paid during the term; the capital is repaid out of the tax-free lump sum which the customer receives on retirement from his pension plan.

As security the bank will take a first mortgage over the property: if a customer defaults, then the bank can sell the property and recover its loan.

Usually the banks charge an **arrangement fee** for providing the mortgage. They often include free life cover for the borrower so that a sum equivalent to the advance is guaranteed by the policy in the event of the borrower's death.

Banks also provide **bridging loans,** most commonly used with mortgages. Very often a customer will want to buy his new house before he completes the sale of his old one. The bank advances the customer the money to buy his new house and this bridging loan is replaced from the proceeds when he sells the old one.

Business loans

Banks lend small and large amounts to business customers of all kinds, from sole traders to multi-nationals. Loans can be secured or unsecured, but usually security is required for large loans.

The chief purposes for business loans are:

- to buy property, premises, or land;
- to buy plant and machinery;
- to buy another business;
- to buy into a professional practice, such as a solicitor;
- to pay for research and development.

Banks provide a wide variety of loans for businesses. Some of them include:

(a) Business development loans

These loans, ranging from one to twenty years, are for development and expansion rather than for the day-to-day running of the business. They are usually secured fixed-term fixed-interest loans.

(b) Franchise finance

Franchises are a growing sector of business today. A person can buy a licence from the franchise owner (the franchisor) to produce and sell products under the franchisor's name. Typical examples are fast food outlets or car repair shops. The franchisor in effect sells the idea, and supplies the material to the person buying the franchise. The franchisor makes money from selling his proven idea, and the buyer buys a business that he knows can be profitable. The banks will provide funds to purchase and run the business.

(c) Finance for special groups

Very often groups such as farmers or solicitors require specialist loans. Arable farmers, for example, obviously need to finance the time between sowing crops and reaping and selling crops. They often need loans to buy new equipment, storage facilities and machinery. The banks all have packages to meet such requirements.

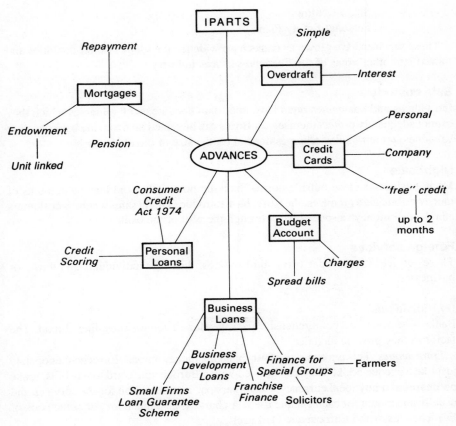

7.10 Bank Advances

(d) Small firms loan guarantee scheme

This is a facility offered to small firms by banks supported by a guarantee from the Department of Trade and Industry, which covers 70% of the funds advanced.

OTHER SERVICES

Alongside their main services banks also provide a range of services. These include:

> Safe Custody
> Night Safe
> Foreign Services
> Unit Trust/Savings Plan
> Insurance
> Investment Management
> Executor and Trustee
> Homebanking

Share Dealing
Personal Equity Plans

These services have grown as banks have widened the scope of their activities and moved into other areas of the financial services industry.

Safe custody

Individuals and businesses often have important documents or valuables which they cannot adequately protect themselves. Boxes can be rented out from the banks to store valuables in their vaults. Charges depend on the size of the object or box.

Night safe

Many businesses close outside normal banking hours. To avoid leaving amounts of money on business premises, the banks have introduced night safes whereby customers can deposit money in special bags through the wall of the bank.

Foreign services

These services come under two main headings, those for individuals and those for businesses.

(a) Individuals

Banks have organised comprehensive packages for customers travelling abroad. The facilities they provide include:

Eurocheques. This is a convenient way of taking money abroad. Eurocheques operate just like a cheque book. They can be used with a Eurocheque Card to pay bills, make purchases and buy local currency. Customers pay a commission for the services and usually an amount for each cheque used. A charge is also made for either the book of Eurocheques or the Eurocheque card itself.

Travellers Cheques/Foreign Currency. All banks can provide customers with travellers cheques and foreign currency. Travellers cheques are safer than foreign currency; if the cheques are stolen or lost it is possible to obtain immediate replacements from a local representative of the issuing company. They are available in fixed denominations either in sterling or other currencies such as dollars. A commission is charged by the banks. Most travellers prefer to carry a small amount of foreign currency in addition to travellers cheques. It is useful, for example, when buying small items at an airport, where facilities for cashing travellers cheques may not be available.

Travel Insurance. Banks provide a comprehensive insurance package to protect customers from

        car breakdown
        personal accident, medical expenses
        lost tickets, travellers cheques, money
        cancelled holidays
        legal costs
        lost stolen baggage and personal effects.

(b) Businesses

Banks provide a range of services for business customers involved with foreign trade. They provide:

Foreign Exchange. This enables a business to purchase goods and materials abroad.

Documentary Credits. Very simply, this is a guarantee by a bank to make a payment on behalf of a customer. It gives both seller and buyer a sense of security, very useful when buying or selling abroad, and where the two parties do not know each other very well.

Documentation. The bank will arrange to have all the necessary documents checked ready for dispatch (e.g. Bills of Lading, Waybills, and Bills of Exchange).

Unit Trust/savings plans

One way in which an individual can make money is by buying and selling shares on the Stock Exchange. This, however, can be a very risky business because the price of these shares can fall as well as rise.

Banks have developed a way of obtaining the rewards to be made from company shares, whilst at the same time minimising the risks of loss: they employ professional investors to buy and sell shares for bank customers.

They do this by offering Unit Trusts to customers. For a lump sum or through a regular savings scheme, a customer can invest in one (or more) of a number of unit trusts. The money of all such customers is added together and invested by professional managers.

The risks of loss are minimised by

(i) using the expertise of the professional managers;

(ii) buying, not just a few shares, but a broad range of shares.

The broad range of shares ensures that if one particular share is not performing well its effects on the unit trust will be offset by the performance of the others.

Banks usually offer two ways of buying into a unit trust

(i) minimum lump sum e.g. often as little as £250.

(ii) regular savings plan whereby over a period a customer can build up a large amount to be invested.

The profits of the unit trust are returned to the investors in relation to the size of their investment after expenses have been deducted. These include management charges (salaries of the professional managers), stamp duty and dealing costs.

There are three basic types of unit trust depending upon the needs of the customer. *Income trusts* are designed to provide a regular income for the unitholder. *Growth trusts* generate little income but provide for capital growth over a long period. The third type of unit offers a *combination* of the two above — a small regular income coupled with some capital growth.

Insurance

As part of their move into the wider area of financial services the banks now provide a complete range of insurance services, either through their own insurance subsidiaries or through insurance companies where special discounts are offered for bank customers.

Insurance can be categorised as either Life Insurance or General Insurance.

(a) Life insurance

We have seen in an earlier section how the banks offer life insurance cover with, for example, personal loans and mortgages. Cover can also be arranged for accident, sickness and unemployment.

Various plans exist which provide cover in the form of an amount of money in the event of death, or at the end of a fixed term whether or not the insured has died during that period.

(b) General insurance

Banks can now offer insurance services covering a wide range of needs. For example:

— *House Insurance.* This is usually linked to a mortgage and provides, for an annual premium, cover in the event of loss or damage to the house. Banks granting mortgages will usually only do so on the proviso that the house is adequately insured.
— *Contents Insurance.* The contents of a home can be insured against fire, theft, flood and other risks.
— *Travel Insurance.* Holiday cancellations, travellers cheques, money, lost or damaged luggage can all be insured.
— *Car Insurance.* As part of the whole insurance package banks can provide insurance not only for customers' cars but also for their caravans and boats. All sorts of benefits can be built into these packages, for example 'safe driver' discounts, monthly premium payments by standing order, claims assistance, and discounts on car rental after an accident.
— *Special Groups.* Special groups such as the self-employed, farmers, and company directors may have particular needs, which the banks can cater for. For example, farmers may need to insure against damage to crops by cattle, and tractor and other farm vehicle accidents.

Investment management

Very often customers lack the time or expertise efficiently to manage their own assets.

Many banks provide an investment management service whereby customers are allocated a member of staff to manage the customer's assets. They advise on investments, types of accounts, liaise with the customer's accountant and generally take on all the administration which the individual customer may not have the time to do. A charge is made for this service.

Usually this service is available only to those customers with a certain level of assets, for example £25,000 in cash or securities. It is, therefore, not for the small saver.

Executor and Trustee

It is very important for people to make wills. Often people do not make a will, or they delay because they feel there is no need. However, the consequences of not making a will can be worrying for relatives, and expensive in the long run.

A will is the only way a person can guarantee that his/her money and other assets will be distributed after death according to his/her wishes.

When making a will a person has to decide who will administer the 'estate', in other words the money and other assets. Wills can be drawn up by individuals, and members of their family can act as administrators or executors. However, if the estate is complicated in any way, or the will not specific enough, severe delays can be caused and much expense involved in resolving matters.

The banks have Executor and Trustee departments whose staff are experts in wills and the administration of estates. A customer can appoint the bank as his executor by including a clause to that effect in the will. If part of the estate is to be set up as a trust, for example for a child, the bank will also act as trustee to look after that trust.

Charges as executor and trustee vary according to the value of the estate or trust and the amount of work involved. They are sometimes levied on a percentage basis, sometimes on a fee basis.

Homebanking
Although there has been talk for years about the importance of homebanking the service is at present only available to a small proportion of bank customers. Although all banks have the computer capability to provide this service the number of systems available at present are restricted to those outlined on pages 131–2.

Share dealing
Banks had provided a buying and selling service for customers wishing to deal in shares which was operated through a stockbroker, with the customer paying a charge to the bank for such transactions on top of the normal broker's commission. This made share dealing through a bank more expensive than directly through a broker.

With the deregulation of the market, the growth of share ownership and developments in computer technology, several banks (and building societies) are now providing a direct buying and selling service. Through a computer system customers can within minutes

- place buy and sell orders
- obtain a contract note (for a buy)
- obtain a cheque (for a sale)
- obtain quotes
- follow the market prices
- ascertain the charges payable

The first banks to offer a full share dealing service through their branch networks are Barclays, whose Barclaycare service is available through all branches, and NatWest, whose system deals with twenty leading shares through 250 of its larger branches.

Personal equity plans (PEP)
These were introduced to allow individuals aged 18 or over to invest in shares and at the same time obtain tax advantages. Through these tax benefits the Government hope to encourage investment in a plan thereby enabling more people to enjoy the benefits of simplified share ownership.

BOB—L

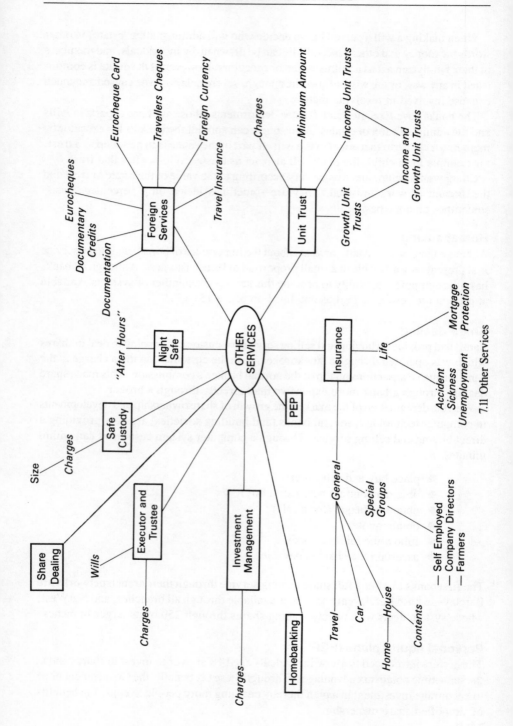

A PEP is a selection of stocks and shares and unit trusts available. Investment in a plan of a lump sum of £3,000 a year or £250 a month can be made, but only one plan a year can be started. The amounts are then invested on the Stock Market. Provided the plan is held for a minimum period of a full calendar year, gains are free from both income and capital gains tax.

The advantages of a PEP are
— investors with small amounts can enjoy an opportunity to invest on the Stock Market
— gains are free from tax provided they are held for a minimum period of one full calendar year
— a new plan can be taken out each year
— funds are managed by professionals
— dealing costs are minimised.

SUMMARY

All the retail banks have similar functions:
- Deposit Taking
- Money Transfer
- Advances
- Other Services.

DEPOSIT TAKING
- This involves acceptance of deposits from personal and business customers.
- A range of accounts are available to suit individual needs
  - (i) *Current Accounts.* These provide customers with instant access. With a cheque book and cheque guarantee card, they comprise an efficient safe method of making payments.
  - (ii) *Deposit Accounts.* These vary between the banks but all offer interest on deposits. These accounts are designed for
    - young savers   - large savers
    - regular savers   - students
  - (iii) *Combined Cheque and Deposit Account.* To obtain the ease of access of the former with the interest-earning element of the latter.
- People save for a variety of reasons
  - for emergencies
  - by tradition
  - to increase wealth
  - for future obligations
  - for security
  - against inflation
  - for convenience
  - for future borrowing.

MONEY TRANSFER

- A major element of the bank's activities is concerned with the transfer of money.
- Money can be transferred in a number of ways
  - Cheque encashment
  - Standing Orders/Direct Debits
  - Cheque guarantee cards
  - Charge/Credit cards
  - Cash dispensers/ATMs.
- Increased competition has resulted in the offer of 'free' banking. Cheque Accounts which stay in credit incur no charges.
- Even when charges are levied, they are often offset by notional allowances for credit balances.

ADVANCES

- Banks need to make profits to stay in business.
- They have developed certain principles of lending to minimise the risk of default (IPARTS).
- The banks offer a wide range of lending facilities to meet the changing needs of personal and business customers.
- These include:
  - overdraft
  - credit cards (personal or company)
  - budget account
  - personal loans
  - mortgages
  - business loans.
- All lending to individuals, societies, sole traders and partnerships up to £15,000 is regulated by the 1974 Consumer Credit Act.

OTHER SERVICES

- Banks offer a complete range of financial services for their customers.
- These include:
  - Safe Custody
  - Night safe
  - Foreign services
  - Unit Trusts
  - Insurance
  - Investment management
  - Executor and Trustee services
  - Homebanking
  - Share dealing
  - Personal equity plans

CHECK OUT QUESTIONS

1. List the four main functions of the retail banks.
2. Give five reasons why people save.
3. How can savings be different from investment?
4. Which account provides instant access to deposits?
5. List four features of the deposit account.
6. List one benefit for each feature described above.
7. Give an example of a bank service for regular savers.
8. Give an example of a bank service for young savers.
9. What types of accounts you would recommend for the following deposits:
   (i) £500
   (ii) £5,000
   (iii) £50,000
10. What are term deposits?
11. Give an example of a term deposit.
12. What effect does Composite Rate Tax have on interest paid to depositors?
13. List four ways in which money can be transferred.
14. What are ATMs?
15. List four services provided by ATMs.
16. How can cheques be made more acceptable as a method of payment?
17. When does interest have to be paid on overdrafts?
18. What alternative to an overdraft would you recommend to cover expenditure of £250 over five weeks? Why?
19. How do banks try to offset bank charges?
20. What is the main difference between a Standing Order and a Direct Debit?
21. What is a PIN?
22. To what does the mnemonic IPARTS refer?
23. List the main details a bank would need to grant a personal loan.
24. Why is security important in bank lending?
25. Give an example of the type of security a bank asks for.
26. How does a budget account work?
27. What Act governs bank lending?
28. Which groups does the Act cover?
29. What is meant by APR?
30. Define credit scoring.
31. Name two types of mortgage.
32. List three types of business loan.
33. How are charges levied for safe custody?
34. What foreign services do banks provide for:
    (i) personal customers?
    (ii) business customers?
35. What are unit trusts?
36. Name the two main types of unit trust.

37. What insurance services do banks provide?
38. What are night safes?
39. What do you understand by the 'Executor and Trustee' service provided by banks?
40. Why are travellers cheques often better to take on holiday than currency?

8

Banks and Competition

On completion of this chapter you will know the
— main sources of competition, their development and role
— range of financial services available and their advantages and disadvantages
— type of customer who would benefit from the services.

Once upon a time 'financial' life was very straightforward. If you wanted
   a method of paying for goods and services or bills — you went to a bank
   a mortgage — you went to a building society
   to save — you went to the savings bank (Trustee or National) or the building society
   a loan — you went to a finance house or a bank
   an insurance policy — you went to an insurance company.
Life was made even simpler by the fact that most of the services supplied, at least by the banks and building societies, were all very similar; they also paid, or charged, the same amount of interest. The range of 'products' supplied by these financial institutions was limited and most were easy to understand.

But take a walk down any high street; you will soon see that today's financial service market is no longer straightforward, simple or similar.

The financial market place has seen a great change over the last two decades. The start of this change was probably the *Competition and Credit Control* document issued by the Bank of England in 1971. One reason for its issue was to promote competition within the banking system.

Prior to the document banks all paid very similar rates, and all agreed that no interest should be paid on current accounts.

Following *Competition and Credit Control,* the banks agreed to give up their collective interest rate policy, and to fix their own base and deposit rates. Bank rates are still very similar today and it would seem that *Competition and Credit Control* did little to increase competition in terms of price; but it was a big step forward in giving customers a wider choice of services and 'prices'.

Certainly after 1971 the personal customer became more important to the clearing banks. Competition spread into the provision of personal loans, credit cards, home improvement loans, insurance and unit trusts. This may also have come from the fact that the clearing banks' share of new personal savings had fallen dramatically; in 1971 the building societies replaced the banks as the major source for personal savings.

In other words the banks were moving towards the idea of 'one stop' shopping for financial services, an idea which took them into the market of other financial institutions. This was the signal for the rapid changes that have taken place over the last fifteen years in the financial service scene.

Additional consumer protection legislation was introduced in 1986 in the Financial Services Act. The basic aims of the Act were to

— regulate the conduct of investment business
— increase competition
— increase customer confidence.

To those ends all investment businesses have to be recognised by one of five **Self Regulatory Organisations** (SROs) who work under the control of the Government's watchdog, the Securities and Investments Board (SIB). The SROs set their own rules which must be followed by members who, before they are admitted must give proof of their financial resources and agree to take part in procedures to deal with complaints and compensation. The five SROs are

AFBD　　— Association of Futures Brokers & Dealers
FIMBRA　— Financial Intermediaries, Managers & Brokers Regulatory Association
IMRO　　— Investment Management Regulatory Organisation
LAUTRO　— Life Assurance & Unit Trust Regulatory Organisation
TSA　　　— The Securities Association

The investments covered by the Act are

● stocks and shares
● unit trusts
● life assurance contracts (in excess of 10 years, i.e. unit linked and endowment policies)
● pensions
● personal equity plans (PEPs).

An investment business for the purposes of the Act is one which arranges, deals in, manages, and advises on any of the above investment products. It should be noted that bank deposits are excluded.

The Act introduces the concept of **polarisation,** which makes investment businesses choose whether they will give 'best advice' from the whole range of products available in the market (i.e. act as an 'independent intermediary'), or whether they will sell investment products from one company or group of companies (i.e. act as a 'company representative'). To operate professionally under the Act the following rules must be observed:

- **know the customer,** so that any advice given is based on the customer's personal and financial circumstances. This means that customer information must be kept up to date;
- **give best advice,** so that only services which are suitable to the customer are recommended;
- **explain the risks,** so that customers are made well aware of any dangers arising from the investment, e.g. share prices rising and falling;
- **best execution** provides the customer with the best terms available, e.g. prices and costs;
- **records** must be maintained of the advice given to customers and the reasons for the advice.

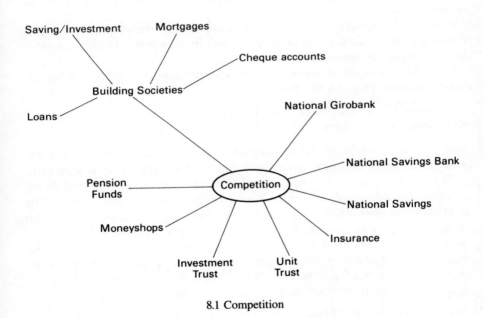

8.1 Competition

THE BUILDING SOCIETIES

The building societies are the banks' largest competitor in the area of deposit taking. Today there is also competition on the lending side of the business, especially for mortgages. The building societies' share of consumer deposits has in the past ten years risen from 38% to 50% whilst the banks' share has dropped from 45% to 33%.

Development

The first building society is said to have been founded in Birmingham in 1775. The early societies were set up to help small groups of people save money to buy land and build houses on it. When the houses were completed they were allocated or auctioned to the members. When all the members had been housed the society was dissolved.

However, around 1850 societies were allowed to borrow from members of the public even though they did not personally want a house built; they merely wanted somewhere to save their money. These 'new' societies were known as *permanent* building societies rather than the earlier *terminating* societies.

Building societies today are *mutual* institutions. They operate to serve the mutual interests of their members, and any surpluses are used for the members' benefit. They are 'controlled' by the Registrar of Building Societies who has powers to investigate their affairs on behalf of depositors and investors, and generally to protect the members' interests.

The society is owned by its members. These members are the people who put their money in a 'share' account. These 'shareholders' are then paid a dividend (interest) on their holding (savings).

The building societies are today the banks' greatest high street competitor for personal customers. They owe this position to:

(i) Interest earning accounts. The rates of interest earned are always competitive with alternative investments.

(ii) Income tax treatment. All building society accounts are paid *net* of basic rate tax to the customer, the society having paid the tax to the Inland Revenue at the composite rate. The composite rate is calculated on the amount that would be paid should each depositor individually pay the tax due on the interest to the Inland Revenue. The result of the calculation is that a lower rate is paid as there are many customers who pay interest on their savings even though they are not liable to pay tax normally. From this it can be seen that, although the net tax system benefits most customers, non taxpayers are at a disadvantage since the tax paid cannot be reclaimed. For many years the composite rate was felt by banks to be unfair competition. Since 1984, the banks have received similar treatment on their 'savings' accounts.

(iii) Convenience. Building societies are open longer than the banks, and Saturday opening has been particularly popular. Today banks are trying to redress the balance by having some limited form of Saturday opening.

(iv) Branches. The number of branches has grown dramatically over the 1970s and 1980s. Their design has in general been more welcoming and friendly than some of the more imposing and formal bank premises. This fact has certainly encouraged the use of building societies by some customers nervous about going into banks.

(v) Simplicity. In the main, building society services are very simple and easy to understand. They are not surrounded by some of the technical jargon that can be offputting to customers. The societies have tried to make it as easy as possible for customers to deposit and withdraw their money.

(vi) Security. The societies are seen as secure as the banks. There have in the past been some failures, particularly among the smaller societies. However, today, depositors' money would probably be secured by the larger societies should a small society have financial problems.

(vii) Mortgage availability. Until the banks entered the mortgage market in earnest in 1981 the building societies had a virtual monopoly of house purchase lending. This fact was a great incentive for people to open an account and save regularly before applying for a mortgage.

Role

The main role of the building society is to take in funds from customers, and to lend money to other customers for house purchase. Building societies therefore act as financial intermediaries between savers and borrowers.

Today, however, the societies are expanding their activities. They provide a wider range of financial services and are becoming more and more like the banks.

The Building Societies Act 1986 was the first fundamental change in the role of building societies since 1874. Under this legislation societies are able to provide a much wider and more sophisticated range of services. Three different classes of lending are now allowed:

- loans for house purchase secured by land
- other loans secured by land
- personal unsecured loans and overdrafts of up to £5,000 (only provided by the largest societies with assets of over £100m)

Money transmission services can now be operated, including cheque accounts and use of BACS (the Halifax and Abbey National are already members of BACS). The largest societies with assets of £100m or more can own, develop and manage land (e.g. both the Halifax and Abbey National are starting to build houses for sale for the elderly and single people) and to cooperate with housing associations. These large societies can also manage personal equity plans. Unit trusts can be run through subsidiaries whilst estate agencies, conveyancing businesses and insurance brokerages can be run by the societies themselves.

Although this Act greatly increased the powers of the societies, it was felt that it did not go far enough and after a period of lobbying such powers were significantly increased in 1988. The main changes were that

- societies are allowed to buy life assurance companies, take over or start stockbroking firms and run unit trusts;
- they are able to buy up to 15% of general insurance companies;
- cheques can be guaranteed above £50;
- the unsecured lending limit is increased from £5,000 to £10,000;
- hire purchase, executorship, trusteeship, share registration, tax advice and financial planning services were all sanctioned.

These new facilities take the building societies far beyond the provisions of the 1986 Act and the fact that the Act was overhauled in such a short space of time is further evidence of the growing importance of the role of building societies in the financial market place.

BUILDING SOCIETY SERVICES

The building society basic service range consists of
— savings facilities
— borrowing for house purchase
— other financial services.

Historically the first two activities have played a major role in the development of the societies, but it is their impact in the third area that has brought them into direct competition with the banks. These services will grow further as the societies move more and more into the banking area.

Each society will have its variations on the basic services in terms of interest rates, limits and 'add on' benefits.

The individual building society services have become more competitive in terms of rates since the 'cartel' arrangement on interest rates was ended a few years ago. Originally the rates of interest charged and paid were agreed at the Building Societies Association, and followed by all societies. With more internal competitive pressure from the bigger societies, and external pressure from the banks especially in the mortgage market, the cartel was abandoned. More active marketing of services could then take place.

Savings facilities

Share account. This is the most common account. Investment in it makes the customer a 'shareholder' or member. Like shareholders in a company the member has a stake in the society; he could in theory lose his investment should the society default. Unlike company shareholders, however, the building society shareholder can only buy from and sell his shares to the society. The share account is a very simple one; it allows customers to deposit and withdraw money at any time subject to any maximum deposit or period of notice that the society may impose. Interest is often calculated daily and is usually credited half yearly. Withdrawals can be made in cash or by cheque.

Extra Interest Share Accounts. The societies have developed a range of services all of which pay higher rates of interest than the share account to attract customers who can deposit larger amounts or who do not need immediate withdrawal. Generally speaking the higher the amount, or the longer the notice of withdrawal period, the higher is the rate of interest. Some examples of these accounts are:

1. High deposit/immediate withdrawal. Here deposits from around £500 attract higher rates and the rate varies according to the account balance. If a withdrawal is wanted no notice is needed.

2. High deposit/notice (e.g. 90 days). Here deposits from say £500 attract a higher rate but a long period of notice is needed. As an alternative to giving notice withdrawal, interest for the period (e.g. 90 days) will be deducted.

As an alternative to having interest credited half yearly these 'high deposit' accounts can have interest paid as a monthly income.

Deposit Accounts. Investors in this account are lending their money to the society. As creditors, they do not become members of the society. The account is rather like the share account, but the interest paid is slightly less. This reflects the fact that the deposit account holder is less at risk if the society has financial problems. In such an event deposit account holders would be paid out before the share account members.

Regular Savings Accounts. This account is for customers who want to save a regular amount. There is no set period for the savings, but an upper limit (e.g. £250 per month) is often applied. These accounts usually attract a slightly higher rate of interest than the share account, and one withdrawal per annum is normally allowed.

Save As You Earn (SAYE). This is a contractual savings scheme where regular amounts up to a maximum of £20 are saved for five years. After that, payments cease but the money can be left in the SAYE account for a further two years. At the end of five years a tax-free bonus is paid equivalent to 14 months' payments. But if the money is left for a further two years the bonus is doubled. The SAYE scheme pays a higher rate than the share account, but the rate falls if the contract is not completed. This kind of savings plan is attractive to higher rate taxpayers.

Children's Accounts. In order to attract savers at an early age many societies have special 'clubs' whose aim is to make saving fun. In addition to paying interest depositors receive magazines and gifts to encourage saving.

Lending facilities

Property Purchase — Mortgages. Mortgage lending for property purchase is the reason for the presence of building societies. Until the banks entered the mortgage market the building societies accounted for over 90% of all monies lent for home purchase. Nowadays their share is declining.

Building societies lend money to both customers and non-customers although in times of shortage of mortgage money preference would be given to existing depositors. Money is lent mainly for the purchase of owner-occupied domestic property with repayments being made over periods up to 25 or 30 years. The money is lent either as a **repayment mortgage** where the capital plus interest is repaid in regular monthly instalments over the full period of the loan; or as an **endowment mortgage** where an insurance policy is taken out on the life of the borrower. This policy is taken out with a sum assured sufficient to pay off the capital borrowed at the end of the period, or on the death of the insured.

Interest on the loan is paid off by regular payments over the term which are added to the endowment assurance monthly premium. The payment of constant interest gives the endowment method one of its advantages in that tax relief stays the same over the term of the mortgage. For repayment mortgages the relief declines as interest payments fall over the term.

Other advantages of this type of mortgage are that customers have

- full life insurance cover throughout the mortgage
- a tax-free lump sum at the end of the mortgage term (after capital is repaid)
- flexibility to transfer the policy between mortgages. In other words when a new mortgage is taken out, the new amount is only to cover the increased mortgage; the term can remain the same. For a repayment mortgage a new mortgage has to be taken out and a new term started.

One disadvantage of the endowment mortgage is that if rates of interest rise, the term cannot be extended as it can in the repayment method. The monthly payments will increase instead.

An alternative to this 'normal' endowment is the low-cost endowment mortgage. This works in a similar fashion, but the sum assured is lower than the final 'capital' to be repaid. The difference is made up over the term by adding 'bonuses' to the policy. This type of mortgage is cheaper than the full endowment mortgage but the tax-free lump sum will be a good deal lower.

The endowment mortgage is becoming more popular with house buyers today due to the additional benefits it provides over the repayment mortgage. Until recently endowment mortgages cost rather more partly because borrowers had to pay extra interest ($\frac{1}{2}$-1%) over the normal mortgage rate. This differential has been reduced in many cases. This, added to tax changes introduced a couple of years ago, makes the endowment mortgage a competitive product. Many societies are providing these mortgages in collaboration with Insurance Companies for whom the policies sold help their endowment assurance business.

Before granting a mortgage the building society will require

- a valuation and survey of the property
- an assurance that the borrowers can meet the monthly repayments (a maximum amount of 2 to 3 times the salary plus an addition of the spouse's income will be lent)
- the customer usually to pay at least 5% of the purchase price
- buildings and fire insurance to be taken out
- a first mortgage to be placed on the property.

Home Improvement Loans. Homeowners often want to improve their homes. These improvements can range from putting in new kitchens and bathrooms to house extensions and all can cost thousands of pounds. Building societies are an important source of lending for these home improvements with the loan often being added to the mortgage.

Unsecured Loans. Under the Buildings Societies Act 1986 as subsequently amended, the societies can now offer their customers personal loans and overdrafts up to an unsecured limit of £10,000.

Homeloan. Homeloan is a Government scheme designed to provide special help for young first-time buyers. Applicants have to save for two years; if at the end of the period £600 has been saved the Government matches it with a £600 loan which is interest free for five years. In addition, if the saver holds at least £300 in the account for the year

ACCOUNT	PURPOSE	CUSTOMERS	ADVANTAGE/ DISADVANTAGE
Share Account	Basic account	Savers who want interest but immediate access	Membership Ease of deposit No withdrawal restriction
Extra Interest Share Accounts	Higher deposits Higher rates	Savers with larger amounts and where saving is for longer term	Higher rates often rising with account balance (disadvantage of notice period)
Deposit Accounts	Savings account	Savers who want interest and immediate access but no risk	Ease of deposit and withdrawal (lower rates)
'Plastic' card Account	Savings with withdrawal and bill payment	Customers who want to earn interest and carry out business through ATM	Cash and services available outside normal hours
Regular Savings	Monthly savings	Monthly savers who do not wish to withdraw on a regular basis	Flexible monthly savings No capital needed Larger monthly sums
SAYE	Monthly contractual savings (5 years)	Savers who want a tax free bonus Suitable for higher rate taxpayer	Tax free bonuses Double bonus for seven years
Children's Accounts	Savings plan with 'giveaways'	Young savers to encourage 'savings' or building societies habit	Encourages saving Makes saving exciting

N.B. Interest payable net of basic rate tax.

8.2 Building Society Services — Savings

before application is made a cash bonus of £40 is payable for savings between £300 and £399, with a maximum bonus of £110 for savings of £1,000 or more. Despite the apparent attractive benefits very little use has been made of the service by young savers.

As the scheme is meant for first-time buyers there is a limit on the price of a home qualifying for the scheme.

ACCOUNT	PURPOSE	CUSTOMERS	ADVANTAGE/ DISADVANTAGE
Mortgage (General)	To purchase house	House buyers	Tax relief (to £30,000) Long term repayment
Repayment Mortgage	Capital and interest paid off regularly	For purchasers who cannot afford benefits of endowment (costs of two types now very similar)	Lower repayment Not dependent on health
Endowment (full cost) mortgage	Interest paid regularly	Purchasers who wish to repay loan and possibly have some capital over at end	Full life assurance Tax free lump sum No extension of term for subsequent house moves (but monthly repayments can rise)
Endowment (minimum cost) mortgage	As above	As above	Full life assurance Tax free lump sum Monthly premium — less than above
Home Improvement Loan	Home extension or improvement	Home owners	Added to mortgage and repayments spread
Unsecured loan (personal or overdraft)	Goods and services	Creditworthy customers	Finances in one place
Homeloan	Government subsidised scheme	Young house buyers	Interest free loan Cash bonus

8.3 Building Society Services — Lending

Other financial services

(a) Cheque accounts
The introduction of a cheque account service has been the largest single step taken by the building societies towards becoming 'banks'.

The first of these cheque accounts was introduced in 1982 by the Leicester Building Society which came to an arrangement with Citibank to provide its customers with such an account, together with personal loans, standing orders and travellers' cheques. Since then a number of societies have provided this service. Each had to link with a bank in order to have its cheques cleared through the Clearing House. The cheque account offered to the society customers was often linked to one of the 'savings' accounts in the following way:

— Customer opens a building society account
— Part of this account money (e.g. £350) is transferred to the bank
— The bank uses the money to open a cheque account (following normal bank procedures)
— Cheques can then be issued
— If the balance in the cheque account falls below a certain amount (e.g. £100) the building society automatically tops up the account to the original sum from the savings account.

With such a system the cheque account should always be in credit, assuming there are enough funds in the 'savings' account to cover any transfers that are necessary. This means that the cheque service itself has no charges.

Like many building societies' services each account has different features but in general each will provide

● cheque books
● cheque card
● free banking
● standing orders and direct debits
● statements
● personal loans/overdrafts (provided by the bank)
● interest (through the building society acount)

The Building Societies Act 1986 allowed societies to provide their own cheque account service and it was only a matter of time before one of the major societies provided such a service and joined the clearing system (the Abbey National in 1988).

A major innovation to the cheque service was introduced by the Abbey National in 1988 when they agreed to provide a cheque card with a limit of £100 to customers earning £10,000 and having their salaries paid into the account. Although the banks had hoped to maintain the £50 limit until a national EFTPOS system was in place such competitive action is almost bound to evoke a response.

(b) Automated teller machines/plastic card accounts
Building societies like banks are expanding their network of automated teller machines.

Although the basic use of the machines for customers will initially be cash withdrawal the societies' ATMs offer a host of add-on benefits, the mix of which differs from society to society. These benefits include:

- extended withdrawal periods (up to 24 hrs a day)
- instant balance statement
- mini statements
- request for full statement
- deposit capability
- bill paying service
- transfer of funds between accounts

With the growth of plastic some customers are having difficulty remembering the numbers which are given to them so in addition some societies, e.g. Halifax, Abbey National and Bradford & Bingley, allow their customers to choose their own PIN. The banks, on the other hand, are not keen on giving their customers such freedom.

One distinct advantage of the building society ATM system is that the accounts to which the transactions are applied are interest earning. Some societies link their ATM

SOCIETY	BANK	SERVICE
Alliance & Leicester	Bank of Scotland	Cheque Account
Halifax	Barclays	Cheque Account
Midshires	TSB	Cheque Account
Town & Country	Co-operative	Cheque Account
Nationwide	Midland	Access
Leeds Permanent	Lloyds/American Express	Travellers' Cheques
National & Provincial	National Westminster	Access
Woolwich	American Express	Travellers' Cheques
Bristol & West	Standard Chartered	Cheque Account
Nottingham	Bank of Scotland	Home Banking

8.4 Some Building Society / Bank Links

service to an existing account. For example Abbey National's Abbeylink uses either a Share or Cheque Save Account. Others have their own special account such as Halifax's Cardcash.

Most of the building societies' ATM networks are provided through shares networks. There are at present two ATM networks.

The LINK network is a federation of financial institutions which has four major partners:

National Girobank
Co-operative Bank
Abbey National
Nationwide Anglia (old Nationwide branches)

In addition to these four, a group of companies including Western Trust & Savings, American Express, Citibank, HFC Trust & Savings, Dunbar, Allied Irish, and twelve building societies have set up Funds Transfer Sharing (FTS) to participate in the LINK network. FTS will operate 230 machines and in addition FTS cardholders will be able to draw funds at any of the LINK machines.

Matrix. The building societies' national network has been set up by Electronic Funds Transfer Ltd and is a network of seven building societies — Alliance & Leicester, Leeds Permanent, Woolwich, National & Provincial, Nationwide Anglia (old Anglia branches), Bradford & Bingley, and Bristol & West.

Cardcash. In addition, the largest society, the Halifax, operates its own ATM network known as Cardcash. This is, in fact, a plastic card account operated through the society's ATMs which allows customers to

— withdraw cash (up to £250 each day)
— deposit notes and cheques
— pay regular bills by free standing order and irregular ones through the machine
— obtain account balances and mini statements
— order a full statement
— earn interest on their credit balances.

The use of **plastic card accounts,** which provide customer service through the ATM network, is a growing feature of building societies. The use of the ATM network is therefore somewhat different from that adopted by the banks which link their ATM/cashcards to a main account, usually a cheque account, rather than allowing customers to open what is in effect an interest-bearing account which has withdrawal and bill payment facilities.

(c) Insurance

Building societies are keen to promote insurance services in order to protect not only their customers but also their own investment in the property. The societies are actively involved as agents in the provision of:

Buildings insurance. This insurance is a compulsory requirement on the granting of a mortgage; societies arrange a high proportion of insurance on the properties on

BUILDING SOCIETY	SERVICE NAME	NUMBER
Halifax	Cardcash	691 (840)
Matrix network		
Alliance & Leicester	ATM	75 (110)
Anglia branches	Moneypoint	42
Bradford & Bingley	Passcard	32 (62)
Bristol & West	Matrixcard	40 (50)
Leeds Permanent	Moneybox	101
National & Provincial	Money Manager	52
Woolwich	Cashbase	99
LINK network		
Abbey National	Abbeylink	284 (420)
Nationwide branches	Flex Account	142 (195)
	Cash Link	
FTS	Link	171

(The figures are at end 1987, figures in brackets are projected figures (where available) for end 1988. Source CIOB)

8.5 The Building Societies' ATM Network

which they lend money. This insurance covers damage which relates directly to the fabric of the building; should the building be damaged beyond repair it would pay for rebuilding a similar property.

Home contents. This insurance covers the contents of the home against a variety of risks including theft, fire, damage, flood and storm.

Life cover. It is advisable that borrowers arrange to pay off the outstanding mortgage in the event of death. This cover can most cheaply be provided by a decreasing term assurance which gives enough cover to pay off the outstanding amount of the mortgage. As the mortgage is paid off over the years, the sum assured will gradually decrease, too.

Life cover (endowment). This insurance provides for a sum to be paid either on the death of the insured person or at the end of a stated period. These insurance policies are often linked directly with the mortgage in the form of an 'endowment mortgage'.

The 1986 Act and the 1988 additions have allowed the societies to own insurance companies and they will in due course start to provide their own insurance policies rather than merely act as agents for other companies.

In addition to these services, available at many building societies, there is a wide range of other activities in which individual societies are involved. These include:

(d) Credit cards (Access, Visa)

Because building societies could not provide their members with unsecured loans (personal loans or overdrafts), several societies linked up with a bank to provide a credit card for their customers, for example:

>Abbey National and Co-operative Bank — Visa
>Midshires and TSB — Visa
>Halifax and Barclays Bank — Visa
>National & Provincial and National Westminster — Access
>Nationwide and Midland — Access

This type of card allows the societies' members to get extended credit to buy consumer durables, an area which lay outside the scope of building society lending until the 1986 Act.

(e) Travel services

Many customers use their building society account to save for their annual holiday. When these holidays are taken outside the UK the members will probably need travellers' cheques. Because of the potential market many societies have linked with a 'travellers cheque' supplier to provide the service, for example:

>Abbey National and American Express
>Leicester and Citibank
>Bristol & West and Visa
>Nationwide and Thomas Cook

(f) EFTPOS (Electronic Funds Transfer at the Point of Sale)

The first attempt by a *single* financial institution to provide EFTPOS to a wider shopping public was when the Anglia Building Society started a scheme in the Northampton area with around 200 terminals in several national store groups.

Six building societies — Alliance & Leicester, Bradford & Bingley, Bristol & West, Leeds Permanent, National & Provincial and the Woolwich Equitable — have opened talks with EFTPOS UK Ltd about the possibility of their joining the national scheme. The LINK group launched a pilot EFTPOS scheme in 1988 enabling LINK customers to use their cards in 23 BP service stations close to the M25 motorway for petrol and forecourt services and also to obtain cash.

(g) Homebanking

As with EFTPOS, much has been said and written about the potential for homebanking. Again there are few schemes yet in operation, but significantly one of the first was set up by a building society. The Nottingham Building Society, together with the Bank of Scotland, has started its Homelink scheme in 1983. It used the Prestel system as the

'gateway' to the accounts. The system allowed customers to:
— view their account statement
— transfer payments between accounts
— pay certain household bills by electronic transfer.

The Nationwide Anglia has introduced a voice response system using a telephone linked directly to the society's computer. This is similar to the Speedlink system described on page 132.

Building societies are obviously already very comprehensive service outlets. But the new legislation has radically changed their role in the financial market place. They have become even more competitive with developments in the following areas:

- provision of *banking* services — cheque accounts.
- an *integrated* house purchase service (conveyancing and agency). Some societies have already started to move in this direction.
- new lending business with a move into *unsecured* lending.
- *associated* financial services — insurance broking, money transmission.
- more extensive business such as insurance, pensions, and stockbroking.

ACCOUNT	PURPOSE	CUSTOMERS	ADVANTAGES/ DISADVANTAGES
Cheque account	Money transmission	'Banking' service customer	Cheque service Free
Automated teller machines	Automated cash withdrawal	'Mobile' customers	Account is interest-earning
			Money can be used at several societies' machines
Insurance	Cover for house and life	Home buyers with mortgage	Security Ease of cover
Credit cards	Revolving credit	Customers who want extended credit	Borrowing facility (but interest high)
Travel services	For overseas travel payment	Customers 'saving' for foreign holiday	Security

8.6 Building Society Services — Other Financial Services

NATIONAL SAVINGS BANK

Development

The National Savings Bank (NSB) was set up in 1861 as the Post Office Savings Bank. It was renamed in 1969 when the bank was separated from the Post Office, to be run by the Department of National Savings.

The NSB operates through the 22,000 post offices and sub post offices which gives it very wide coverage over the country. Customers can transact bank business for longer periods than in the normal clearing banks, including Saturday mornings. The post office 'branch' network gives the NSB an advantage over any other 'financial' organisation. But NSB customers have to share the post office resources with people wanting to do business with the post office itself or with the National Girobank which also uses the post office as outlets.

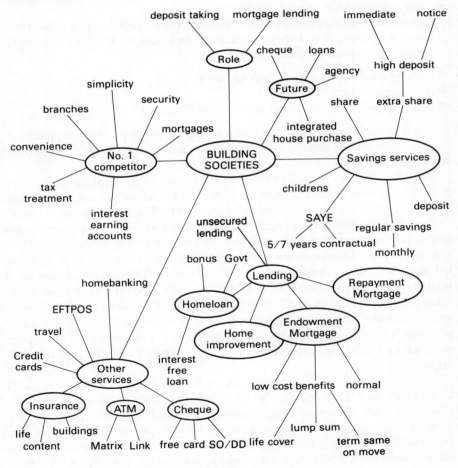

8.7 The Building Societies

Role

The main role of the NSB is to provide a banking service geared to small personal savers. It offers only limited services, providing a savings source which pays a competitive rate of interest.

The NSB's funds are lodged with the National Debt Commissioners and are invested in Government Securities. In this way the NSB helps to finance the Government's borrowing requirement. As a result all deposits in the NSB are guaranteed by the Government.

Services

(a) Ordinary account

This account is a passbook account which can be opened by anyone aged 7 or over, or by clubs and societies and formally constituted trusts. The minimum deposit on the account is £1 and the maximum £10,000.

Although up to £100 a day can be withdrawn on demand, a disadvantage of the system is that if more than £50 is withdrawn on demand the bank book will be retained for checking. The reasons for this are to

- prevent fraud should a bank book be stolen
- encourage savings
- deter the use of the account as an 'in and out' account.

Larger amounts can be obtained within a few days by making a specific application. Such accounts are paid either by a crossed warrant similar to a cheque, or in cash payable at a named post office.

'Regular Customers' can withdraw up to £250 at a *named post office* without having to hand in the bank book. To qualify for a 'Regular Customer' account the customer has to hold an account at the named or 'chosen' post office for at least six months.

There are two interest rates payable on the ordinary account. These rates are announced around November and are *guaranteed* for the whole of the following year. This gives customers the benefit of knowing what rates they will receive; should general rates fall, the NSB ordinary account customer would benefit. The guaranteed rates pay a smaller rate for balances less than £500 with the higher rate for balances over £500.

Interest is calculated on each whole pound deposited for each complete calendar month, although money does *not* earn interest in either the month of deposit or withdrawal. This can obviously be very disadvantageous to the customer; if a deposit was made on 3rd January and withdrawn on 27th February no interest at all would be earned.

Interest is credited to accounts on 31st December and the first £70 of interest (£140 for husband and wife) is free from all UK Income Tax and Capital Gains Tax.

Various special services are available to ordinary account customers. They can make *standing order* payments free of charge provided that the payments are not more than once a month and there is sufficient balance to cover the payment. A *paybill* service can also be used to pay bills which are normally payable at the post office, such as electricity, rates, road tax and TV licence, up to a limit of £250.

ACCOUNT	PURPOSE	CUSTOMERS	ADVANTAGES/ DISADVANTAGES
General	National Bank providing saving services	Customers who do not want 'full' banking service Less sophisticated customers	Large number of outlets — post offices Tax benefits Government guaranteed Longer opening hours
Ordinary account	Basic saving service	Any personal customers Short term/easy withdrawal	Passbook Easy withdrawals up to a limit (but book can be retained for checking) Large amounts within days Guaranteed rate of interest (but interest quite low, and up to 2 months' interest can be lost) Tax-free interest Standing orders (but only one payment per month allowed)
Investment account	Longer term savings	Any personal customers Non taxpayers Commercial organisations	As per savings Interest credited gross (but one month's notice needed for withdrawal)

8.8 National Savings Bank

(b) Investment account

This account is intended for customers who wish to save longer term. Accounts can be opened for individuals, clubs and societies, formally constituted trusts and also for commercial organisations.

This last type of customer is additional to the ordinary account range. Other differences are:

- one month's notice of withdrawal required;
- interest calculated on a daily basis;
- interest earned on each whole pound for each day of deposit.

The main benefit of an NSB Investment Account is that the rates are usually slightly higher than similar bank and building society services and that the interest is paid gross.

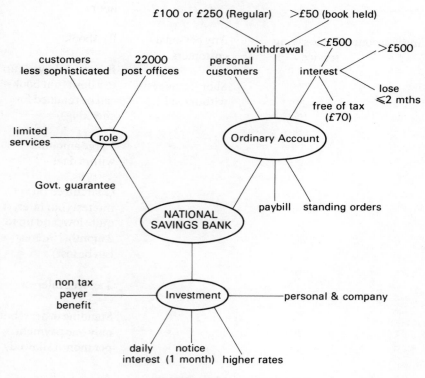

8.9 National Savings Bank

NATIONAL GIROBANK

Development

The National Girobank was set up in 1968 as part of the Post Office and was formerly known as the National Giro. Like the NSB it operates through local post offices. The

National Girobank had a shaky start in that it did not attract the numbers of personal customers originally hoped for. But it is now providing an effective and increasingly comprehensive banking service for both personal and business customers.

The Girobank has, however, been more successful in providing services to business customers — especially those who collect money direct from the public such as gas and electricity. In 1978 the National Girobank was given Listed status by the Bank of England and in 1979 became a member of the Clearing House.

Role
The Girobank was set up to provide a simple money transmission service, and to extend the use of current account banking to the personal sector — principally for lower income groups who are reluctant to use the large clearing banks.

Services

(a) Money transmission
The word giro means circle; for the girobank 'circle' means the computer which holds all the giro accounts in one place. Once the information has reached the computer at Bootle, Merseyside, money can be transferred easily between one account and another; this system provides the quickest method there is of payment.

All the public utilities (electricity, gas, water boards) include a giro transfer form at the foot of their bills, pre-printed with their Giro account number. To pay a bill a customer only has to insert their own Giro account number and sign and date the form; or pay in cash over the post office counter. Post Offices also hold Girobank directories giving the name and account numbers of giro account holders. This allows money to be transferred after insertion of the appropriate numbers.

Non-account holders can also use the giro system. They have to complete an appropriate form with the receivers' account number and hand this to the post office with the payment. A small fee is payable for this service.

This money transfer service is known as *Transcash*, and is the backbone of the National Girobank's activities.

(b) Current accounts
This service is similar to a bank cheque account but is somewhat more restrictive. Applicants for a National Giro current account must be 15 or over. Applicants under 18 need an indemnity from a suitable adult, usually a parent. The personal customer current account provides:

- Cheque encashment — one personal cheque up to £50 can be cashed every other business day at two named post offices;
- A cheque guarantee card — customers can apply for a card after 6 months or when they open the account if an existing bank cheque guarantee card is already held. This card allows the customer to cash a cheque every other working day up to £50 at any post office or up to £100 at a named office. The card also guarantees cheques for purchases in the normal way;

- Standing orders and direct debits;
- Free banking when in credit;
- Statement of account on every credit or after ten debits;
- Payment of bills through the post in supplied envelopes.

The girobank will also now allow customers of clearing banks to cash a cheque supported by a cheque or Visa card for up to £50 a day at the post offices. This service will help bank customers in rural areas who do not have easy access to a branch or cash dispenser. A charge of 50p will be made for the service during the weekdays (which doubles for a Saturday transaction).

ACCOUNT	PURPOSE	CUSTOMERS	ADVANTAGE/ DISADVANTAGE
General	National bank providing easy money transmission	Customers who want current account but wary of clearing bank Corporate customers who collect money	Large number of outlets — post offices (but compete with post office services & staff) Simple and easy system
Money Transmission	Computerised system allowing rapid transfer between accounts	Customers (private and business) who need to pay or collect money	All accounts at one centre Simple and easy Bills paid via giro credits
Current Accounts	Similar to clearing bank cheque account	Customers needing a cheque account without full clearing bank services	Effective cheque service (but more limited cheque encashment service)
Deposit Accounts	Standard savings account	Customers who want to link saving with a current account	Allows money to be transferred to current account
		Customers who want higher interest	Money earns interest but is easily switched to cover cheques

8.10 National Girobank

(c) Deposit accounts

This is a standard 'savings' account which can be linked to the current account with free transfers being made between the two. Customers can keep sufficient balance in their current account for their normal day to day transactions, and keep the rest of their money on deposit and earning interest. Any extra expenditure can be covered by transferring money from deposit to current account. The bank also offers a higher rate deposit account with rates varying with the account balance.

(d) Credit card

A Visa card, *Girobank Classic,* is available to customers.

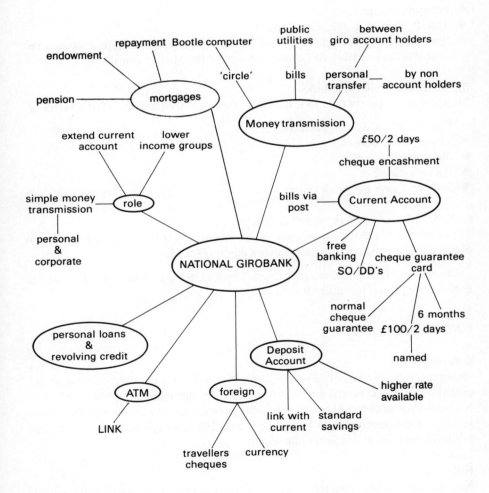

8.11 National Girobank

(e) Home loans

The Girobank has now entered the mortgage market, providing its customers with a range of facilities including repayment, endowment and pension mortgages, and bridging loans if needed.

(f) Corporate lending

The bank has plans to enter the market for small corporate loans, thereby increasing the areas in which it competes with the banks.

(g) Foreign travel

For customers travelling abroad the National Girobank provides:

- Foreign currency;
- Travellers cheques (Thomas Cook's);
- 'Post Cheque Service' (this allows special cheques supplied by Girobank to be cashed at post offices in Western Europe and around the Mediterranean).

(h) Automated teller machines

The Girobank is part of the LINK network. It provides the standard ATM services of:

- Cash withdrawal (£100 per day);
- Cheque book ordering;
- Statement request;
- Balance enquiry;
- 24 hour/7 days per week access.

(j) Personal loans and revolving credit

Customers who have had an account for six months can make postal applications to obtain either a personal loan or revolving credit (*Flexiplan*).

The National Girobank has a programme to widen its range of services. This service expansion will also include unit trust sales.

NATIONAL SAVINGS

Development

National Savings covers services provided by the state, or under state supervision and control. They are designed for, but not confined to, the small unsophisticated saver. National Savings includes the deposits in the National Savings Banks, and the various services of the Department of National Savings. The funds raised are mainly used by Central Government and the public sector.

Role

National Savings has a dual role — one as a source of revenue for the Government and the second as a means of saving for the public.

Services

There are several 'savings' products available for purchase at post offices and banks. Their main characteristics are that they are:

- Offered in the main for the personal savings of private individuals (clubs, charities and friendly societies are the only other significant market);
- Government guaranteed;
- Geared to attract money in small amounts from individuals;
- Given some form of tax exemption;
- Subject to quite low maximum limits;
- At fixed rates of interest;
- Non-transferable. They cannot be bought and sold on the market (with the exception of Government Stocks);
- Highly liquid (they can be redeemed on demand even though some penalty is likely);
- Simple to purchase;
- Subject to rising competitive rates of interest, which disadvantage savers.

We will look now at the main National Savings services.

(a) National Savings Certificates (NSC)

The National Savings Certificate was introduced in 1916 and represents a direct loan by the saver to the Government. The certificate issue is regularly revised to make sure the rates of interest are in line with other investments. When a new issue is made the previous issue is discontinued. Each issue is subject to a maximum holding, for example the 33rd Issue maximum is £1,000, but each individual can, in addition, hold up to the maximum on each *previous* certificate issue.

Each certificate represents a number of units. For example, in the 33rd Issue each unit is £25 and for maximum holding there is 40 units.

Certificates can be bought by almost anyone including children from the age of seven. (For children under seven certificates can be bought on their behalf.) They should be held for a minimum stated period, for example 5 years. Over this period the bonds increase in value with the idea that the rate of return peaks at the end of the period. An example of the rate of interest on an issue is shown on page 200.

From this it can be seen how valuable it is to hold the certificates for 5 years to obtain the highest rate of *tax free* return. Certificates can be held beyond the term, and interest will continue to be paid at a competitive rate. The benefits to savers of NSCs are:

- tax free (income and capital gain);
- liquidity — they can be cashed at any time (if within first year only the purchase price is repaid);
- guaranteed rate of return.

(b) Index Linked National Savings Certificates

The aim of this saving certificate is to offer the investor a rate of return *above* the rate of inflation. It does this by paying an extra rate of interest on top of the annual inflation

DATE OF REPAYMENT	COMPOUND INTEREST EARNED FROM DATE OF PURCHASE
On or after 1st anniversary of purchase but before 2nd	5.50% pa
On or after 2nd anniversary of purchase but before 3rd	5.75% pa
On or after 3rd anniversary of purchase but before 4th	6.00% pa
On or after 4th anniversary of purchase but before 5th	6.50% pa
at 5th anniversary of purchase date	7.00% pa

8.12 Rate of Interest on NSCs

rate. This extra rate increases the longer the certificate is held up to the optimum 5 year period. Certificates can be held longer than 5 years and still receive inflation-proofing plus extra interest. Certificates can be held in amounts (at present) from £25 to £5,000 (4th Issue) and purchases are made in multiples of £25. The maximum holding is in addition to holdings in all issues of Savings Certificates.

Certificates can be cashed at any time after the first year and receive the inflation proofing plus extra interest. Certificates cashed in the first year are repaid at the purchase price only. On encashment the saver receives

amount originally invested	+	rate of return equal to inflation	+	guaranteed extra interest
				Year 1 3.0%
				Year 2 3.25%
				Year 3 3.5%
				Year 4 4.5%
				Year 5 6.0%

All repayments are again free of UK income and capital gains tax. This is an advantage to investors although the greatest advantage is that the savings are inflation proofed.

(c) Premium Savings Bonds (Premium Bonds)

These bonds were introduced in 1956 and provide investors with a form of savings coupled with the chance of winning a large prize. They can be bought by anyone aged over 16; parents, guardians and grandparents can purchase them for anyone under 16.

Bonds are at present bought in multiples of £5 with a minimum purchase of £10 and a maximum holding of £10,000. Although no interest is paid, each £1 of the bond entitles the holder to one chance in a prize draw which takes place weekly with a higher prize draw monthly. Bonds are eligible for the prize draw 3 months after purchase. The winning numbers are selected by ERNIE (Electronic Random Number Indicator Equipment) from over 1,700 million bond numbers in a random manner.

Although each bond number can win only one prize in every draw there is no limit to the number of wins any bond can have. Eligible bonds take part in each prize draw.

WEEKLY	MONTHLY
1 of £100,000 1 of £50,000 1 of £25,000	1 of £250,000 5 of £10,000 25 of £5,000 165,000* of £50 to £1,000

(*the exact number varies each month)

The main disadvantage of Premium Savings Bonds as a method of saving is that no interest is payable; unless a prize is won the real value of the savings will fall in line with inflation. On the other hand the prize draw does give the chance of winning a big amount and these winnings are free from all UK income and capital gains tax.

The bonds are also very liquid. They can be encashed for their face value and funds received within a few days of the encashment request.

(d) Yearly Plan Certificates (regular monthly savings)

This scheme allows savers to make regular monthly savings of between £20 and £200 for twelve months. After this period they receive a Yearly Plan Certificate. This certificate is then held for up to five years over which time it receives a guaranteed tax-free rate of interest. This service replaced the Government SAYE Scheme.

Suppose a saver makes 12 monthly payments of £20. At the end of the year a certificate for £240 plus interest (6%) will be sent. The certificate, if held for a further four years, will then receive additional guaranteed interest paid at a higher rate.

These certificates can be encashed at any time although in the first year only the monthly premiums will be returned. Savers can continue to pay their monthly premiums beyond the first year and be issued with further Yearly Plan Certificates.

(e) Deposit Bonds

These bonds are designed for people who want to invest lump sums at an attractive rate of interest. The interest is paid *gross*, which makes the bond attractive to non-taxpayers. Bonds can be bought by individuals (solely or jointly), by or for children, clubs, charities, friendly or provident societies, registered companies and corporate bodies and by trusts, in amounts of £50 with a minimum of £100 and a maximum of £100,000.

BOB—N

Interest on the bonds varies depending on market conditions. It is calculated daily and added to the investment on the anniversary of purchase.

Bonds should be held for at least twelve months since earlier repayment will result in only *half* the published rate of interest being payable. To obtain repayment, three months' notice of withdrawal is needed.

(f) Income Bonds

These bonds are designed to provide a regular income from invested capital. They can be purchased in multiples of £1,000 with a minimum and maximum investment of £2,000 and £100,000 respectively. The bonds are similar to the Deposit Bonds in that

- Similar individuals and groups can purchase;
- Interest rates are variable, but competitive interest is paid gross;
- Interest is calculated daily;
- Three months' notice of repayment (half interest if repaid in first year).

The main difference is obviously that, instead of paying the interest annually, the investor receives the interest as a monthly income. It comes either by warrant through the post or goes directly into a bank or National Savings Bank account.

(g) Indexed Income Bonds

These new bonds are very similar in design and intent to the Income Bond but the minimum investment here is £5,000. The key difference is that the income received is guaranteed for a period of 10 years. The income is increased by the inflation rate. This means that investors receive protection against changes in interest rates together with protection against rising prices. This is how the bond operates:

1. In the *first* year an income is paid at an agreed rate (e.g. 8%).
2. On the *first anniversary* the monthly income for the next year is increased to match the increase in prices over the previous year.
3. This monthly income is guaranteed for the whole of the *second* year and is then increased to meet that year's inflation. This continues for 10 full years.

(h) Government Stock

The Government Stock often referred to as gilt edged security or simply 'gilts' — Stock Exchange Securities issued by the Government — can be purchased by post from the Bonds and Stock Office of National Savings. This is an alternative to buying through a stockbroker. As the rates of commission are very attractive for smaller investments the service is a good one for the less sophisticated investor.

Gilts usually have a life of between 5 and 20 years. Dividends are paid twice a year and when they reach the end of their life they are **redeemed** or repaid by the Government at their 'nominal' or face value. Most gilts pay a guaranteed fixed rate of interest, although some are index-linked for both dividends and capital. The benefits of gilts are

- dividends are guaranteed regardless of change in interest rates
- index-linked gilts offer a lower guaranteed rate of return but the rate is increased with the rate of inflation
- there is the opportunity of tax-free capital gain.

ACCOUNT	PURPOSE	CUSTOMERS	ADVANTAGE/ DISADVANTAGE
General	Savings services (State)	Small unsophisticated saver	Government guaranteed Tax benefits Useful for small amounts Easily bought and sold
N.S.C.	Loan to Government	Personal savers who can save for 5 years	Tax free Guaranteed return
N.S.C. (Index Linked)	As above	As above	Ensures rate above inflation
P.S.B.	Form of savings with prize possibility	Personal customers who like to 'gamble' on a large win	Regular Prize draw Large sums to be won Liquid assets (but no interest paid and value of savings can fall)
Yearly Plan	Regular savings scheme	Savers who can make monthly contributions and can leave money in scheme for 5 years	Guaranteed rate — tax free Flexible savings — vary amount from year to year
Deposit Bonds	Lump sum investments	Personal and corporate customers who can invest lump sums	Interest paid gross Benefits non-taxpayers Interest competitve and variable (but three months' notice needed)
Income Bonds	Regular income from capital	As above	As above but interest paid as monthly income

Indexed Income Bonds	As above	As above	Bond guarantees income against inflation for 10 years
Government Stock	Gilt edged government security	Less sophisticated investor who wants to purchase 'stock' easily	Commissions attractive (but stocks available are limited) Guaranteed rate of return Capital gains tax free Government security Easily marketable

8.13 National Savings

The range of stocks which can be purchased are limited to those held on the National Savings Stock Register. All are 'marketable securities' since they can also be bought and sold on the Stock Exchange. Almost anyone can hold stock, and the stock can be sold at any time at current market price or held until *redemption,* in other words, the date on which the stock is repaid in full by the Government.

Interest on the stock is paid without deduction of income tax. Income tax is payable, but there is no capital gains tax payable when the stock is sold.

INSURANCE

Insurance companies are a major competitor for personal savings and life insurance is the largest single regular source of saving.

Development

Insurance has been, from its beginnings in the sixteenth century, a major activity of UK financial institutions. Originally it dealt mainly with marine and fire insurance although around the turn of the seventeenth century the first life offices came into being. Since then, various mutual and joint stock companies have developed and these (together with Lloyds of London) meet most modern insurance needs. Insurance covers a wide range of activities including:

Life	Property
Marine	Aviation
Transport	Motor Vehicle
Third Party Liability	Personal, accident and sickness

The competition offered by the insurance companies to the banks came mainly in the area of life assurance, although personal accident and sickness insurance also compete for savings resources. However, as banks have moved more and more into the general insurance business, such as motor, home contents and building, the competition has increased both in range and intensity. Insurance companies have themselves widened their own financial services range and are now competing in areas such as unit trusts and personal pensions.

Role

The main aim of life assurance is to provide protection for dependants in the event of the death of the insured which could include:

- Death of the breadwinner

  The death of any member of the family who contributes to the family income. If both parents earn, then the family needs protection against the death of either parent.

- Death of the home-minder

  It is possible to depend financially on someone without receiving income from them. A person who looks after the home and children is a valuable resource. Unless you can get a relative to take over the role of looking after the children, then it will be expensive to employ a regular child/home minder.

- Death of both parents

  Some parents may not wish their children's future to be dependent on charity or the Local Authority. A cash sum may enable a relative to take on the children and keep the family together.

Life assurance also provides a source of savings should the assured survive the term of the insurance. In order to meet these aims two things are usually **assured,** namely:

- that the company will have to pay out if the insured person dies or if he lives for an agreed time; and
- that the premiums paid will be fixed over the whole period of the assurance.

Services

The terms and conditions for life cover vary from insurer to insurer. In general, however, companies provide life assurance services to provide cover in the event of death, a form of savings, and a regular income. For the first two events the cover can vary from Term Assurances of a few weeks to Endowment Policies of 25 years to whole life policies on which premiums can be payable until death.

To calculate the regular payments (premiums) to be paid over the period, the assurance company takes into account the

    age of the insured person
    sex
    state of health
    occupation (for 'risky' jobs)
    sum assured
    term

Using average life expectancy figures, it can work out a premium that, averaged over all the policies it issues, will provide more in income for the company than it pays out.

All life policies set out the following in the Insurance Contract:

- *The proposer* — this is the person who takes out the policy and pays the premiums;
- *The life assured* — this is the person covered against death;
- *The beneficiary* — the person who collects any sums assured paid out;
- *Sum assured* — The amount for which the life is covered;
- *Date of any payment* — this can be either the death of the assured or some stated date;
- *Amount of premium* — this is usually fixed for the whole period over which premiums are paid.

(a) Life cover policies

These are fairly simple policies which agree to pay out a sum on the death of the life assured.

Whole Life. This policy matures (i.e. is paid) only when the life assured dies no matter when that may be. Premiums on this kind of policy can be paid up to the time of death or can be limited to a period of years, for example up to age 65. This policy can be taken out either as a 'with' or 'without' profits policy. A 'with' profits (or bonuses) policy agrees to pay the sum assured plus any profits added to the policy by the company. These profits are the insurance companies' equivalent of the rate of interest paid on other types of saving.

These 'profits' are generated not only by the premiums that the insurers charge, but by the investments that the insurance companies make in government securities, property and so on. Insurance companies are one of the leading 'financial investors' in the British economy. In addition, many companies add a 'terminal' bonus to the policy when the policy matures or on the death of the life insured.

A 'without' profit policy on the other hand pays only the stated sum assured. With this kind of policy no additional return is made to cover inflation. What appears to be adequate cover today could in twenty years turn out to be rather small.

Because of the added bonuses on a 'with' profits policy, premiums are substantially higher than the without profits version.

Term Assurance. These are temporary policies which provide cover for a specified period of time. If the assured person lives beyond that date, no money is paid out. This kind of assurance is fairly cheap especially if the insured person is young and needs cover for only say 5 to 10 years. It is useful for couples with young children who need life cover for their dependants but cannot afford the more expensive policies. With this policy there is no saving element and no surrender value. Protection is the benefit.

Probably the most popular form of term assurance is a **decreasing term policy**. This is used to provide cover for a repayment mortgage. It pays off the balance on the mortgage if the assured dies before the end of the mortgage period. Obviously the more payments that are made to repay the mortgage, the lower is the life cover needed that is *decreasing* cover over the *term*.

Convertible Term Assurance. These policies are term assurances which let the policy holder convert the policy at some future date to a whole life or endowment policy, without needing further medical evidence. The policies are again attractive to younger 'savers'; they tend to need life cover now but would like to switch at some time in the future to a wider but more expensive policy.

(b) Savings policies

There are two main kinds, endowment policies and regular savings policies.

Endowment Policies are the most popular form of life assurance. They pay out the sum assured on the death of the assured or at some stated date (whichever is the sooner) and provide not only protection for dependants but also an effective method of saving. The policies are often 'with profits' and are usually taken out to provide a lump sum at a certain date, for example for retirement.

Over the past five years there has been a growth in the popularity of **endowment mortgages.** Here a mortgage is granted and the proceeds of an endowment policy are used to pay off the capital at the end of the mortgage (or on the death of the assured if earlier).

Regular Savings Policies have been introduced by many insurance companies to cater for people who want to save a regular sum each month. The plans combine life cover with a savings plan geared to provide a lump sum at the end of a term of years. The emphasis is on savings and the life cover provided, although useful, is relatively small.

The plans are for a minimum of ten years in order to qualify for the payment of a tax free lump sum. The monthly premiums are flexible within any limits set by the insurance company. The lump sum payment is made up of a guaranteed sum assured plus any bonuses added to the policy. The policies attract a surrender value.

Many of the regular savings schemes are now linked to a unit trust investment. The premium provides for insurance cover and a balance used to buy units. In the first year only a little of the premium is available to buy units, because the early premiums are set aside to pay for the life cover and setting-up charges.

The insurance cover on these plans is again quite small, but by linking the plan to an insurance policy they qualify the lump sum payment for tax benefits.

(c) Income policies (annuities)

This is to some degree assurance in reverse. Here the individual gives the company a lump sum and in return is paid a regular income by the company. Annuities are most suitable for elderly people who are prepared to exchange a capital sum for a guaranteed income.

There are several types of annuity:

Immediate. Here the company makes the income payments as soon as it receives the lump sum. These payments cease either after an agreed period, or on the death of the annuitant. The younger the annuitant the larger has to be the sum paid to the company. Where the annuity ceases on death there is a large capital loss if the annuitant dies after receiving only a few payments.

Deferred Annuity. Here a sum is paid and the annuity only starts at some agreed future date, again either for a fixed period or until death. Since the company has use of the money for some years before payments are made, the amount of the annuity paid is higher for any given sum than for the immediate annuity.

POLICY	PURPOSE	CUSTOMER	ADVANTAGES/ DISADVANTAGES
Whole Life	Sum payable on the death of the insured	Savers who wish to provide for dependants	Sum payable on death Premium less than endowment (but premium could go on for long periods and there are no benefits for life assured) Surrender value
With Profits	Bonuses added to sum assured		Sum assured increased to provide savings growth Inflation covered (but premiums higher)
Without Profits	Original sum assured paid		Opposite of above Final sum may not be sufficient for original aim
Term Assurance	Temporary policies to cover life for certain period	People who want 'short' term life cover	Cheap Provides for dependants (but no sum payable at end) Can be linked to mortgage
Convertible Term	Policies which can be changed to whole life or endowment	People who want cheap cover now but wish to change in future to a more comprehensive policy	Flexible and cheap No medical evidence needed on 'conversion'

Endowment	'Savings' policy which covers life over a period	People who want an effective savings plan with life cover for dependants	Usually with profits Provides good growth Linked with mortgage Surrender value
Regular Savings	Regular savings 10 year period	People who want capital growth in return for regular saving	Insurance cover Tax free lump sum Surrender value
Annuities	Income provided in return for lump sum payment	Customers who want to receive regular incomes	Regular income (but potential loss if early death — not with Annuity Certain)

8.14 Insurance Companies

Reversionary Annuity (or Joint or Last Survivor). Here the annuity is paid on the lives of two people (usually husband and wife) and is payable until the final death.

Annuity Certain (Guaranteed). This annuity provides for a stated number of payments to be made. If the annuitant dies before payment has been completed, the beneficiaries of the estate receive the money.

(d) Surrender value
Insurance companies provide competition in the savings area and also to a lesser degree in the lending area. Companies can provide funds for its policy holders by means of a policy surrender, or loan against the policy.

Policy surrender. For certain policies (e.g. whole life or endowment) the policy holder can stop paying premiums and request the return of some of the funds he has 'saved'. The amount returned is known as the *surrender value* of the policy. It is calculated by

premiums saved   + any bonuses which have   − amount for the life cover
                                        been added (part only)   provided

The surrender of a policy although providing a lump sum, is not the best way of raising money particularly in the early years of a policy. Most policies do not acquire a surrender value until they have been in existence for two years, as the early premiums are used to set up the policy. If they are cashed within the first four years some tax relief may have to be repaid.

A major drawback of surrender is its finality. All cover is lost and should a similar policy be taken out in a few years' time the premiums paid would be higher due to the life assured being older and therefore a greater risk.

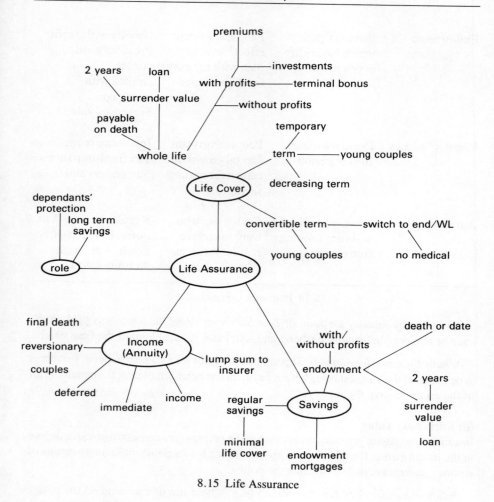

8.15 Life Assurance

An extra benefit of an existing life policy is that its surrender value is good security for a bank loan.

Loan against the policy. This is an alternative to surrendering the policy. Here the insurer will work out the surrender value and make a loan against the value. Although interest has to be paid on the loan, the policy remains in force and the assured remains covered.

The loan can be paid back usually as and when the borrower is able. It may even be repaid at the end of the term from the final 'payout' of the policy.

Paid up policy. If a policy has a surrender value there is a further option to full surrender if the policyholder does not wish to continue paying premiums. This is to arrange for the policy to be made **paid up.** Here premiums are stopped and the policy is frozen. The advantage is that any bonuses that have been added to the policy will be maintained and some future bonuses will be added. When the policy matures a reduced sum assured will be paid.

UNIT TRUSTS

Development
The first unit trust was created in 1931. Although the idea caught on rapidly the last twenty years has seen even more awareness of the benefits of unit trusts by the general public. This is partly due to the involvement of the clearing banks as unit trust managers in the late 1960s. Today there is a wide range of trusts available to the investing public connected to banks, insurance companies and professional savings (unit trust) companies.

Role
There are all kinds of unit trust plans designed to meet the needs of specific markets, but the basic roles of a unit trust are to

- allow individuals to share in a bigger and more diversified portfolio of investments than they could afford themselves;
- involve small savers in longer term investment in stocks and shares;
- collect funds from a number of investors and to invest the money in securities.

Investing directly on the stock market needs specialised knowledge and large sums of money. Most of the public lack these. Unit trusts have been developed in order to meet the needs of the investor with a smaller amount of money to invest.

A unit trust enables a large number of investors with a small amount of money to pool their resources into a central fund. The fund is controlled by professional managers who invest in a wide variety of securities available on the stock exchange, thus achieving a spread of investment which is both secure and rewarding.

There are three parties to a Unit Trust, namely

The Trustee
The Managers
The Unitholder.

(i) *The Trustee* must be approved by the Department of Trade, usually a Bank or an Insurance Company, and must by law be independent of the Unit Trust Managers. The role of the trustee is really one of a watchdog. His job is to make sure the terms of the Trust Deed are observed in all respects and to hold the cash and securities belonging to the fund. He normally plays no part in choosing the investments, other than to be satisfied that the managers' investment policy is within the terms specified by the Trust Deed.

(ii) *The Managers* of a Unit Trust have the job of investing the money subscribed by the unitholders in such a way that the aims of the fund are met. The expertise and experience of the investment managers produce returns which are generally better than the stock market average. Another attraction is that the unitholder always has a *market* for his units: the managers are always prepared to buy them back regardless of quantity or of the state of the market.

(iii) The unitholder is a saver who wishes to invest in the stock market but through lack of knowledge and experience, or perhaps because his investment is not large enough to spread over a wide selection of stocks and shares, finds it more convenient to invest in a Unit Trust.

Before a unit trust can begin operating the managers and trustees must come together and draw up the Trust Deed. This legal document must satisfy all the requirements of the Department of Trade and receive its approval. The unit trust then becomes an *'authorised'* unit trust. The trust deed lays down:

- the rights and responsibilities of the parties concerned;
- the provisions enabling new investors to join;
- the maximum charge that can be made by the managers for administering the fund; and
- the method by which the buying and selling price of units is calculated.

Managers are required by law to calculate the prices at which they will buy (bid price) and sell (offer price) units in accordance with a formula laid down by the Department of Trade. The bid and offer prices of most active unit trusts are calculated daily and quoted in the financial press. This provides a firm basis on which units can be bought and sold by the public.

Services

A quick glance at the financial pages of a newspaper will show the variety of unit trust plans available to the investing public. The following are just some of the plans on offer in the press.

M & G International Income Fund
MLA General Trust
Mercury Japan Fund
Hambros International Situations Trust

From this it can be seen that there are two main types of unit trust funds: **General Funds** which spread the invested money through all sectors of the economy, and **Specialist Funds** which place the investment in a special sector or country. When the investor has decided in which type of fund to invest he can choose whether he wants income or capital growth from the investment, or a mixture of both.

Most unit trusts offer two different types of unit. First there is the **accumulation unit**; here the regular return from the investment is ploughed back into the plan to increase the value of the investment. Second there is the **income unit** where the return is distributed to the unit holder at regular periods. If income is important to the investor there is a danger that the fund may not perform well enough to provide the income.

To overcome this problem, the investor may select a *withdrawal fund* which guarantees a stated payment. These guaranteed payments are made out of the investment income, but if this is not enough part of the capital is repaid. Although giving the advantage of a guaranteed income there is some danger that, over the years, the value of the capital investment is reduced.

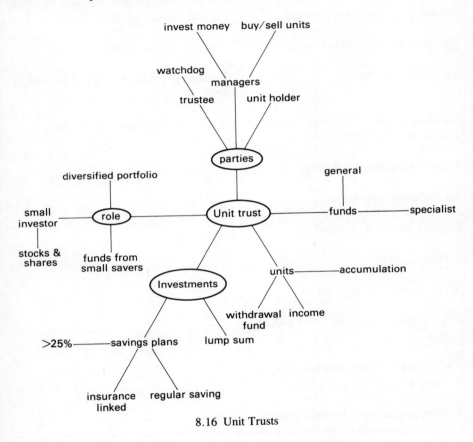

8.16 Unit Trusts

(a) Lump sum investments
Investment in unit trusts can be by means of a *lump sum payment* which is used to purchase units at the offer price. There is usually a minimum purchase; it is possible that additional units can be bought at some later date, again subject to a minimum amount. Some lump sum investments are also linked to a life policy which guarantees payment of the lump sum, or the value of the units, whichever is the greater.

(b) Savings plans
A significant proportion of unit trust investment is today placed through the regular *savings plans* many of which are linked to an insurance policy. The insurance linked savings plan outlined earlier is probably the main development in the unit trust service package. Today more than 25% of unit trust investment is made through this particular method.

ADVANTAGES	DISADVANTAGES
Spread of investment — less risk	Investment can go up or down
Specialist investment management	Long term investment
Ease of investment	Possible loss if have to sell when market low
Units easily bought and sold — trust managers must repurchase	Wide variety of funds (confusion)
Relatively liquid investment	
Capital growth potential	
Regular income if required	
Dealing costs low	
Wide variety of funds (choice)	
Management charges less than using broker	
Authorised trusts enjoy favourable tax treatment	
Trustee protects unit holders' interest	

8.17 Advantages and Disadvantages of Unit Trusts

INVESTMENT TRUSTS

Development
Investment trusts were an earlier version of the unit trust idea designed to encourage small investors into the Stock Market. Today they manage funds of more than £20 billion (compared with £29 billion for unit trusts). The first ones were founded soon after the introduction of limited liability for joint stock companies. Historically, investment trusts provided capital for overseas development. Their activities are not well known to the general public as there are restrictions on their advertising, but they are an interesting alternative to stock and share investment.

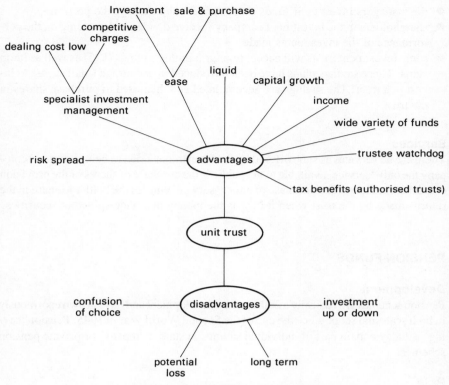

8.18 Advantages and Disadvantages of Unit Trusts

Role

Their role is similar to the unit trust in that they allow a spread of stock and share holding for investors. But the shareholders tend to have larger holdings than the unit trust investor and hold them for longer.

The basic difference between a unit and investment trust is that the investment trust is a limited company (not a trust). These are some of the other differences:

- it raises money through the issue of shares and debentures
- the money available to invest in other company securities is limited to shareholders' funds plus any borrowing it makes
- investors in the investment trust buy *shares* in the company and in that way take part in the stock and share investments of the company. The share price is quoted on the Stock Exchange and shares are bought and sold in the normal manner.
- it does not buy and sell its own shares (unit trusts buy and sell their units).
- it does not raise money by attracting small savings.

The similarities of the two are that:

- they provide 'indirect' investment on the stock market

- the managers invest their funds in 'securities' and manage the portfolio
- shareholders in the investment company receive dividends depending on the performance of the investments made
- some investment trusts will accept regular monthly savings (£25) as well as lump sums. These savings plans have been introduced to encourage small savers to invest in a trust. The savings are accumulated and then used to purchase shares in the trust.

Services

There are no services as such offered by the Investment Trust as being a limited company the only 'service' available to the public is the purchase of shares or the provision of a debenture loan. The purchase of either 'service' entitles the holder to share in the returns made by the trust when it invests the money in a wide spread of securities.

PENSION FUNDS

Development

Pension schemes are basically a 20th century development and have grown enormously in both scale and scope since the end of the Second World War in 1945. Pension 'saving' is today a main part of individual savings in state, company, or private pension schemes.

Role

The obvious role of any pension service is to provide an income when the contributor retires. The pension funds are financial institutions set up to receive payments from members, invest those funds and eventually pay pensions for the employees of a particular organisation.

Some of the largest pension funds are operated by British Gas, British Rail, the Post Office, the British Coal Corporation, ICI, Barclays and National Westminster Banks. These large employers usually operate and manage their own pension schemes. Smaller companies often use outside agencies such as insurance companies to manage their pension funds.

Funds from which the pensions are paid are built up from contributions paid in by employers and employees (although some schemes are free of employee contributions) plus income from the investments made.

Pension funds are major 'institutional' investors. They have huge funds available for investment in securities, shares, property and land.

Services

The main service provided by a pension fund is the final pension. But with the increase in life expectancy and the demand for pensions, more and more is being saved for pension provision. The three main pensions available are:

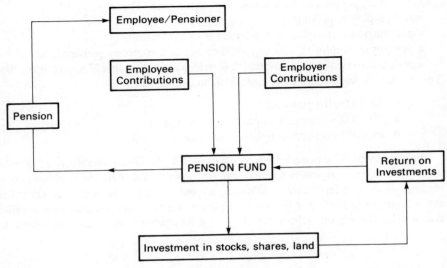

8.19 Flow of Pension Funds

(a) State pension

In this scheme men aged 65 and women aged 60 receive a pension provided that they have ceased full-time employment. Funds to pay their pensions are provided largely through compulsory national insurance contributions. Additional amounts are provided by taxation or from the Treasury. An additional state pension is also payable — the earnings related scheme. Under this increased benefits are bought by increased contributions made on a sliding scale depending upon earnings. Employees can 'contract out' of this scheme provided an earnings-related scheme is provided by the company.

(b) Occupational schemes

These are schemes provided by the employer and are funded as previously described. Details of each scheme vary, but the maximum pension that can be provided is two-thirds of final salary. The employee can, however, usually choose to *commute* part of his pension: in return for a smaller pension he will receive a lump sum payment when he retires. This sum can be quite substantial; often it is an alternative to building up a capital sum in another savings institution particularly as pension contributions from income are not subject to income tax. Death benefits are provided where the employee dies before reaching retirement age. These benefits can be up to four times the annual salary, in addition to which reduced pensions are payable to dependants. Occupational schemes are the main area in which the pension funds operate.

(c) Personal pension plans

These schemes are operated by a variety of institutions including banks and insurance companies and are becoming more popular. They are designed mainly for the 'self-employed' or employees who do not have an occupational scheme.

Only certain people can by law take out such a plan. These are
— a self-employed person;
— a partner or sole proprietor in a business or profession;
— a director or employee who is not a member of a company pension scheme;
— a person with two jobs, one of which provides an income that is non-pensionable.
The market for such schemes is large with an estimated

- 80,000 self-employed
- 750,000 without a company pension scheme
- 450,000 part-time employees without a scheme

The market for these plans has been encouraged by the Government through means of tax concessions. Eligible individuals can pay up to 17½% of their net relevant earnings (gross income less business allowances) into a scheme and are given tax relief at the standard rate. If an individual is a higher rate taxpayer a higher rate of relief is available. These tax benefits can make saving for a pension an attractive investment.

FINANCE HOUSES

Development
The first finance houses were set up in the 1860s to provide credit for colliery owners who found they could not always afford to buy railway wagons to move their coal. The finance companies bought the wagons and hired them to the collieries. Finance houses are today providing similar services with their loan and leasing plans.

Although finance houses originally dealt mainly with companies they did move strongly into providing finance for consumer durables in the 1960s consumer boom. More recently however with a flattening out of consumer demand together with stricter lending legislation (Consumer Credit Act) finance houses have returned more to their traditional company business.

Although there are hundreds of companies acting as finance houses and providing 'loans' to the general public the 30 major companies are members of the Finance Houses Association. This Association represents over 90% of all finance house business.

Many banks have interests in finance houses:

Bank	Finance House
Bank of Scotland	North West Securities
Barclays	Mercantile Credit
Lloyds	Bowmakers & Lloyds and Scottish (61%)
National Westminster	Lombard North Central
Royal Bank of Scotland	Lloyds and Scottish (39%)
T.S.B.	United Dominions Trust

Role

Although historically they provided 'hire purchase' facilities, finance houses are now involved in a wide range of credit operations for personal and corporate customers. Many of them also take 'deposits' to help to finance their lending operations.

Services

Finance houses are the major specialists in providing instalment credit facilities. Other sources include some retailers who make finance available from their own resources to purchasers of their goods. In recent years, the major banks have provided consumer credit through personal loans and facilities offered by their credit card subsidiaries.

Where a finance house is providing credit for, say, a motor car it is normal for the motor dealer to arrange the transaction with the finance house once the customer has chosen the vehicle. The finance house and the customer sign an agreement, and the customer then pays by instalments direct to the finance house.

In other cases a retailer and the customer may have a financial agreement but the retailer will *sell* the debt owed to him under that agreement to a finance house. The customer pays the instalments to the retailer, he may not even know that the finance house has provided the funds. This form of financing is known as *block discounting*.

A private individual can also negotiate direct with a finance house, as do many business organisations.

Instalment credit may take several forms:

Hire purchase. This is perhaps the best known. Under a hire-purchase agreement the customer hires goods for an agreed period and can buy them at the end of the period for a very small sum. When all the instalments and the 'option fee' have been paid the customer actually owns the goods.

Conditional sale. In this case the price of the goods is payable over an agreed period. But the goods remain the property of the seller for some stated period (usually until the last payment has been made).

Credit sale. Under a credit sale the buyer owns the goods from the outset, but undertakes to pay for them over an agreed period.

Revolving loan. Here the customer borrows a multiple of an approved monthly payment; for example 20 times a monthly payment of £30 (£600). The customer can then buy whatever goods he chooses up to that amount. Each month he will make the agreed payment — in this instance £30. A proportion of this goes to pay the interest charged monthly to this account; the rest goes to pay off the capital borrowed. The customer can 'top-up' his borrowings to the originally agreed limit.

Personal and commercial loans. These are simply loans of money repayable, with interest, by equal instalments over a fixed period. Instalment credit of this type has become more common in recent years and is widely used by consumers and industrial and commercial customers.

Leasing. In leasing, the customer chooses the industrial plant, machinery or other equipment he needs for his business. The finance house then buys the equipment and leases it (that is hires it) to the customer at an appropriate rental which he has to pay over an agreed period. At the end of this period the customer may decide either to obtain new equipment or to go on using the original leased equipment at a very small rental. The unique feature of leasing is that it completely separates *use* from *ownership*; the customer uses the machinery as he pleases, but the lease never makes him the owner. In practice leasing is not much used by private individuals, except in certain areas such as TV rental.

(a) How instalment credit works

In most types of instalment credit agreement, the customer makes a minimum down-payment, usually a stated percentage of the cash price of the goods. The down-payment is deducted from the cash price, and the balance is provided by the finance house, which adds its own 'credit charges'. The resulting sum is divided by the total number of instalments to find the amount of each payment.

The following is an example:

	£
Cash price of goods:	1,350
Less: Down-payment of 33⅓ %	450
Balance of the cash price	900
Add: Credit charges for 2 years calculated on the balance of the cash price at 12% 'flat' per annum	216
Total sum payable by 24 monthly instalments of £46.50	1,116

(The APR — annual percentage rate — of charge in the above example is 23.8%.)

(b) Consumer hire purchase

A feature of the finance houses hire purchase lending is that they rarely meet the public with whom they do business. They usually work through the supplier of the goods who arranges for his customer to pay by HP.

Buying on hire purchase is relatively easy since it does not involve the customer in having to obtain credit from a third party such as a bank. The loan can be arranged at the time of purchase with the supplier — a car or caravan showroom, or an electrical shop.

The advantages of hire purchase to the customer are:

Certainty. Once a customer has signed a fixed term agreement he or she can plan to make pre-arranged payments at regular intervals. The credit charge cannot normally be varied once the agreement has been signed. Unlike some other forms of borrowing, there is no risk of a personal budget being upset because of a change in interest rates or a demand for repayment.

Protection. In many cases the customer can look to the finance house as well as to the supplier for assurance regarding the quality of the goods.

Standardisation. Standard printed documents are used, which means that the transaction can be arranged quickly without too much formality.

Legal costs. Normally, there aren't any.

Quality. The customer may be able to acquire better goods than would be possible if the full cash price had to be found immediately.

Maintenance of savings. By making use of instalment credit the customer may be able to keep hard-earned savings for an unforseen emergency: most people are happier knowing that they have something set aside for a rainy day.

Immediate use of the goods. The customer can obtain and use the goods immediately the down-payment is made, rather than wait until the total price has been paid.

The main *disadvantage* of HP credit is that the rates of interest are substantially higher than for a bank loan. These higher rates are due to the fact that the finance house often has to rely on the skill of the suppliers when making a loan and although they make the normal lending enquiries they are more at risk than banks who usually have greater knowledge of their customers.

(c) Personal loans

Finance houses also provide personal loans both unsecured and secured for a wide variety of purchases including home improvements, holidays, school fees, consolidation of other debts. Customers for these services come from:

- existing customers (perhaps HP) who are mailed;
- customers who reply to press advertising;
- customers introduced by brokers or suppliers, e.g. home improvement.

(d) Industrial hire purchase

This side of the finance houses' business is growing in importance and accounts for more business than the consumer hire purchase side. Industrial HP is commonly available for the purchase of industrial and agricultural equipment, plant and machinery. One variation to consumer HP is that it is becoming more common for loans to be subject to a variable rate of interest over the period of the loan.

The benefits of hire purchase to a company are

> Working capital is not strained;
> Bank overdrafts not used;
> Budgeting made easy by instalments;
> Contracts are simple and flexible; and
> Possible tax advantages.

(e) Leasing

Although companies normally never become the owners of the plant and machinery or equipment that they lease, leasing is now the most popular method of obtaining the use of such items. In its basic form the user pays a 'rent' to the owner for the use of the equipment. There are two types of leasing agreement: **operating leases** where the manufacturer or supplier offers the lease and not only provides the goods but agrees to service and repair them. These leases are used by manufacturers to help the sale of their products. In **finance leases** a leasing company (for example finance house) buys the equipment; although it remains the owner it passes the equipment to the 'purchaser' to use. The leasing company is not concerned with the goods themselves or in their servicing but merely with providing the finance for their purchase.

Leasing is an attractive method of obtaining the use of goods as

- it does not use up liquid assets
- there are no worries of ownership — for example depreciation or replacement
- rentals are set at the outset (after several years they can fall to a minimal level)
- arrangements are flexible and contracts can be tailormade to suit the company's needs
- budgeting is eased by spreading capital costs over several years and removing peaks of expenditure.

(f) Deposit service

Finance houses obtain funds by borrowing from banks (often supplied by parent banks), borrowing in wholesale money markets, and borrowing from the public (and local authorities and commercial concerns). The last method is a most important method. It involves the finance house in advertising for deposits from the public and so coming into direct competition with other sources of saving such as banks and building societies.

(g) Savings accounts

These personal customer savings schemes usually need some period of notice from one month to twelve months with the rates of interest paid increasing with the period of notice. The rates paid although competitive are variable at short notice as the rates are set according to the prevailing market conditions. The accounts are usually intended for larger savers with some accounts having a minimum deposit of £500. For withdrawals notice is needed although up to £100 can often be withdrawn without notice. In addition to this straightforward savings scheme, finance houses also offer special schemes which require high minimum deposits e.g. £5,000 and a period of notice which may be as short as seven days. Such schemes are designed for professional advisers who have access to clients' funds, companies, as well as individuals.

(h) Wholesale deposits

Finance houses also compete for 'wholesale' deposits from banks, building societies, pension funds and commercial companies. These deposits are taken in large amounts, e.g. £25,000, for any period from overnight to say three years. The rates of interest paid are very competitive and are determined by market conditions which make them very variable.

MONEYSHOPS

Development

'Moneyshops' were established in the early 1970s. They were set up by American banks to compete in personal lending for customers who wanted a simpler and more 'approachable' method of raising money. The moneyshops provided basic banking services with

> longer opening hours
> comfortable and informal offices
> appeal to private individuals
> provision of personal, home improvement, and mortgage loans, insurance and savings services.

Role

The moneyshop provides an alternative method of banking mainly for the private customer without the formality associated with the major banks.

Services

Although the accent is upon lending, some moneyshops do provide a wide range of financial services, provided in different ways. Citibank for example not only provides services through its retail outlets (branches), it also has arrangements with third parties which increase its market potential. For example it has links with Marks & Spencer (credit card) and Leicester Building Society (Leicester card).

Other moneyshops such as Western Trust & Savings deal mainly by post. This can be appealing to customers who are reluctant to ask personally for a loan. But the retail outlet is the *only* service of business for some moneyshops, such as Boston Trust. This variety is typical of the moneyshop approach. They are concerned with winning a place in the market and making banking business easy to transact for their customers. The services offered by the moneyshops are 'normal' banking ones but they are often packaged differently.

The services include:

- cheque accounts — no charge
                  — interest earning
- Savings accounts — time (notice of withdrawal needed)
                  — fixed term
- personal loan
- revolving credit
- standing orders/direct debits
- travel services — travellers' cheques
- insurance

SUMMARY

- Competition growing
- Competition and Credit Control 1971

Building Societies
- Main competitor to banks

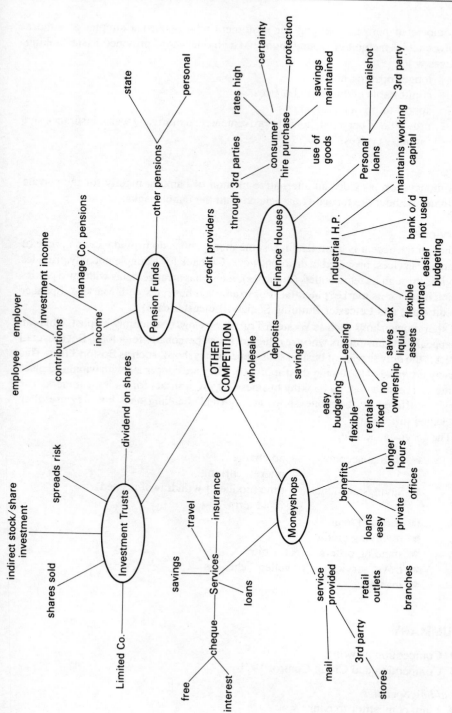

8.20 Other Competition for the Banks

- Prime position due to
  - interest earning accounts
  - tax treatment
  - convenience
  - branches
  - simplicity
  - security
  - mortgage availability

- Role
  - financial intermediary
  - accept deposits and lend for house purchase

- Savings services
  - share
  - extra interest share
  - deposit
  - regular savings
  - SAYE
  - children's

- Lending
  - repayment mortgage
  - endowment mortgage
  - home improvement
  - homeloan

- Other financial services
  - cheque (often free)
  - ATMs (Link and Matrix)
  - insurance
  - credit cards
  - travel services
  - EFTPOS
  - homebanking

National Savings Bank
- Uses post offices (22,000)
  - longer opening hours
- Role to provide banking (saving) service for modest personal savers

Services
  - Ordinary account—
    (2 levels of interest)
  - Investment account—
    gross interest
  - tax free (£70)
  - notice

National Girobank
- Simple money transmission service
- Extends current account usage (lower income groups)

Services
  - money transmission
  - current accounts
  - deposit account
  - base service
  - similar to clearing bank service
  - easy transfer with cheque
  - interest earned on 'idle' money.

  - foreign travel
  - ATMs (Link)
  - Personal loans and revolving credit

National Savings
- Savings service for small unsophisticated saver
- Services have characteristics of
  - government guarantee
  - attracting funds in 'small' amounts
  - some tax exemption
  - low maximum limits
  - non-negotiable
  - liquid
  - simple to buy
  - subject to rising rates

- Services include
  - National Savings Certificates
    - standard
    - index linked
  - NSC tax free guaranteed return
  - Premium Savings Bonds
    - prize but no interest
  - Yearly Plan Certificates
    - flexible savings, guaranteed rate
  - Deposit Bonds
    - gross interest, non-taxpayer benefits
  - Income Bonds
    - standard
    - index linked
    - provide monthly income
  - Government Stock
    - National Savings Register

Insurance
- Largest single source of regular personal savings
- Role to provide cover for dependants and/or a source of long term savings, or regular income
- Life cover policies are
  - whole life
  - term assurance
  - decreasing term assurance
  - convertible term
  - with or without profits
  - cover for fixed period
  - for mortgages
  - change to endowment/whole life

- Savings policies are
  - endowment
    - with or without profits, pay out sum on fixed date of death
  - endowment mortgages now becoming very popular
  - regular savings policies
    - emphasis on saving with minimal life cover
    - some linked to unit trust

- Income policies are
  - annuities
    - pay an income in return for a lump sum
  - immediate annuity
    - reversionary annuity
  - deferred annuity
    - annuity certain

- some policies have surrender values (after 2 years)
- loans can be made against surrender value

Unit Trusts
- Role   — allow small savers to participate in stock/shares
                                           — collect from number of savers and invest in securities
                                           — diversified portfolio
- Three parties   — trustee — watchdog
                                           — Managers — invest money/buy and sell units
                                           — unitholder — saver

- General funds spread invested money through variety of sectors
- Specialist funds concentrate on special sector or country
  - Accumulation units   — money ploughed back
  - Income units   — return paid as income
  - Withdrawal fund   — guarantees income
  - Lump sum investments
- Savings plans often linked to insurance
- Insurance linked more than 25% of unit trust investment

Investment Trusts
- Similar to unit trust
- Investors buy shares in Investment Trust
- Does not buy/sell units
- Investors have larger holdings for longer time.

Pension Funds
- Provide income on retirement
- Funds are major institutional investors e.g. British Gas
- Pension payments come from
  - employers' contributions
  - employees' contributions
  - investment income
- Three main pensions
  - state
  - occupational   — pension funds
  - personal pensions   — self employed or non pensioned employees.

Finance Houses
- Role to provide hire purchase and credit operation for personal and corporate customers

- Credit in form of
  - hire purchase
  - conditional sale
  - credit sale
  - revolving loan
  - personal or commercial loan
  - leasing

- Consumer hire purchase advantages
  - certainty
  - protection
  - standardisation ·
  - legal costs
  - quality
  - savings maintenance
  - immediate use of goods

- HP rates higher than bank loan
- Personal loans for variety of purposes to customers via mailshot or third party introduction.

- Industrial hire purchase for equipment, plant, and machinery
- Advantages
  - working capital not strained
  - bank overdrafts not used
  - budgeting easier
  - contracts simple and flexible
  - possible tax advantage

- Leasing — most popular method
  - operating leases used by manufacturers and suppliers to promote sales
  - finance leases provided by finance houses direct

- Leasing advantages
  - does not use up liquid assets
  - no worries of ownership
  - rentals set at outset
  - flexible to meet company needs
  - budgeting is easy

- Funds obtained from
  - bank borrowing
  - wholesale borrowing
  - public borrowing

- Deposit services include
  - savings accounts
  - wholesale deposits

Moneyshops
- American in origin geared mainly to private customers
- Provide basic banking service based upon
  - longer opening hours
  - comfortable and informal office
  - appeal to private individuals
  - provision of 'easy' loans

- Services provided via
  - retail outlets (branches)
  - third parties — retail stores
  - mail 'order'

- Services include
  - cheque accounts
  - savings accounts
  - loans — personal
    — revolving
  - standing orders/direct debits
  - travel
  - insurances

CHECK OUT QUESTIONS

BUILDING SOCIETIES
1. Why are the societies a major competitor in the personal business market?
2. Name at least four savings services.
3. What are the advantages/disadvantages and customer targets for the services?
4. Are building society savings schemes suited to the non-taxpayer? Explain.
5. List the lending services.
6. What are the benefits of an endowment mortgage?
7. What are the differences between a repayment and endowment mortgage?
8. Name at least five other financial services offered by the building societies.
9. How do building societies 'clear' their cheque account cheques?
10. Name the two ATM networks.
11. What major developments are likely in the next couple of years?

NATIONAL SAVINGS BANK
12. Why is the passbook retained for withdrawals of more than £50 from an ordinary account?
13. How would you qualify to be a 'Regular Customer'?
14. What is the main problem regarding interest calculation on Ordinary Accounts?
15. How much interest is credited free of Income and Capital Gains Tax?

NATIONAL GIROBANK
16. What are the two roles of the Girobank?
17. What is its basic service?
18. How does the cheque account withdrawal differ from the clearing bank system?
19. What is the main advantage of the Deposit Account?
20. Name two other services offered by the Girobank.

NATIONAL SAVINGS
21. List four main characteristics of National Savings services.
22. What are the benefits to savers of NSC?
23. What is the main advantage of index-linked NSC?
24. What is the main advantage of Premium Bonds?
25. How do Yearly Plan Certificates operate?
26. What are Deposit and Income Bonds?
27. To whom are Government Stocks attractive?

INSURANCE
28. What are the differences between Term and Whole Life Insurance?
29. What is the main purpose of a Decreasing Term Assurance?
30. What are the benefits of an endowment policy?
31. What is meant by surrender value?
32. Name the four types of annuity.

UNIT TRUSTS
33. What are the roles of a unit trust?
34. What are General and Specialist Funds?
35. Name the two types of unit.
36. What has been the major recent development in unit trusts?

INVESTMENT TRUSTS
37. How do investors invest in an Investment Trust?

PENSION FUNDS
38. What are the three types of pension?
39. How do pension funds build up their assets?

FINANCE HOUSES
40. What is the main role of a finance house?
41. Name three forms of instalment credit.
42. Give three advantages of consumer hire purchase.
43. How do finance houses obtain customers for personal loans?
44. Give three benefits of using industrial hire purchase.
45. Name the two types of lease.
46. Give three reasons why leasing is attractive.
47. Where do finance houses obtain their funds?

MONEYSHOPS
48. Why are Moneyshops attractive?
49. Describe three means by which Moneyshops provide their services.
50. Name four moneyshop services.

Appendix
The Output Study Method

This book is written following the principles used in the OUTPUT study method. It is an approach to studying designed to make studying not only more effective but easier and more fun. This appendix is reprinted from *Studying the Professional Way* by Keith Elliott and Don Wright.

THE OUTPUT STUDY METHOD
In this chapter we introduce you to the OUTPUT study method. It will enable you to become more effective in your learning and more successful as you study the professional way. It is based on a blend of research and 'chalkface' experience which suggests that you are most likely to be effective in your learning when during your study period you —

● have a clearly defined target
● study with clearly framed questions in mind
● are active, rather than passive
● create notes and convert them from one form to another
● conclude by testing your recall of the material, to determine if the target was achieved and the initially framed questions answered.

The OUTPUT method is so called because it integrates all these features and so enables you, the student to convert inputs of time and effort into outputs of more effective learning resulting in improved academic performance.

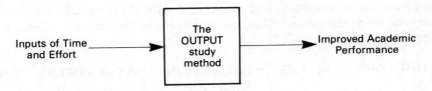

1. THE OUTPUT STUDY METHOD
The method itself consists of five parts
Map Out
Search Out
Look Out
Print Out
Check Out

(a) Map Out

It has been said of Christopher Columbus that when he set out he did not know where he was going, when he got there he did not know where he was, and when he returned he did not know where he had been. This first stage is designed to prevent you from falling into that 'Columbus Syndrome'.

When you **Map Out** a journey you should know your constraints, that is how much time you have for it, to enable you to decide whether you can complete it in one attempt or divide it into shorter stages.

Similarly here, when starting to study you need to **Map Out** what you are to study by looking at the overall picture of the study topic. This will involve a fairly quick survey of the material to provide a general idea of its complexity, content and format. From this you can then break up the material into manageable chunks which can be covered in the time slots available.

In the light of this initial **Map Out** a target can be set that is clear and attainable.

MAP OUT GIVES AN IDEA OF CONTENT AND COMPLEXITY AND SO ENABLES TARGETS TO BE SET.

(b) Search Out

It is vital to be purposive when studying. The second stage therefore is to **Search Out** your existing knowledge of the subject area, and the information gleaned from the quick **Map Out,** to frame questions that you will want to answer to enable you to achieve your target.

This stage gives your studying a clear sense of direction.

SEARCH OUT CONCENTRATES STUDY ACTIVITY AND MAKES IT ACTIVE AND PURPOSIVE.

(c) Look Out

This is the stage which moves you on to achieve your target. Here you are on the **Look Out** for the information that will enable you to answer your questions. You will focus on the basic facts and individual details, the relationships and links between them, and the overall structures which give meaning and coherence to these relationships.

LOOK OUT FOR THE INFORMATION THAT ANSWERS YOUR QUESTIONS.

(d) Print Out

This stage is concerned with building up a structure of relevant notes. As memory fades over time it is important to **Print Out** information of the relationship and structures identified at **Look Out.**

The separation of **Look Out** from **Print Out** emphasises the importance of identifying the key points and the general thread of the argument or analysis before engaging in note making activity.

PRINT OUT BUILDS UP A STOREHOUSE OF INFORMATION.

(e) Check Out

At this final stage of the OUTPUT study method you should **Check Out** that you have hit your target by ensuring that you recall the material and that you have answered your questions. By doing this you lay a secure basis of understanding and make revision a continuous all year round activity. This **Check Out** is therefore so crucial it should take up about one quarter of your study time.

The knowledge that the study period will conclude with a **Check Out** session will create a sense of purpose and increase concentration.

CHECK OUT CEMENTS UNDERSTANDING AND EASES LEARNING AND RECALL.

This is a brief outline of the OUTPUT study method.
It is a method which is adaptable to all the main areas of study skills.

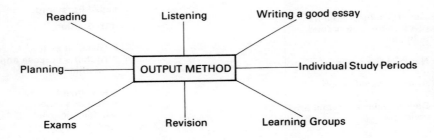

A.2 The OUTPUT Study Method

In this book we illustrate its application and relevance to all of these.

Reading — Books/Articles	Chapter 2 (this chapter)
Listening	Chapter 3
Reading — Graphs, Tables, & Diagrams	Chapter 3
Notemaking	Chapter 4
Writing a good Essay	Chapter 5
Revision	Chapter 6
Exams	Chapter 7

However, as the major source of private study information, for most students, comes from reading, we turn first to

2. THE APPLICATION OF THE OUTPUT STUDY METHOD TO READING

(a) Map Out

Obviously much of your reading will be of recommended texts. Before you start to read specific chapters it is worthwhile to apply **Map Out** to the book as a whole.

(i)   *Map Out — the book*. All books have a clear structure and follow some sort of plan. An initial 'flick through' will give you a good idea of this plan and so help you to understand as you read. Before dipping into chapters themselves it is worth while to skim the —

- title page
- preface
- table of contents
- index

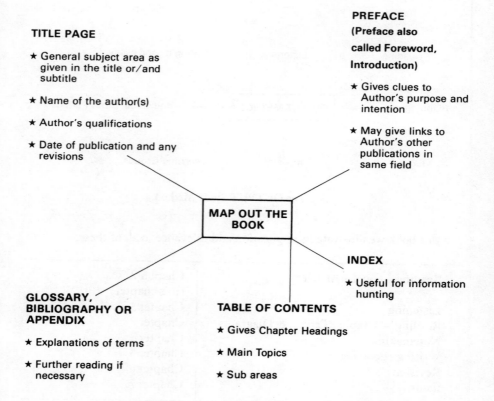

TITLE PAGE

★ General subject area as given in the title or/and subtitle

★ Name of the author(s)

★ Author's qualifications

★ Date of publication and any revisions

PREFACE
(Preface also called Foreword, Introduction)

★ Gives clues to Author's purpose and intention

★ May give links to Author's other publications in same field

MAP OUT THE BOOK

INDEX

★ Useful for information hunting

GLOSSARY, BIBLIOGRAPHY OR APPENDIX

★ Explanations of terms

★ Further reading if necessary

TABLE OF CONTENTS

★ Gives Chapter Headings

★ Main Topics

★ Sub areas

A.3 Map Out the Book

So when flicking through from the front not the back look at the book as a whole. Try to
- Note the headings of the main sections and chapters, and chapter headings
- Check if there are any summaries at the end of any sections or chapters
- Look at any visual aids such as charts, graphs, tables or pictures
- Read a few sentences.

This sampling will give a flavour to **Map Out**. The complete **Map Out** should take about 10 minutes and certainly no more than double that, even if it is a recommended text.

(ii) *Map Out — chapters or articles*. It is always good practice to **Map Out** each chapter or article before you read it to enable you to get an idea of its structure, overall content and how it fits into the book as a whole. When mapping out an article or book chapter you are 'flicking through', looking particularly for —

- Any foreword, or quotation at its outset
- The first paragraph which may give you the author's own survey of what is to come
- Any subheading that helps to show you the route to be taken. You will often see that different subheadings are given different levels of importance by their degree of prominence.
- Any italics that show key concepts or vital areas.
- The final paragraph or conclusion which may summarise the essence of what has been said.

At this stage you are noting the degree of complexity of the material and whether it is completely new or familiar to you. This information is very important as we shall see when we come to the relationship between **Look Out** and **Print Out**.

Finally you are deciding whether the material can be covered in one study period or spread over several. This will enable you to set a realistic target for the time available.

(b) Search Out

A number of questions based on the date and balance of the layout will arise during **Map Out**:

- Is this up to date?
- Have there been any major changes since publication?
- Why is paragraph 3 so long? Is it the most significant?

You can add to these questions others raised by the structure of the article or chapter itself.

- A good tip here is to **Search Out** the headings or subheadings to turn them into questions.

Questions may also arise if there is a **Search Out** of past examination questions and essay titles. The sort of specific questions that can arise from all these sources might include.

● What does it mean?
● Why is it important?
● Where is the evidence for this view?

Questions of association are MOST important.

● How does it link with earlier chapters or other articles?
● Is there a link between what you are about to read and what you have already read?
● Is it related to another section of the course or another subject you are studying?

You should try to frame questions such as these even if at first you find it an awkward task. It does come easily with practice especially if the tip to turn the headings of sections and chapters into questions is followed.

The importance of questions of association cannot be over-emphasised because, not only is the danger of 'pigeon-holing' prevented but you will be encouraged to integrate your work, and this will lead to associations at the 'deeper' level of relationships and structures, rather than at the 'surface' level of rote learnt facts.

(c) Look Out

This is the stage when you start to read. At the initial **Map Out** stage you will have found out whether the material to be covered is familiar to you or brand new, simple or complex.

For new or complex material we would recommend that you should read straight through without rereading or making notes. On this first reading you should concentrate on looking for the —

● main ideas and key points
● the relationships between them

You should then read the material again in order to —

● answer the rest of your questions
● understand the details
● make notes

If you are familiar with the material, or it is obviously very simple, then at LOOK OUT you should —

● skim quickly through the text without notes then
● on first detailed reading make notes

NATURE OF THE MATERIAL	FIRST READING	SECOND READING
Familiar or Simple	Quick 'Skim'	Detailed Reading with Notes
New Complex	Detailed Reading	Detailed Reading with Notes

Why make notes only AFTER a skimmed or detailed first reading?
The reason for this is that if you make notes on your first reading —

- you do not yet know what the main points are or the overall thread of the argument
- you will therefore concentrate on detail rather than see the whole picture
- you will tend to forget your questions
- it will distract you and slow you down
- you will tend to copy words from the book rather than use your own expressions so that when the notes are later used for essays you can face charges of plagiarism
- you will make more notes than you need

So when you are on the **Look Out** during first (skimmed or detailed) reading try not to make notes until you move onto the next stage.

(d)   Print Out
This is the stage of Notemaking, a process which not only records information but RESULTS IN MORE EFFECTIVE AND RAPID UNDERSTANDING.

- The **print out** of notes can take place now you have got the key ideas(s) firmly in your mind from your first skimmed or detailed reading.
- You can read through for the second time and concentrate on the supporting details, examples and illustrations
- It is a good idea to underline with a pencil or circle the main points and perhaps to put a star by any example of importance. You could even use a fluorescent pen but please only do these things if it is your own book
- Once this has been completed you can transfer your selected main ideas, and the supporting details and examples into note form
- The different notemaking techniques that can be used will be analysed in our next chapter

Now that you have finished your notes, you are in a position to move onto the crucial final stage of the OUTPUT study method.

(e) Check Out

This is a key component not only of reading technique but of study skills generally. So many students when they finish reading fail to **check out** that they have grasped the essentials of the text. You should always **Check Out** that you have understood what you have read because —

- revision should not be a 'rush' activity at the end of the year but a continuous 'checking-out' process
- it is part of a continuous revision process
- it creates ACTIVITY and reinforces the target set for your study period
- memory fades so it is crucial to cement understanding straightaway
- it builds confidence as you prove you understand
- understanding fresh material is easier because old material was 'checked out'. Your memory is like a rolling snowball, which expands by continuous reinforcement of old material and the addition of new.

You should spend approximately ONE QUARTER of your study time on this vital final stage. Therefore if you have a 3 hour study period, plan to take up the last 45 minutes on checking that you have understood

- the basic points
- the relationship between them
- the overall structure that gives meaning to these relationships
- links with earlier work
- interrelationships with other courses

(i) *Check Out Activity Methods.* There are a number of activities that can be used to **Check Out** your understanding and to see if you have hit your target. You can —

- talk to yourself. Read out your original questions created at **Search Out** and try to answer them
- record them on tape for a playback check out
- complete a short summary without notes and with books closed.
- plan or complete a Tutor-set essay on the topic
- answer a past exam question, in simulated examination conditions especially with regard to time
- take a blank piece of paper and create a new form of notes. We fully develop this point in our Notemaking chapter
- explain to each other in your Learning Group the key points of the text that you have all read

You can now start to apply the OUTPUT study method in your studies. You will find it will make a major difference to you. It is summarised in Figure 2.2, and it would be a good idea to go through it and **Check Out** so that you have it clearly in your mind before you turn to the exercise.

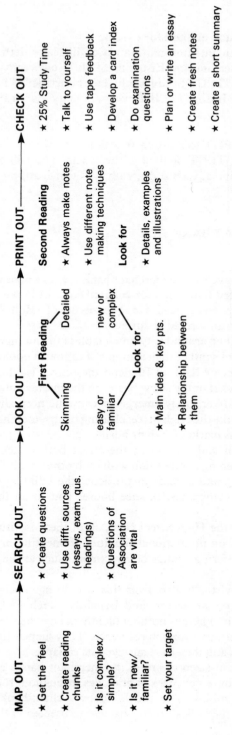

MAP OUT ⟶ **SEARCH OUT** ⟶ **LOOK OUT** ⟶ **PRINT OUT** ⟶ **CHECK OUT**

MAP OUT

★ Get the 'feel

★ Create reading chunks

★ Is it complex/ simple?

★ Is it new/ familiar?

★ Set your target

SEARCH OUT

★ Create questions

★ Use difft. sources (essays, exam. qus. headings)

★ Questions of Association are vital

LOOK OUT

First Reading

Skimming   Detailed

easy or   new or
familiar   complex

Look for

★ Main idea & key pts.

★ Relationship between them

PRINT OUT

Second Reading

★ Always make notes

★ Use different note making techniques

Look for

★ Details, examples and illustrations

CHECK OUT

★ 25% Study Time

★ Talk to yourself

★ Use tape feedback

★ Develop a card index

★ Do examination questions

★ Plan or write an essay

★ Create fresh notes

★ Create a short summary

Purpose + Activity + Recall = Effective Learning

A.4 The OUTPUT Study Method Applied to Reading

Exercise 2 The OUTPUT study method for reading

Reading is a major source of student information and we will deal with the specific skill in the next Chapter on Reading and Listening Skills. However, you can at this stage start to apply the OUTPUT Study Method to the article "What makes a Merchant Bank Tick" by Joe Irving, T.S.B. Review, January March 1982, Vol. 1 No. 9.

Exercise 2.1. Applying OUTPUT to reading an article

Apply all the stages of the OUTPUT method to the article. You will be able to compare some of your thoughts, at each stage, with ours which appear after the article.

WHAT MAKES A MERCHANT BANK TICK

By Joe Irving

Years of political cartooning have left the merchant banker with a poor image. In the public mind he is an overfed figure in a fur-collared coat, a Lew Grade sized cigar in his mouth and a top hat on his head. He squeezes out of a Rolls-Royce on the solicitous arm of a smartly-uniformed chauffeur.

The odd cigar may still be lit up around City lunch tables but any surviving top hats are traditional to certain jobs rather than symbols of capitalist opulence. The topper to the gilt-edged dealer or Bank of England messenger is what the tall white hat is to the *cordon bleu* chef or the straw boater to the master butcher. The true picture of a merchant banker rarely emerges because he normally neither seeks nor needs publicity. Unlike the High Street clearing banks, merchant banks do not have to rely on the mass market for their business.

The clearers need the man and woman in the street both as lenders and borrowers. They are in sharpening competition with each other, with the TSBs, and with other deposit-taking and savings institutions, the building societies, National Savings, insurance companies, finance houses and so on for savers' money.

To maintain their share of the High Street cake, all of these institutions are spending vast sums of money on promotional activities of one kind or another. Between them they are now offering a range of investments such as the saver has never seen before.

The merchant banks stand virtually aloof from this in-fighting. Their business is in the more exclusive corporate sector, and Britain's merchant banks are themselves an exclusive bunch. There is nothing like them anywhere else in the world; they are few in number but strong in resilience. They helped finance the growth of the British Empire, and they have survived its collapse.

Yet compared with the giant-sized clearers, the merchant banks are small. While the High Street banks have networks of branches throughout the country and count their customers in millions, the much older merchant banks operate from only a few offices, with the bulk of their business transacted in the City of

London. Interestingly, these historic financial institutions were started by foreigners in the latter part of the eighteenth century as sidelines to their merchanting activities. As time went on, the banking side dominated the merchanting, and eventually the latter was phased out altogether by some merchants so that they became bankers instead.

Such names as Kleinwort Benson, Hambros, Hill Samuel, Rothschilds and Lazards with whom the TSB has a business link, are household names. But to the average man their activities are a closed book. Ask him if he has visited an accepting house lately and he will very likely blush.

A merchant bank is an accepting house when it is doing a certain kind of business accepting responsibility for the payment of a bill of exchange. For this the bank receives a commission. It is part of a merchant bank's primary function the financing of international trade.

A bill of exchange is much the same as a cheque. It is an order by one party to another to pay a third party a named sum of money at a certain date. A bill of exchange is a good way of settling international trade deals between companies which know nothing about each other. For instance, a British manufacturer will send off a consignment of clutch linings to a hitherto unknown concern in Nigeria once he is assured that he can get his money through a merchant bank. The bank will have accepted the debt on the understanding that it will be reimbursed in, say, three months' time, plus a bit extra for its trouble.

The bank pays the debtor in the form of an 'acceptance credit' which can be traded on the London discount market. The discount houses, of which there are only 11, are another branch of the financial markets which few people know much about.

In spite of their low profile compared with other big commercial concerns, the merchant banks are not slow to take advantage of new trends and opportunities. Although these specialist bankers may not be any more partial to toppers as workwear than the rest of us, they do wear a number of other hats. And they don't come out of the same wardrobe.

The mix of activities varies considerably, even among the elite of the merchant banking world the 17 members of the Accepting Houses Committee. Any collection of banking services can quickly become out of date, with new requirements needing new services. At no time has this been more true than the past year or two. Witness the rapid changes which are taking place in 'retail' banking. Starting almost from scratch, the clearing banks and the TSBs between them have sliced off a significant share of house mortgage business from the building societies. Next year could see them building up their share to 18 per cent or more.

Whether they aim to stay in the market at that level is anybody's guess. Some believe that the banks will pull down the shutters on mortgage business when the economy picks up and there is a bigger demand and better returns to be had from financing new and reviving industries. Others are not convinced that the banks will do as they have done in the past, and give up business which has fallen into their laps surprisingly easily. It may be much harder to elbow out the more alert building societies next time.

Meanwhile, no one is looking forward to economic recovery more than the merchant banks. They thrive on industrial dynamism and economic growth. As well as financing the flow of goods which developing industries produce, they supply much of the cash they need for new factories, equipment, offices and other buildings. Their role is particularly valuable, and indeed often essential in projects which require specialised financial knowledge. Sometimes these may be so big that they can be financed only by an international consortium, and it is the merchant bank's job to put this together.

On a more normal scale of financing the bank will advise on ways and means. New companies need start-up capital and for these the first port of call is usually the merchant bank. Many applicants inevitably leave empty-handed, usually bitterly disappointed and often very annoyed. The inventor or budding entrepreneur who thinks he has a winner in his briefcase is difficult to convince that the cost/risk ratio is too much out of balance. Merchant banks, of course, are not infallible, and none of them can cross their hearts and say they have never made a misjudgement.

Backing risk projects, however, has been the essence of merchant banking since it began hundreds of years ago. Putting up venture capital is essentially putting your money where your judgement is, and like a race meeting, there are always more losers than winners.

However, Britain's top merchant banks and the system under which they operate has not survived as long as it has by backing losers. So once a merchant bank puts its energy, expertise and resources behind a new project, there is more than a sporting chance of it coming off. For its money and its trouble the bank will usually take a stake in the business at the outset or insist on its loan being in the future convertible into the company's stock. Normally the bank will not interfere in the day-to-day running of the business, but it will step in with financial advice whenever necessary.

Existing companies, too, can feel a lot more comfortable with a merchant bank at their elbow. With both declining and expanding concerns there comes a time when expert outside help is imperative. Either way the bank may provide a rejuvenating injection of cash of lift-off capital into a new phase of progress. The bank may provide the money itself or organise loans from other sources. With the money may come suggestions on ways to alter the corporate set-up, particularly on the financial side, and advice on long-range planning.

One of the few times when merchant banks get in the news, is when they are masterminding a capital issue or a take-over. Bringing a company to market by a public issue of its shares is an operation that calls for a finely-tuned rating of the company's worth and prospects. If the banks get it wrong the only people to benefit will be the stock market speculators. The bank itself, as principal underwriter, with an undersubscribed issue takes on the surplus stock.

Underwriting capital issues is a major source of income for merchant banks, and one serious misjudgement can damage a bank's reputation for a long time. Capital-raising by share issues is bound to increase sharply once industrial expansion gets under way, but this could be some time off.

Ian Fraser, chairman of Lazards, says: 'I see no increase in capacity for the next two or three years. Industry is at present working well below capacity, and there is a great deal of slack to be taken up before there is any real expansion. However, once the economy starts to pick up, some firms will be going into the market for more capital.'

Meanwhile, the City's merchant banks are keeping their doorknobs polished and their 'welcome' mats brushed. They are also dusting off their action suits for an upsurge in takeovers and mergers when the business scene starts looking up. This is another activity where the skill of the merchant bank, on one side or the other, can be crucial to the outcome if a takeover bid leads to a bitterly contested battle, as it often does.

In recent times merchant banks have become increasingly involved in the expanding field of investment counselling and dealing. They manage pension funds and other institutional and individual portfolios. Will they be tempted to expand into the High Street savings scene? The answer is no, at least for a number of years. Postal and plastic card banking may eventually enable the merchant banks to try for a share of the market without the expense of opening local branches, but that is probably a long way off.

In the meantime Ian Fraser sees no major changes taking place in the present decade. He says: 'Merchant banks are always going through an evolutionary process. One class of business goes and another takes its place. But I see no substantial departure from the basic traditional activities over the next ten years.'

Joe Irving has worked for newspapers in various cities, including Newcastle and Manchester. During the past 20 years in London he has been on the City staff of *The Guardian* and *The Daily Telegraph* before moving to *The Sunday Times*.

Some of the points that you may have considered are shown below. They form a guide not an exhaustive list.

MAP OUT This provides a quick survey of the article which showed —

● that it can be read at one sitting.
● it is written in continuous prose in a journalistic style
● an explanation of the main areas of Merchant Bank activity.
● a final paragraph which emphasises the stability of merchant banks — they are not subject to rapid change. (Quote from a Chairman of Merchant Bank Lazards).
● the author is a journalist with City experience.

SEARCH OUT Here you would produce a list of questions to keep your reading ACTIVE and PURPOSIVE.

● What is a Merchant Bank?
● Is this the same as an Acceptance House?
● How do the relevant Banks differ from clearing banks?
● What is their main area of activity?

● Is this an historical role and how does it fit into the 1980's scene?
● Why do we need Merchant Banks?
● Are there many Merchant Banks and what are their names?

LOOK OUT Our first reading gave us information

● that this article covers an area about which students are often unsure
● that the content is unfamiliar and should be read twice.
● that on FIRST reading to read straight through without rereading or making notes
● to concentrate on main ideas, key points and relationships
● to show the importance of not making notes at this stage, by the fact that the article is written in a journalistic style with related facts being spread throughout the article
● much of the article also deals with Bank activity other than Merchant Banks
● which could ensure that the questions highlighted at search out have been answered.

PRINT OUT We are able to make notes now because

● on SECOND reading you are aware of the content and flow and are able to keep the notes concise and to the subject
● you need to record the information to aid recall and revision
● we need to record Merchant Bank operations

CHECK OUT Here you can establish whether you fully grasped the essentials of the article by —

● Using any of the recommended Activity Methods
● Preferably using one that at first you were unsure of e.g. talking to yourself on tape.

Which one did you use?

You can now see how valuable the OUTPUT study method is when reading. We apply the method to Listening in the next chapter after we have further developed ways of improving reading skills. So it is to the development of reading and listening skills that we now turn in Chapter 3.

Copies of Studying the Professional Way can be obtained from Skills of the Eighties, 22 Burrell Close, Prenton, Birkenhead, Merseyside. Price £3.95.

Index